ADVANCE PRAISE FOR
THE DECISIVE DECADE

"*The Decisive Decade* is cautionary and optimistic. Ward shows a path for America and the Free World to win the contest with the Chinese Communist Party. He calls for rebuilding American economic, industrial, and technological might, and identifies the technologies, industries, countries, and regions that are most consequential. This book is a call to action for all, but especially for business executives. Just as American military officers plan and execute the combat missions to win battles, corporate officers must plan and execute business strategies that enhance our security, promote prosperity, and help the Free World prevail in the most consequential competition of this century."

—From the Foreword by LT. GENERAL H.R. MCMASTER (US Army, Ret.), Former US National Security Advisor

"Building upon his groundbreaking work *China's Vision of Victory*, Jonathan Ward lays out a comprehensive American grand strategy for competition with China in *The Decisive Decade*. Dr. Ward shows the critical role of economic power in US strategy both in our past victories and in our present competition with China. His exploration of the crucial role of American business and finance in strategic competition, the conversion of economic might into military power, and a revitalized American-led order all ring urgent and true. *The Decisive Decade* should be read by both parties in Congress, as well as in American boardrooms, in Allied governments, and across the United States. This is the first book-length effort to show us how to flat out win this contest with the People's Republic of China."

—SENATOR JON KYL

"*The Decisive Decade* is a wake-up call to all Americans. Jonathan Ward offers not only a diagnosis of the urgent problem but also a prescription for future success if we act now. Mobilizing America's key strengths, especially our economic dynamism and global alliance system, can enable us to create the world we want to leave our grandchildren."

—MIKE BROWN, Former Director, Defense Innovation Unit, US Department of Defense; Former CEO, Symantec Corporation

"*The Decisive Decade* is the clearest, most coherent and comprehensive articulation of the breadth and depth of our existential challenge with China and the means to a solution. A rare compendium of the diverse threats—economic, diplomatic, and military—and the need for a decades-long government and business world commitment to a campaign. This is not just the Cold War redux. It is more and it is multidimensional. Jonathan Ward makes it clear that superlatives and declarations in national and defense security strategies have not and will not be enough. The call to action is for Washington, Silicon Valley, and Wall Street."

—ADMIRAL JONATHAN GREENERT (US Navy, Ret.),
Former Chief of US Naval Operations

"Jonathan Ward has written a stimulating and provocative account of the US-China relationship in the coming few years, with data and statistics that will help inform readers, particularly on the US-China business relationship. Whatever your conclusions may be about these issues, you will find plenty to make you think in this lively and engaging book."

—RANA MITTER, Professor of the History and Politics
of Modern China, University of Oxford

"In *The Decisive Decade*, Ward reminds us that America and its allies have all the tools necessary to defend liberty against Beijing's hollow despotism. The ingredient urgently needed now, which Ward has in spades, is the will to act."

—MATT POTTINGER,
Former US Deputy National Security Advisor

"An insightful analysis of one of the most important geopolitical relationships in the twenty-first century. Ward builds upon his exposition of the Chinese Communist Party strategy that guides the rise of China and presents a compelling course of action for the United States."

—JOHN W. GARVER, author of *China's Quest: The History of
the Foreign Relations of the People's Republic of China*

"With *The Decisive Decade*, Jonathan Ward offers a diagnosis and a prescription. The industrial base which has made the United States so powerful since Pearl Harbor must be redesigned and reinvigorated to guarantee our continuing success against rising challenges—like the Chinese Communist Party. Prevailing will require a network approach between the public and private sectors that prioritizes competition, balance, innovation, human talent, and the power of our capital markets. This book is an excellent blueprint."

—GENERAL JOSEPH L. VOTEL (US Army, Ret.),
President and CEO of Business Executives for National Security;
Former Commander, US Special Operations Command

PRAISE FOR AUTHOR'S PREVIOUS BOOK, *CHINA'S VISION OF VICTORY*

"A powerful work."

—GENERAL DAVID PETRAEUS (US Army, Ret.),
Former Commander of Coalition Forces in Iraq and Afghanistan
and US Central Command, and Former Director of the CIA

"A Master Class on China."

—JACK DEVINE, US Central Intelligence Agency (Ret.),
author of *Good Hunting: An American Spymaster's Story*

"Jonathan Ward's stimulating *China's Vision of Victory* is one of the first books to make an explicit argument for containment of China by the west."

—*Financial Times*

"Insightful, compelling, and long overdue."

—ADMIRAL SCOTT H. SWIFT (US Navy, Ret.),
Commander of US Pacific Fleet, 2015–2018

"As the United States debates the future of its China policy, *China's Vision of Victory* deserves the widest reading."

—ASHLEY J. TELLIS, Tata Chair for Strategic Affairs,
Carnegie Endowment for International Peace

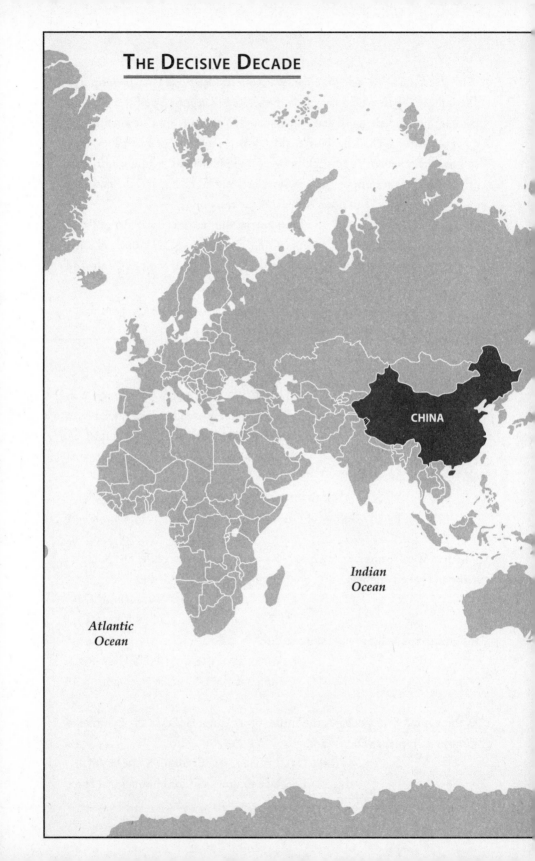

THE DECISIVE DECADE

CHINA

Indian
Ocean

Atlantic
Ocean

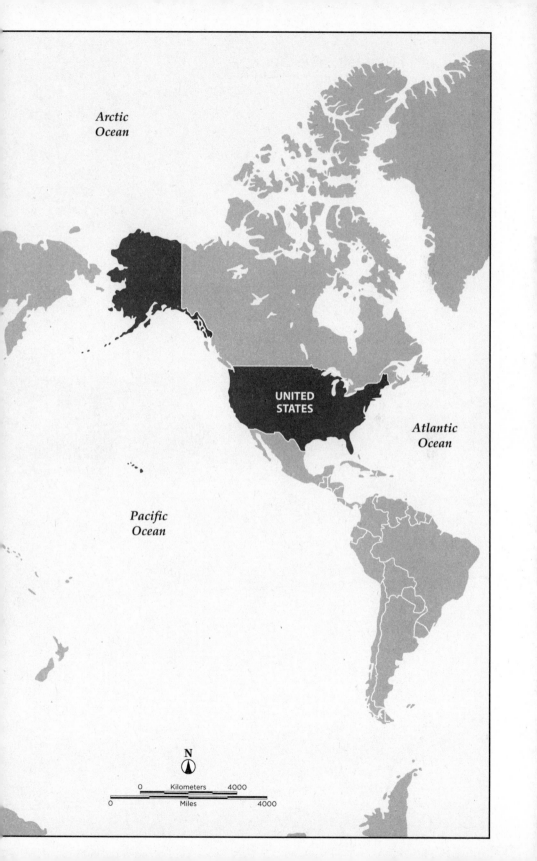

Arctic
Ocean

UNITED
STATES

Atlantic
Ocean

Pacific
Ocean

N

0   Kilometers   4000

0   Miles   4000

THE
DECISIVE
DECADE

ALSO BY JONATHAN D. T. WARD

China's Vision of Victory

THE
DECISIVE
DECADE

American Grand Strategy
for Triumph Over China

JONATHAN D. T. WARD

DIVERSION
BOOKS

Diversion Books
A division of Diversion Publishing Corp.
www.diversionbooks.com

First Diversion Books edition, April 2023
Hardcover ISBN: 9781635768459
eBook ISBN: 9781635769500

Maps by Tim Kissel

Printed in the United States of America
10 9 8 7 6 5 4 3 2 1

To My Fellow Americans:
May You Come to See Your Importance to the World

Josh,
Fight the Good
Fight with all
thy Might!

Your Friend,
Jonath

Might!
Your Friend!
Dean

CONTENTS

FOREWORD

by Lt. General H.R. McMaster (US Army, Ret.), Former US National Security Advisor

To Citizens and Business Leaders across the Free World:

With the unprovoked Russian invasion of Ukraine in February 2022, our post–Cold War holiday from history officially ended. The brutalization of Ukraine at the hands of a revanchist Kremlin and its military, enabled by the moral, diplomatic, financial, and propaganda support of the People's Republic of China, revealed to all that we are in an era of geostrategic competition with ruthless authoritarian powers. Just prior to the Beijing Olympics, dictators Vladimir Putin and Xi Jinping professed "no limits" to their "friendship" as they declared a shift in the balance of power in the world toward their authoritarian regimes and away from the United States and the Free World. Dr. Jonathan Ward's new book, *The Decisive Decade,* defines the US-China global competition as a strategic contest that will be won or lost based on economic power.

Before Russia's renewed assault on Ukraine, the global pandemic intensified the competition with the Chinese Communist Party (or CCP). The CCP's actions during the pandemic should have removed any lingering doubts concerning its leaders' intention to extend and tighten their exclusive grip on power internally and achieve "national rejuvenation" at the expense of other nations.

As Jonathan Ward pointed out in his previous book, *China's Vision of Victory*, the CCP is pursuing strategies designed to maintain control and gain economic and strategic advantage. These strategies have names like "Civil-Military Fusion," "Made in China 2025," and "the Belt and Road Initiative." The goals are to establish Chinese hegemony, create exclusionary areas of primacy across the Indo-Pacific region, achieve preponderant advantage in advanced manufacturing and the emerging data-driven global economy, dominate global logistics and communications infrastructure, and rewrite the rules of international trade and political discourse. In the pages that follow in *The Decisive Decade*, Ward makes a strong case for stopping actions that "enable the economic ascendancy of our primary adversary." Ward demonstrates that governments and businesses have underappreciated that geostrategic risk associated with the Chinese Communist Party.

Across all those strategies, the CCP employs what we might call the three C's—a combination of cooption, coercion, and concealment. China coopts countries, international corporations, and elites through false promises of impending liberalization, insincere pledges to work on global issues, and especially the lure of short-term profits and access to the Chinese market, investments, and loans. Cooption includes debt traps set for corrupt or weak governments. It makes countries and corporations dependent and vulnerable to coercion. The Party coerces others to turn a blind eye to its most egregious human rights abuses and to support its foreign policy. And it applies cooption and coercion to subvert international organizations.

The party's success depends on concealing its intentions and portraying its most egregious actions as normal practice. "Free trade" Xi Jinping signs a draft Comprehensive Agreement on Investment with Europe while shutting down market share for retailers who object to slave labor. "Environmentalist" Xi Jinping promises carbon neutrality by 2060 while China finances and builds scores of coal-fired power plants internationally. "Human rights" Xi Jinping gives speeches on rule of law while he interns millions in concentration camps, extends the Party's repressive arm into Hong Kong, imprisons journalists and freedom activists, and holds hostages. "Compassionate" Xi Jinping speaks of a "community of common destiny" and of "peace, concord, and harmony," and asserts that the "Chinese nation does not carry aggressive or hegemonic traits in its genes" while his government subverts international organizations, his army bludgeons Indian soldiers to death on the Himalayan frontier, his cyber forces continue massive campaigns of espionage, his air force menaces Taiwan, South Korea, and Japan, and his navy, coast guard, and maritime militias exert ownership over the South China Sea.

Russia's brutal assault on Ukraine and CCP aggression expose the importance of factoring geopolitical risk into business and financial decision-making. The case of Germany's dependence on Russia for oil and gas revealed the folly of relying on hostile authoritarian regimes' critical supply chains as well as the high cost of ignoring warning signs. Germany failed to learn from Russia's use of energy to coerce Ukraine, Belarus, Armenia, Tajikistan, and Kyrgyzstan. Chairman Xi Jinping has used economic coercion against South Korea, Sweden, Australia, Lithuania, and many other nations while pursuing a "dual-circulation economy" that depends little on overseas markets, finance, and technology while deepening dependence of other nations on Chinese manufacturing and upstream components and materials. Companies must also recognize the reputational risk associated with investing or doing business with a police state that is victimizing its own people and forces its companies to act as arms of the government. China's genocidal campaign against the Uyghur population, for example, should be a human rights and environmental, social, and governance (ESG) issue in boardrooms.

The Decisive Decade will be of particular value to business and financial leaders because they will understand better their role in the most consequential competition of the coming century. American business played a vital role in the world-changing conflicts of the past century. From the role of American manufacturing power and industrial might in defeating Nazi Germany and Imperial Japan in World War II to the victory over Soviet Communism in the Cold War, economic security proved essential to national security. Ward tells stories about the vital roles that companies and business executives played in those competitions as well as the sad tales of companies that took on unmanageable risk in China or compromised their values as they enabled a hostile government's effort to gain preponderant power.

As China surpassed the United States as the top destination for new foreign direct investment in 2021, one could imagine CCP leaders evoking the quotation erroneously attributed to Vladimir Lenin: "The capitalists will sell us the rope with which we will hang them." Except it is worse; the Free World is financing the CCP's purchase of the rope. Nations and corporations should take something like a Hippocratic Oath for doing business in or investing in

China. In particular, Free World political, corporate, and financial leaders should vow to cause no harm or hurt in three ways:

1. Do not transfer sensitive technology that gives the CCP military advantage or unfair economic advantage.
2. Do not help the CCP stifle human freedom and perfect its police state.
3. Do not compromise the long-term viability of companies in exchange for short-term profits.

As Dr. Ward demonstrates, the contest with China will not only change the shape of the world economy, but it is also already transforming the role of the American corporation in US national security and global strategy. Those companies who understand and get ahead of that change will do well and those who continue to take on risk and hope for a fundamental change in the CCP will lose out. The question that should be heard in American boardrooms is: What is the right choice for my shareholders, my country, and humanity?

The Decisive Decade is cautionary and optimistic. Ward shows a path for America and the Free World to win the contest with the Chinese Communist Party. He calls for rebuilding American economic, industrial, and technological might, and identifies the technologies, industries, countries, and regions that are most consequential. This book is a call to action for all, but especially for business executives. Just as American military officers plan and execute the combat missions to win battles, corporate officers must plan and execute business strategies that enhance our security, promote prosperity, and help the Free World prevail in the most consequential competition of this century.

Lt. General H.R. McMaster (US Army, Ret.)
Former National Security Advisor
Stanford, California

INTRODUCTION

There will come a time when we in the United States of America will fully recognize the challenge that we face from the People's Republic of China and its ruling Chinese Communist Party. There will arrive a moment when we realize the depth and nature of the conflict that we have with the most potent challenger that we have faced in decades, the most capable challenger since the Soviet Union or even since the Axis Powers of the Second World War. When that time comes, whether through deadly manifestations of China's military ambition—which is rising in the Pacific—or through the gradual consensus-building that has begun to take shape among governments across the world, we will need to understand how we can win.

That day may come soon. Before Pearl Harbor, before September 11, there were many who could have told us about the threats we faced from overseas. But only when America is ready—not only as a government, but also as a people, as a nation—can we engage and overcome our most important challenges.

Let us imagine, for a moment, that we have reached that point, the point where it is clear that we face monumental dangers, in our country and around the world. Perhaps it arrived when Vladimir Putin and Xi Jinping spoke in unison about their "unlimited" partnership at the Beijing Olympics in 2022, carried out on the world stage in the midst of a genocide taking place in China and announced just weeks ahead of Putin's invasion of Ukraine. Perhaps it arrived with the Chinese Communist Party's military antagonism by sea, air, and land against its neighbors in Asia from India to Japan to Taiwan, or the threats of "possible nuclear attacks in the future" against our ally Australia.[1] Perhaps it coincided with the threat by official Chinese Communist Party media to curtail medical equipment exports to the United States at the start of the COVID-19 pandemic and so that America would be "plunged into the mighty sea of coronavirus."[2] Perhaps it has taken all these together to awaken us. Or, it may be that we shall only awaken through events yet to come. But America, together with our friends and Allies across the world, is today in a process of awakening to the enormous scope, scale, and maleficence of the challenge posed by China. When our awakening is complete, when it comes time that we are ready, we will need to understand what to do and how to win.

This book endeavors to help us do just that. Its purpose is to explain the nature of our competition with China and its fundamental properties, and to provide a useful framing for the many, many people who will ultimately work to lift our country out of a time of danger and toward a new path: a path to victory. We have done this before.

This is a book, like my first book, *China's Vision of Victory*, which is meant for all Americans, and for our friends and Allies around the world. *China's Vision of Victory* put in front of thousands of readers—for the first time—many of the primary strategy documents that explain the Chinese Communist Party's global ambitions and their quest for unsurpassed power, held since the founding of the People's Republic of China. That book brought the reader on a journey that few had been on before. It was a journey through numerous Communist Party documents and strategies, laid bare and assembled so any reader could see China's ambitions through the Party's own eyes. It was also a journey through a multitude of topics that constitute global grand strategy. The reader explored military, diplomatic, ideological, and economic topics from undersea warfare to state-owned enterprises, from nuclear strategy to economic coercion in Asia and Africa, from historical conflicts with India and America, to present-day military concepts in the Pacific Island chains. It was a journey through which readers came to understand not only the strategic thinking of China's leadership but also the various component pieces that will decide the course of the world in our lifetimes. This book, like that one, must deal with a host of issues and arenas. We must understand the stakes from sea to space. We must see how different industries, technologies, nation-states, and military systems can play essential roles in a path to American and Allied victory. Above all, we must see how victory, like a giant global puzzle spanning space and time, can begin to fit together. We must see what the fundamental concepts are that can guide us, what the areas of focus are where we can apply ourselves, and how to bend this contest to our advantage, overcome China's myriad plans and activities, and ultimately win.

Toward that end, let me explain three things that we should see from the beginning.

First: the current decade, the 2020s, is the decisive decade in US-China competition. If we are able to organize and execute a successful American grand strategy now, then we can begin to manage our long-term challenge from China and reshape the world in such a way that China and its supporters never reach their ambitions. If we fail, however, to manage this decade, then we are unlikely to have a second chance to preserve American leadership and to fully prevent Beijing from achieving many of its goals. This contest will shape the twenty-first century, and we must use the time we have left in this decade to set the course for an American ascendancy that will last for the remainder of the century. In the longer term, we must work with our friends and Allies to create a second Great Divergence in history. The First Great Divergence, beginning in the 1800s, was one between industrial and non-industrial societies that shaped the course of history and the power structure of the world. A second Great Divergence must be a divergence between the world's democracies and the world's dictatorships, wherein the world's free countries head off the challenge posed by Beijing and its supporters. To shape the century ahead, America must make monumental changes in strategy during the 2020s and sustain them well beyond this decade.[3] When Americans think and strategize not with short-term timeframes, but toward 2030 and beyond, we will gain a powerful advantage. This is true for business, national security, and our national politics—all essential elements in our contest with China.

Second: we will ultimately win or lose this contest through economic power. Our private companies are therefore essential. China's role in the world economy, its status as a responsible trading partner, is already under consistent review from the United States government across both Republican and Democratic administrations. However, America must go further in order to tilt the economic balance of power permanently in our favor and ensure that the twenty-first-century world economy does not rely on and is not dominated by our primary strategic adversary. Without the support and engagement of our business leaders, finance leaders, and major companies, we won't have a chance in our long-term contest with Beijing. Bringing American business to the right side of history, as has been done in the past, will be necessary. Our companies cannot assist our adversary's economic ascendancy any further. Today, our businesses exist in a state of conflict with the US national interest, transferring technology and injecting capital into our primary antagonist, in ways that will ultimately harm both themselves and their country. The scandals and embarrassments of what American companies must do to accommodate China, its human rights abuses, and its totalitarian political system are now the stuff of daily news. This must change. Our business leaders must understand that they are vital to American victory in the economic contest with Beijing.

American economic power has arguably been the deciding element of the major contests of the past hundred years. In the decade before Japan attacked the US Navy at Pearl Harbor, America had up to *ten times* the industrial power of the Japanese Empire.[4] Robert D. Kaplan describes his father, a veteran of the Second World War, recalling "the moment" when he knew America would win:

> At a rail junction near Cairo, Illinois, the sun was setting in rich colors over the prairie. Other trains were then converging from several tracks onto a single line that would take the troops to points along the East Coast, where ships to Europe awaited. Across a wider arc, the only thing he saw were trains and more trains, with soldiers looking out through every window as each train curved toward the others against a flat and limitless landscape lit red by the sun. "Just looking at that scene, that's the moment when I knew we were going to win the war," he said to me.[5]

This expression of raw industrial and logistical power applied to a century-defining war demonstrates the awakening of the "sleeping giant" by Japan and Germany.[6] But today it is perhaps far easier to imagine such a scene taking shape in China, which is now the "top ship-producing nation in the world by tonnage" and which fields the world's largest navy in quantity.[7] China, with its dominance of rail, maritime, steel, and heavy industry, is now responsible for nearly 30 percent of the world's manufacturing power.[8] It is China, not America, whose troop trains, ports, and industrial potential would likely define a global conflict. China's leaders understand the use of economic might for strategic ends. Do we?

A lack of clear, strategic economic thinking has plagued American policy-making in the past, but it has never been more vital than it is now, with the contest at hand.[9] As former US secretary of defense Robert Gates explains: "National Security Advisers Henry Kissinger, Brent Scowcroft, and Zbigniew Brzezinski were world-class geostrategists, but even they didn't write or think about the different forms of power—and none of them paid much attention to economic and financial tools."[10] The advantages of being a capitalist country in competition with a socialist system during the Cold War caused our premier strategic thinkers—like heirs and heiresses to immense fortunes—to take economic power and economic supremacy for granted, as they applied the overwhelming resources of the United States of America to our most pressing strategic problems. The most important change in the world today is that we no longer hold a position of uncontested economic supremacy—and, if we fail to act, *it may in fact be our adversary that holds this position over us.*

To win this contest, we must fundamentally transform the world so that America and our Allies secure and hold an indomitable share of global economic might. Doing so requires a two-pronged strategy of economic containment toward China alongside the revitalization and evolution of American industrial and technological power. We must work to secure North America as the superior center of economic gravity vis-à-vis China and integrate our Alliances into a Free World economic community.

Third, we must also understand the fundamentals: the ambitions of the adversary and the nature of this competition. At the root of victory is grand strategy. In the Cold War, we had containment, the brainchild of America's leading Sovietologist, George F. Kennan, who famously intuited and explained the Soviet threat in his "long telegram" and then defined a strategy to win the contest with Soviet Russia. Containment challenged and tested America. It took different shapes and forms, had different successes and failures, but was largely passed across presidencies—from Truman, Eisenhower, Kennedy, and ultimately to Reagan—to fight and win the long Cold War. There was a kind of beauty to containment. Its simplicity, coherence, and durability, the fact that it could be worked on, adapted, evolved, and yet retained its fundamental properties. In the hands of master statesmen and numerous professionals, it delivered a victory for America after half a century of focused struggle against what was then the most formidable opponent we had yet known. All of this should remind us that American grand strategy has been a space for great genius, intuition, and pragmatism. Above all, it is a tradition that gets results. With containment, arguably our most brilliant and successful grand strategy, the burdens, hard as they might have been to bear, neither destroyed nor distorted us. In the words of Henry Kissinger:

> Containment was a doctrine that saw America through more than four decades of construction, struggle and ultimately, triumph. The victim of its ambiguities turned out not to be the peoples America had set out to defend—on the whole successfully—but the American conscience. Tormenting itself in its traditional quest for moral perfection, America would emerge, after more than a generation of struggle, lacerated by its exertions and controversies, yet having achieved almost everything it had set out to do.[11]

Managing and defeating the Soviet Union was about managing a world in which two disconnected blocs sought relative influence and global power. The friction between these two blocs was immense and dangerous. Yet, we were able to understand our adversary clearly, intuit our fundamental advantages over it, and sustain and evolve our strategy over multiple decades, bringing about a peaceful, though generally unanticipated, end to the Cold War.

In the case of China, we live in a world that is defined today not by competing blocs but by economic integration. This integration is not only between nations around the world—the result of decades of post–Cold War globalization—but perhaps most importantly at present, this is most pronounced between the US and China, which have the world's largest bilateral trading relationship, albeit one that exists disproportionately in China's favor.

America's choice to engage China economically, bringing it into the global trading system, making it party to the world's most important economic and political institutions from the World Bank to the World Trade Organization, and integrating our economies in every possible manner, rather than choosing to contain China or place conditions on economic engagement in the post–Cold War era, is the source of our troubles today. And yet, an important battle is already being fought and won to change decades' worth of failed American strategy toward China. American leaders and policymakers have turned our country away from a self-defeating, myopic strategy of engagement with China, which began with Henry Kissinger's secret visit to Beijing in 1971, and toward a strategy of global competition with Beijing. This change from engagement to competition represents what former national security advisor H. R. McMaster has called "the most significant shift in US foreign policy since the end of the Cold War."[12] Yet, though our foreign policy is changing, we still lack a long-term vision of victory. We still lack a twenty-first-century global grand strategy that is shaped around the challenge posed by our most significant rival. The current shift in American foreign policy paves the way for an essential evolution. If we can understand the nature of this contest and refashion a world in which China's ascendancy has stalled, while the Allied order is rebuilt in such a way that it becomes insurmountable for Beijing's ambitions, we will turn the tide and leave our opponent behind, much as we did with the USSR. In this case it means not simply managing the friction between two disconnected blocs, but effecting the right levels of separation and divergence between two opposing systems, and producing a new ascendancy for America and the world's democracies.

To begin our journey, we should recognize that our contest with China will take place in a series of fundamental arenas, which this book explores in detail.

To win this contest, America must understand four arenas of victory.[13] Each arena is not equal to the other. Without victory in one above all, the possibility of victory may never come to pass. We can win in two or three and still lose, but if we win the right ones, we will win the contest as a whole. If each arena is won, and victory is sustained and held, the world can be rebuilt and the defining geopolitical challenge of our century will end in a second era of prosperity and power for the world's free nations. America must know these arenas, understand their contours and consequences, and we must be victorious in each of them:

The Economic Arena
The Diplomatic Arena
The Military Arena
The Arena of Ideas

Economic power is the primary arena of American strategic victory. In the case of strategic competition with China, it is the overriding arena of victory that will enable victory in other realms. In this decisive decade—the decade that will determine the *course* of our *entire* global competition with the People's Republic of China—we must first win and hold the Economic Arena. Without this, victory in the others cannot be sustained.

So, to begin, let us turn first to the Economic Arena.

It is not the critic who counts; not the man who points out how the strong man stumbles, or where the doer of deeds could have done them better. The credit belongs to the man who is actually in the arena, whose face is marred by dust and sweat and blood; who strives valiantly; who errs, who comes short again and again, because there is no effort without error and shortcoming; but who does actually strive to do the deeds; who knows great enthusiasms, the great devotions; who spends himself in a worthy cause; who at the best knows in the end the triumph of high achievement, and who at the worst, if he fails, at least fails while daring greatly, so that his place shall never be with those cold and timid souls who neither know victory nor defeat.

—Theodore Roosevelt, 1910

PART ONE

THE ECONOMIC ARENA

On February 24, 2022, Russian missiles began to rain down on Ukraine. Armored columns soon followed. Russian president Vladimir Putin's invasion had begun, shattering decades of major power peace in Europe and returning the world to an era in which authoritarian powers are willing to openly use their armies to advance their aims. Just weeks before, the governments of Russia and China had issued a joint statement at the Winter Olympics in Beijing. Putin and Chinese Communist Party Chairman Xi Jinping announced a "no limits" partnership in which "there are no 'forbidden' areas of cooperation," outlining a shared desire to confront and fight against the American-led international order. Building on several years' worth of speeches by Vladimir Putin, and on a China–Russia "comprehensive strategic partnership of coordination" two decades in the making, the statement issued by the world's two largest dictatorships included joint opposition to "further enlargement of NATO" and a Russian pledge to recognize that "Taiwan is an inalienable part of China." In a thinly veiled swipe at America and its Allies in Europe and Asia, the statement also declared that "Russia and China stand against attempts by external forces to undermine security and stability in their common adjacent regions, intend to counter interference by outside forces in the internal affairs of sovereign countries under any pretext . . . and will increase cooperation in the aforementioned areas."[1] China and Russia's joint challenge to the United States, to the world's democracies, and to the existing international order was mutually declared in its full depth and breadth.

The American economic response to Russian aggression in Ukraine was swift and powerful. As Putin's military advanced toward Kiev and Kharkiv, the United States ushered in a new era of Western economic warfare, the likes of which we have never seen in the globalized post–Cold War world. Russia's leaders, by all appearances, believed they were prepared for economic measures taken by the US and our Allies. Attempting what Chatham House scholar David Lubin terms "Fortress Economics," the Russian government had built up several hundred billion dollars in foreign exchange reserves, aiming to withstand the sanctions that America could deploy once the invasion commenced.[2] Little of that preparation mattered. The initial fall of the ruble and contraction of the Russian economy demonstrated that Russia's precursory actions were inadequate.[3] After decades of utilizing sanctions against countries such as North Korea and Iran, policymakers in America and Europe were thinking bigger when it came to the Economic Arena.

Even since 2018, when the world economy was rocked by the beginning of the US-China trade war and America began to ask how far economic engagement with China should go, we have not seen anything implemented on the scale of what took shape in the early weeks of Russia's invasion of Ukraine. Prior to the war, as the Russian invasion grew more likely, the US and our Allies began to design state-killer sanctions that could produce enormous effects on a trillion-dollar, G20 economy. Russia, as a major producer of energy and agricultural goods; as the world's largest country by landmass; as the world's largest nuclear force other than the United States, is a far different target than North Korea or Iran. Our economic toolkit had to be deployed on a larger scale. As the British government said in January 2022, new Allied sanctions would target "any individual and business of economic or strategic significance to the Kremlin." Then-British foreign secretary Liz Truss explained prior to the war that, "Currently, the economic sanctions are fairly narrowly drawn, so we could only target companies with a direct involvement in destabilising Ukraine. . . . What we are looking to do is widen that, so any company of interest to the Kremlin and the regime in Russia would be able to be targeted, so there will be nowhere to hide for Putin's oligarchs, for Russian companies involved in propping up the Russian state." She added that, "Nothing is off the table. . . . What the legislation enables us to do is hit a much wider variety of targets."[4] America and its Allies prepared to apply powerful economic sanctions, not on a mere "rogue state," but on another major power. In the days following Russia's invasion of Ukraine, the world's democracies ushered in an era of economic warfare in a globalized world.

Two elements are most important in the actions taken against Russia in the Economic Arena. First are the policy actions initiated by Allied governments working together and led by the United States. Second are the actions taken by leading American and European multinational corporations in response to the crisis in Ukraine. The combination of macro- and microeconomic pressure on Russia has begun to lower the curtain on an era of unobstructed economic engagement between democracies and autocracies. It has also shown us what is possible and necessary on the road ahead with the People's Republic of China.

First, the US government's utilization of strategic rather than pinprick sanctions—cutting Russian banks from the international financial system, terminating Russia's access to SWIFT, and a bipartisan congressional vote to end Russia's "most favored nation" status as a trading partner of the United States—all demonstrated the US government's ability to act decisively against an adversary when it comes to financial market access and bilateral trade. Second, corporate flight from Russia marked a change in many companies' understanding of globalization and geopolitical risk: the realization that international security, moral character, and geopolitical realities must sometimes prevail over business interests. Companies that have remained silent on genocide and other human rights atrocities in China chose to leave Russia in a matter of days or weeks after the invasion of Ukraine. Business leaders have now seen the consequences of real geopolitical risk and the problems of building businesses in authoritarian nations with genuine military ambitions. The effects on Russia have been profound: its loss of access to American and global capital, foreign technology, and to the world's leading global brands has built upon years of smaller-scale sanctions levied against it following its annexation of Ukraine's Crimea in 2014. Russia's commercial and financial isolation now exists on such a scale that its place in the world economy was transformed in just a matter of weeks. Hundreds of the world's leading brands ceased or suspended business operations in Russia, leading to the kind of commercial isolation of a major power that we have not seen since the Cold War world was split between two competing economic blocs. The benefits to Russia of thirty years of globalization and commercial engagement were essentially halted in thirty days of worldwide reckoning with Putin's military ambition.

In the aftermath of Putin's invasion, as Western companies step out of Russia, Chinese companies are staying in, consolidating influence and potentially long-term economic control over the world's largest nuclear power. As Exxon, Shell, and British Petroleum began partnership terminations, exits, and divestments in Russia, leaving behind multibillion-dollar stakes in oil and gas fields, China's state-owned oil majors—China National Offshore Oil Corporation, China National Petroleum Company, and Sinopec—began working jointly to pick up stakes in their energy and land-rich northern neighbor.[5] As shipping majors MSC and Maersk ceased container shipping to Russia, Boeing suspended maintenance support for Russian airlines, and brands from General Motors to Ford to Coca-Cola suspended or ceased business operations in Russia, many of China's top companies continued business as usual.[6] Chinese ambassador Zhang Hanhui reportedly convened a meeting of Chinese business leaders in Moscow in March 2022, calling on them to "fill the void" in the Russian market.[7] The suspension of shipments and operations by Apple, Samsung, Nokia, and Ericsson created substantial opportunities for Chinese smartphone and telecommunications providers such as Oppo, Xiaomi, and Huawei-spinoff company Honor, which, according to *Fortune* magazine, captured much of the market share left behind by Western multinationals.[8] Researchers led by Jeffrey Sonnenfeld at Yale have shown that as of 2022 even China's most famous global companies—some of whom are still listed on American stock exchanges or in joint ventures with major American companies—continue to do "business as usual" in Russia many months after the invasion of Ukraine. Alibaba is "still operating in Russia," ANT Group remains in a joint venture with the Russian Sovereign Wealth Fund, Didi (Uber's global rival) "explicitly reversed [its] decision to exit Russia," Haier (formerly GE's consumer appliance division) is "planning expansion in Russia," JD.com's "Russian store is still fully operational," China's Semiconductor Manufacturing International Corporation (SMIC) "defies US sanctions by continuing to export to Russia," and Tencent is making a "major investment" in one of Russia's key technology firms.[9] As multinationals from the world's democracies leave Russia in exodus, the Russia–China economic relationship will deepen, accelerating the return of a world defined by two rival economic blocs.

America and our Allies have begun to see what we are able to do in the Economic Arena. Our adversaries have witnessed the extraordinary potential of our economic toolkit. While the economic consequences for Russia are a clear demonstration of Allied capabilities, the response to Russia is a case of punitive action in reaction to military aggression. What is needed is the ability to deal with a challenger that dwarfs the Russian Federation—our path must be more thorough and strategic. What is needed is not just the ability to apply punitive action, but rather the complete transformation of the global economy through a new economic strategy.

A NEW
ECONOMIC STRATEGY

At the start of the 2020s, conventional wisdom holds that America is set to lose the economic contest with China. Leaders and thinkers from the public and private sectors have determined that it cannot be won. Worse, many of the world's leading businesses, investment banks, and consulting firms have mistaken China's economic ascendancy for a spectacular opportunity. Rather than grasping the potential transformation of world order and turning point in history that jeopardizes the security and prosperity of the United States, our Allies, and the world's democracies, business leaders often see unmatched market opportunities in China. In the words of Starbucks founder Howard Schultz in 2022, "We're going to open up one store every nine hours in China. We have 6,000 stores in China. By 2025, China will be bigger than the US, so Starbucks is ready for this moment in time."[10] As Nike CEO John Donahoe remarked in 2021, "Nike is a brand that is of China and for China."[11] From investment banks to global consulting firms, projections on China envision a world in 2030 where this nation has surpassed the United States as the world's largest economic power. Under "Five reasons to invest in China," J. P. Morgan Asset Management, a division of America's largest bank, states: "We estimate that by 2027 it will overtake the United States to become the largest economy in the world. This is two years earlier than we had estimated pre-pandemic."[12] Jamie Dimon, J.

P. Morgan's chairman and CEO, states that, "[Although] America will still be the most prosperous nation on the planet, they'll be smaller than China."[13] Others concur. In the words of former US treasury secretary Henry Paulson, "[U]nless something changes dramatically, China will remain the world's fastest-growing major economy, surpassing the US in size in the foreseeable future."[14] From *Fortune* magazine to the World Economic Forum, leading international institutions have projected or parroted that China will eventually become the world's largest economy, matching its billion-plus population size and prime position in global trade in goods.[15]

It is hard to contemplate how America, a nation of 330 million people, could maintain the economic lead over a nation of 1.4 billion. As economists at British investment bank Standard Chartered wrote in their 2019 projection that China would become the top economy by 2030, "Our long-term growth forecasts are underpinned by one key principle: Countries' share of world GDP should eventually converge with their share of the world's population."[16] Even Elon Musk, arguably the world's greatest industrialist, agrees: "A thing that will feel pretty strange is that the Chinese economy is probably going to be at least twice as big as the United States' economy, maybe three times." Grasping the problem better than many in the business world, he adds that "the foundation of war is economics. If you have half the resources of the counterparty then you better be real innovative. If you're not innovative, you're going to lose."[17]

The point has made its way to Washington, affecting the assessments of leading American strategists, and creating a climate in which balancing limited American resources against expanding Chinese economic and military power appears to be the only way forward. In the words of former State Department official A. Wess Mitchell, "[T]he defining characteristic of the emerging international landscape is the array of constraints that it presents to the exercise of American power. The rise of China confronts the United States with arguably the most capable adversary it has faced in its history as a global power. Most projections show China having, by 2030, an economy that will be between 1.5 and 2 times the size of America's and a population more than four times as large."[18]

The consequences of this should be lost on no one. If China succeeds in surpassing the United States as the world's leading economy, it would be the first time since the War of 1812 that America would have to contend with a military adversary that wields greater economic power, and the first time in well over a century that we would have a rival of any kind for overall economic power. While our bankers and business leaders may mistake this outcome for opportunity, Americans must not. The most important task of American grand strategy must be to ensure that we remain the world's leading, and yes, largest economy.[19] While banks and businesses project these outcomes to the world and national security strategists deal with the consequences for America, there is no greater believer in the necessity of this outcome—China as the world's largest economy—than the Chinese Communist Party. The global grand strategy of the Chinese Communist Party rests upon the goal of economic supremacy.

Whether it is the pronouncements of Chinese Communist Party diplomats and propagandists, or the intuitions of the founders of the People's Republic of China, those who shape China's path and vision have long been focused on building economic power. As Foreign Ministry Spokesman Lijian Zhao tweeted in December 2019, "China will overtake US in ten years. China's win is unstoppable."[20] Even Mao Zedong, chairman and founder of the People's Republic of China, believed that economic supremacy was an essential objective for the "New China." While Mao was hamstrung by communist orthodoxy and unable to act upon this vision—that was left to Deng Xiaoping—he always viewed China as a place of immense economic potential and believed that this would be a critical advantage in China's long-term contest for power with the United States. As Mao stated in 1955: "Our objective is to catch up with America and then to surpass America. America only has one hundred million people or more; our population is over six hundred million."[21]

Counterarguments exist, from China's long-term demographic decline—whose most serious consequences are likely to take place in the 2030s, rather than in this decade—to softening growth rates and expanding Communist Party control over China's leading entrepreneurs and strategic industries.[22] However, what remains is a fundamental convergence between the desire for Chinese economic growth held by Western businesses and investment institutions and the strategic objectives of the Chinese Communist Party, which believes that economic ascendancy is the key to global power and to strategic victory over the United States. American grand strategy must break this convergence, align American businesses and investment houses with our near- and long-term national security, and triumph over the Chinese Communist Party in the global Economic Arena. How can this be done? The answer rests in a two-pronged strategy: economic containment of the People's Republic of China together with US and Allied economic growth. Our long-range strategy must be to maintain and increase our share of global wealth and gross domestic product (GDP) while slowing China's economic growth.

Historically, the American share of global GDP has been as high as 40 percent in 1960 after the Second World War and baby boom, and maintaining economic superiority over the Soviet Union by a wide margin for the duration of the forty-five-year Cold War.[23] While this percentage has dropped to a smaller share today, it has not been a matter of continual decline but rather influenced by strategy, policy, and international conditions. For example, GDP share jumped to 34 percent from 25 percent from 1980–85 and again from 25 percent to 30 percent from 1995–2000. Even with China's rise in the early twenty-first century, the United States continues to hold the largest share of global GDP, roughly 23.9 percent with a GDP of $23 trillion in 2021.[24] China comes in second at roughly 18.4 percent with a GDP of $17.7 trillion in 2021.[25] Figures on national wealth demonstrate wider divergence between the United States and China: 30.2 percent of the world's total for the United States ($126.3 trillion in national wealth) compared to 17.9 percent for China ($74.9 trillion) in 2020.[26] The United States holds a meaningful but waning advantage in national GDP and a larger advantage when it comes to national wealth in total.

Our economic strategy must focus on *increasing this relative advantage.* If we are able to do this, not only will we maintain our most important advantage for the duration of the contest ahead, but we will also break the foundations of China's Vision of Victory, the Chinese Communist Party's grand strategy to become the world's dominant power from a preeminent position in the global economy. Success in the Economic Arena—which lays the foundations for victory in our larger contest—can be measured in terms of GDP and national wealth as a share of the global total and also relative to our adversaries in Beijing. Even as China's growth rates slow, it has added the equivalent of nearly the entire Australian economy each year (on average) since 2016. In 2021, picking up from slower COVID growth rates, China added *a total of $3 trillion* *to its national GDP, the equivalent of two Australias in one year.*[27] China may be growing more slowly now, but it grows from a larger and larger economic base. We are still in the lead, but we are losing ground.

The 2020s are when our advantage may be lost for good.

In order to achieve our goals, we must focus on two aspects of economic competition: containment and growth. We must remind ourselves of the fundamental weakness in China's long-term strategy: China's ascendancy depends on its access to the global economy, and above all to the American and Allied economies. This access is ours to grant or deny. China's rise is in our hands, and given the Chinese Communist Party's atrocities and ambitions, this rise need not continue. The US-China contest for the twenty-first century is likely to be won or lost in this decade. The 2020s present America with a potentially fatal outcome but also with an exquisite strategic opportunity. The fatal outcome is what follows should China become the world's leading economy, gaining unprecedented resources with which to wage and win long-term competition with America and our Allies. This advantage—which we have held in every existential contest of the past hundred years—would be transferred to our primary adversary.

Here is our exquisite opportunity: in the 2020s and 2030s, the global economy will go through a whole-of-economy transformation in technological and industrial power the likes of which has happened only three times in the past two hundred years. If we are able to seize this moment—what many have termed the "fourth Industrial Revolution" or "Industry 4.0"—we will be able to transform our productive capability and create an economic edge that allows a nation of three hundred million to outcompete a billion under authoritarian rule.[28] Maintaining this edge could allow us to achieve a strategic end state that few envision: a second Great Divergence in history. The Great Divergence was a period following the first Industrial Revolution when European empires gained an industrial advantage over other empires across the world and became the preeminent powers for the period that followed. This was the result in large part of advances in technology and industry that created superior economic and military power. With a second Great Divergence—not between Europe and the world but between democracies and authoritarian nations—the United States and our diverse range of Allies, particularly the world's democracies from

Europe to Asia, could decisively win the contest for the twenty-first century and leave Beijing far behind. Economic divergence can defeat the outcome that the Chinese Communist Party wishes for—China's ascendancy to economic preeminence and thus to dominance through superior economic and ultimately military power. Economic divergence can also create a new American ascendancy, reverse the decline that many believe we are going through, and build a new American and Allied century.

The contest ahead is a contest for the outcome of twenty-first-century history. It is not one that America can afford to lose. If we can win the Economic Arena, achieve a new economic divergence between China and the democracies, then we can reverse the turning point in history that Beijing envisions, and secure a new century in which power is held by nations defined by rights and liberty. To do this, economic containment of China, along with American and Allied growth, are the essential planks.

The world economy is a battlefield. Multinational corporations compete for market share and expansion. Commerce does not reliably prevent war between states—two World Wars in an interconnected Europe is testament to this. The split economies of the Cold War world in which two superpowers avoided full-scale military conflict presents an important counterpoint. Private businesses are essentially free to build ties with other nations regardless of rising geopolitical risks or national security challenges. For the Chinese Communist Party, state-owned and state-backed enterprises are the essential battle units of Chinese economic strategy. For the United States and our Allies, it is the private sector company, the American or Allied multinational corporation. Given the current state of affairs—engagement with China by leading American companies and investment institutions—our vital corporations have drifted far from their necessary role in American security and prosperity, and toward dependency and exploitation by Beijing. American corporate exposure and involvement in China is creating risks and perils to the United States and to global stability. We must bring American business and American national security into alignment, as they have been aligned during our most challenging and consequential past contests.

THE BUSINESS OF VICTORY

The American Multinational Corporation vs. the Chinese State-Owned Enterprise

L ook again at this description of America in 1942. It was a moment, before victory was assured, but after the country had awakened to a challenge that would decide our destiny and also that of the world. The father of Robert D. Kaplan, perhaps the leading American author on foreign affairs, knew in this moment that we would win:

> At a rail junction near Cairo, Illinois, the sun was setting in rich colors over the prairie. Other trains were then converging from several tracks onto a single line that would take the troops to points along the East Coast, where ships to Europe awaited. Across a wider arc, the only thing he saw were trains and more trains, with soldiers looking out through every window as each train curved toward the others against a flat and limitless landscape lit red by the sun. "Just looking at that scene, that's the moment when I knew we were going to win the war."[29]

American logistical and industrial power—Roosevelt's Arsenal of Democracy—underwrote the destruction of the fascist powers in Europe and Asia and the establishment of several generations of American-led peace among the world's major powers. None of this could have happened without our companies, our entrepreneurs, our industrial workforce, and our business leaders: "They wore business suits, dungarees and flannel shirts, spectacles and Stetsons, Homburg hats and hard hats, lab coats and welding leathers and patterned headscarves. They were the American businessmen, engineers, production managers, and workers both male and female who built the most awesome military machine in history: the arsenal of democracy that armed the Allies and defeated the Axis."[30] As described by Arthur Herman, author of *Freedom's Forge: How American Business Produced Victory in World War II*: "Together they produced two-thirds of all Allied military equipment used in World War II. That included 86,000 tanks, 2.5 million trucks and a half million jeeps, 286,000 warplanes, 8,800 naval vessels, 5,600 merchant ships, 434 million tons of steel, 2.6 million machine guns, and 41 *billion* rounds of ammunition—not to mention the greatest superbomber of the war, the B-29, and the atomic bomb."[31]

Companies like Alcoa, Boeing, Chrysler, Douglas Aircraft, Dow Chemical, Dupont, Ford, General Electric, General Motors, Goodyear, and Grumman Aviation, and entrepreneurs like Andrew Higgins—whom General Dwight Eisenhower called "the man who won the war for us"—converted American economic potential into overwhelming military might.[32] Our world-leading industries, the resources of our continent and our people, and the providence of our geography enabled us to achieve total victory in the Second World War. Take the example of America's automotive industry: "Here was a network that could mobilize talent, information, and resources from iron and steel to plate glass, copper, lead, leather, and motor oil, for the defense effort."[33] The critical importance of individual companies cannot be overstated. Many of them are still with us today, having played their role in vital moments in American history. For example, "General Motors alone would make 10 percent of every-thing America produced during World War II, including thousands of aircraft engines, hundreds of different parts for Boeing, Martin and North American, and entire airplanes for Grumman."[34] American economic power has arguably been the deciding element of the major contests of the past hundred years. In the decade ahead of the Second World War, America's economic advantages were profound. In 1937, the United States had *seventeen times* the national income of Japan, and *three times* the national income of Japan and Germany combined, in addition to far outstripping both in industrial power.[35] It was up to us to mobilize, to utilize, and to execute a global plan based upon an overwhelming advantage in resources and mobilization.

What if we had not had superior networks that, in Herman's words, could mobilize talent, information, and resources? What if we had not had the fundamental industries that formed the bedrock of American advantage? What might the twentieth century have looked like instead?

Today, we are rapidly losing, and in some cases have already lost these critical advantages. And China has worked methodically to gain these same advantages over us. China's intellectual property theft, coercion of our businesses, subsidization of its own industries and companies, and in some cases, the destruction of entire American companies and decimation of American industries have taken a toll on us and our readiness for either competition or conflict. Through decades' worth of "engagement" with China, America has transferred manufacturing and industrial capacity, technology, and capital to our primary adversary, a process that we may eventually regard as one of our greatest mistakes in history. Kaplan's epiphany was perceiving the massive scale of American troop trains, transports, and logistical power.

Today it is easier to imagine a scene of such industrial scope and scale taking place *not here in America, but in China.*

In the United States, it was the Second World War that galvanized the conversion of economic might into military power. But in China, the Communist Party has been busy with a massive military build-up despite a long period of global peace: "Since 2014, China has launched more warships, submarines, support ships and major amphibious vessels than the entire number of ships now serving in the United Kingdom's fleet. . . . Between 2015 and 2017, China launched almost 400,000 tonnes of naval vessels, about twice the output of US shipyards in that period [according to the International Institute of Strategic Studies]."[36] China is the uncontested leader in the world's rail, maritime, and steel industries and is responsible, by some estimates, for nearly 30 percent of the world's total manufacturing output, almost double that of the United States.[37] Its state-owned and state-backed super-companies and mega-banks dominate not only the country's enormous internal market, but have extended their reach across most of the world. All of these entities, unlike those of the American private sector, must work at the behest of the Chinese Communist

Party and participate in its global grand strategy. It is China today, not America, that has grasped the meaning of industrial might for military power, and the importance of foundational strategic industries.

Take, for example, US trade representative Katherine Tai's assessment of China's rise in the global steel industry:

> Even with the phase-one agreement in place, China's government continues to pour billions of dollars into targeted industries and continues to shape its economy to the will of the state, hurting the interests of workers here in the US and around the world. Let's look at the steel industry. In 2000, there were more than 100 US steel companies. We produced 100 million metric tons of steel annually. And the industry employed 136,000 people in communities across the country. Soon after, China started building its own steel plants. Its production capacity ballooned, depriving US steel companies of valuable market opportunities. Low-priced Chinese steel flooded the global market, driving out businesses in the United States and around the world. . . .
>
> Today China produces over 1 billion metric tons annually and accounts for nearly 60 percent of global steel production. China produces more steel in a single month than the United States and most other countries in the world produce in an entire year. In the US, employment in the steel industry has dropped 40 percent since 2000.[38]

Even as Beijing subsidizes its own industries, engages in global intellectual property theft, and executes its global economic strategy, many of our own American companies, once the backbone of the Arsenal of Democracy, have now become political and economic captives—hostages in the China market. This is a problem of our own making.

In 2018, according to the US Department of Commerce, China was the third largest market outside of America for US multinational enterprises—bringing in a total of $580.1 billion in sales, second only to sales in the United Kingdom and Canada.[39] In 2019, the figure was $573.4 billion, as reported by the US Department of Commerce's Bureau of Economic Analysis.[40] While hundreds of billions of dollars sounds enormous, and while the US-China trade relationship—and trade deficit—have been the subject of enormous discussion in recent years, consider this: the total *earnings* of US multinationals in China is only $38.2 billion. That's roughly the equivalent of the cost of three US aircraft carriers or one to two nuclear power plants. *It is just 2.6 percent of multinational profits worldwide.* For America, a nation with a $23 trillion GDP and $126 trillion in total national wealth, $38.2 billion does not even make a full percentage point of our total economic power. Even the total of $573.4 billion is just 2.5 percent of our GDP and less than half of 1 percent of our total national wealth.

Let's go deeper into these numbers. Of total sales by US multinationals in all countries worldwide in 2019, China is only 7.4 percent. When we add Hong Kong, that figure reaches 9.6 percent, larger but still a small amount of global totals. When we look at *majority-owned* foreign affiliates in China—entities where our companies actually have *ownership control*, as opposed to 50/50 joint ventures or minority stakes—the numbers drop substantially: $378.8 billion in sales and $28.7 billion in earnings. Of total assets held by American multinationals worldwide, amounting to a total of $30.7 *trillion*, China is only 2.5 percent at $778.5 *billion* (Hong Kong brings this figure to 4.4 percent). When we look at majority-owned enterprises, China accounts for far less in total assets: 1.6 percent of worldwide totals. China's percentage totals are small in size when compared to the majority of multinational concentrations in Europe, Japan, and the rest of the planet. This does not even include multinational statistics in the United States itself. For Net PPE (property, plant, and equipment), in other words *real, physical assets,* US multinationals (majority owned) had $67.8 billion in China, compared to $1.42 trillion worldwide, meaning China amounts to only 4.8 percent.

Individual companies have taken on enormous exposure to China— Apple, Boeing, Caterpillar, General Motors, Starbucks, and Nike are commonly known examples—and single industries such as semiconductors are dangerously based on a global supply chain and market ecosystems that must be reformed.[41] However, the whole ball game of US-China economic relations may not be nearly so grand as it often seems. The US-China trade relationship should also be put in the context of total American economic power. Let's look at exports to China. According to the US trade representative, the United States exported $106.4 billion in goods to China in 2019—just 6.7 percent of our total exports to the world. As a share of GDP, US exports were only 7.4 percent that year, rendering exports to China less than half of 1 percent of US GDP.[42] Imports from China are generally three to four times larger than exports—and the total volume of trade is growing—but this is still small in the context of our entire economic output. Countless experts and institutions puzzle over US-China "decoupling." Numerous businesses and lobbying groups push against tariffs and decry rising US-China geopolitical tensions. However, America's economic exposure to China need not constrain our strategic choices. We can pull back engagement with China in the interest of a greater need—the need to win the Economic Arena.

Today's American corporations have taken on dangerous and enormous risk in their quest for China's billion-person market. We have been here before. Not in the Cold War era when the world was split in two economic blocs, but in the decade ahead of the Second World War. At that time, leading American corporations were embedded in Nazi Germany, participating in the growth and industrialization of the German economy as Hitler began his road to war. In turn, German corporations, guided by the nature of the Nazi Party industrial state, were busy courting US industry and finance in order to strengthen their industrial capabilities after the First World War, which had devastated Germany. Despite mounting evidence of the nature of Germany's Nazi regime, American companies from General Motors to Standard Oil were busy doing business in the country and building up its strategic industries, their assets ultimately contributing to German wartime advantages.[43] American business leaders from IBM's Thomas Watson to Henry Ford were enmeshed in the ceremonies, performances, and politics of the Third Reich, presaging the trap that many of our business leaders today have fallen into in China. It was only after war broke out, after factories were seized and assets stolen, that American business wound up, for the most part, on the right side of history. Only from the ashes of their businesses in Germany did our companies become the heroes of the Arsenal of Democracy.

In the early twentieth century, in what was also a globalizing world of commerce, companies, and trade, many people falsely regarded economic "interdependence" as a way to avoid or prevent military conflict. Nobel Prize winner Norman Angell's book *The Great Illusion*, for example, supposed

that economic interdependence in Europe would obviate the chance of conflict between nation-states given the costs to all involved. Angell's book
was first released in 1909, just five years before the outbreak of the First
World War. His Nobel Peace Prize was conferred in 1933, the same year that
Hitler proclaimed the Third Reich and built Germany's first concentration
camps. Often in an interwar period, the success of global commerce leads
to delusions of stability between states. Business leaders were then, as now,
carried away by wishful thoughts of commerce as a means to pacify dangerous
nation-states. IBM's Thomas Watson's keynote address at the International
Chamber of Commerce in Berlin in 1937 was "World Peace Through World
Trade." On that same visit, Watson was honored by the Nazi regime with a
medal "to acknowledge the services of 'friendly foreigners' to the German
people" and "publicly expressed his gratitude to Hitler."[44] IBM's machines
would soon be used in the Holocaust.[45]

Companies today in China have already found themselves caught amid
Beijing's darkest practices: the human rights abuses and atrocities of the Chinese
Communist Party. Partnerships between US multinationals and their Chinese
counterparts mean that our companies are also tied to China's genocide and
military build-up. For example, in its report "Uyghurs for Sale: 'Re-education,'
Forced Labor, and Surveillance Beyond Xinjiang," the Australian Strategic
Policy Institute identified over eighty "well-known global brands in the tech-
nology, clothing, and automotive sectors" that have Uyghurs working under
conditions that "strongly suggest forced labour" in their factories in China.
According to this study, these companies are "potentially directly or indirectly
benefiting from the use of Uyghur workers outside Xinjiang through abusive
labour transfer programs as recently as 2019." Here is a partial list: Abercrombie
& Fitch, Acer, Adidas, Alstom, Amazon, Apple, BMW, Bosch, Calvin Klein,
Cisco, Dell, Gap, General Motors, Google, H&M, Hitachi, HP, Jaguar, L.L.
Bean, Lacoste, Land Rover, LG, Mercedes-Benz, Microsoft, Mitsubishi, Nike,
Nintendo, Nokia, Oculus, Panasonic, Polo Ralph Lauren, Puma, Samsung,
Sharp, Siemens, Sketchers, Sony, TDK, Tommy Hilfiger, Toshiba, Uniqlo,
Victoria's Secret, Volkswagen, Zara, and Zegna.[46] A congressional report in
March 2020 further substantiates these investigations, listing Adidas, Calvin
Klein, Campbell Soup Company, Costco, Espirit, Esquel Group, H&M, Kraft

Heinz, Nike, Patagonia, and Tommy Hilfiger, among others, as companies suspected of benefiting from forced labor in Xinjiang.[47]

In short, China's genocide has become America's—and the world's—supply chain.

The United States government has warned CEOs and business leaders about these practices, but companies and lobbying groups push back, and companies continue to prioritize the China market. In July 2020, the US Department of State, Department of the Treasury, Department of Commerce, and the Department of Homeland Security (DHS) issued the Xinjiang Supply Chain Business Advisory, which stated: "Businesses, individuals, and other persons, including but not limited to academic institutions, research service providers, and investors . . . that choose to operate in Xinjiang or engage with entities that use labor from Xinjiang elsewhere in China should be aware of reputational, economic, and, in certain instances, legal, risks associated with certain types of involvement with entities that engage in human rights abuses, which could include Withhold Release Orders (WROs), civil or criminal investigations, and export controls."[48] Then secretary of state Mike Pompeo announced that, "CEOs should read this notice carefully. . . . Be aware of the reputational, economic, and legal risks of supporting such assaults on human dignity."[49] In July 2021, the Biden administration updated the Xinjiang Supply Chain Business Advisory, including the following language about genocide and crimes against humanity in Xinjiang:

> The People's Republic of China (PRC) government continues to carry out genocide and crimes against humanity against Uyghurs and members of other ethnic and religious minority groups in the Xinjiang Uyghur Autonomous Region (Xinjiang), China. The PRC's crimes against humanity include imprisonment, torture, rape, forced sterilization, and persecution, including through forced labor and the imposition of draconian restrictions on freedom of religion or belief, freedom of expression, and freedom of movement.
>
> Businesses, individuals, and other persons, including but not limited to investors, consultants, labor brokers, academic institutions, and research service providers (hereafter "businesses and individuals") with

potential exposure to or connection with operations, supply chains, or laborers from the Xinjiang region, should be aware of the significant reputational, economic, and legal risks of involvement with entities or individuals in or linked to Xinjiang that engage in human rights abuses, including but not limited to forced labor and intrusive surveillance.[50]

While the notice is "explanatory only and does not have the force of law," it explains that,

> Given the severity and extent of these abuses, including widespread, state-sponsored forced labor and intrusive surveillance taking place amid ongoing genocide and crimes against humanity in Xinjiang, businesses and individuals that do not exit supply chains, ventures, and/or investments connected to Xinjiang could run a high risk of violating US law. Potential legal risks include: violation of statutes criminalizing forced labor including knowingly benefitting from participation in a venture, while knowing or in reckless disregard of the fact that the venture has engaged in forced labor; sanctions violations if dealing with designated persons; export control violations; and violation of the prohibition of importations of goods produced in whole or in part with forced labor or convict labor.[51]

Yet, despite the recognition that China's companies and practices are tied to military build-up, global geopolitical ambitions, and even what *both the Trump and Biden administrations* have firmly concluded are crimes against humanity, American business has not yet aligned with the cause of human rights and US national security. In November 2020, the *New York Times* reported that Nike, Coca-Cola, and Apple lobbied to "weaken" the Uyghur Forced Labor Prevention Act, a congressional bill that would ban imported goods made with forced labor in Xinjiang, the province where China's genocide is taking place.[52] The US Chamber of Commerce also issued its objection to the Uyghur Forced Labor Prevention Act, stating that "the Chamber believes that H.R. 6270, the 'Uyghur Forced Labor Disclosure Act of 2020,' and H.R. 6210, the 'Uyghur Forced Labor Prevention Act,' would prove ineffective and may hinder efforts to prevent human rights abuses." The Chamber of Commerce argued that "past attempts to utilize domestic US securities law to combat human rights abuses provide a cautionary tale," noting that attempts to prevent the mining of conflict materials in the Democratic Republic of the Congo, "in many cases worsened the situation on the ground in that country," and that "the absence of a qualified inspection and audit systems made it nearly impossible for companies to ensure accurate disclosures. This in turn caused many companies to implement a de facto embargo against material sourced in the region which then hurt legitimate miners."[53]

Rather than the world of *Freedom's Forge* or the Arsenal of Democracy, American businesses and business organizations today often push back against US government efforts to secure supply chains or change the structure of global trade. In addition to their exposure to human rights abuses, American companies have also become embedded in the development and optimization of China's economic power, as well as in some of Beijing's most important global strategies. Caterpillar, for example, a US Fortune 500 construction and engineering company, has been active in its collaboration with Beijing's global trade and infrastructure program, the "Belt and Road Initiative." One US Congressional hearing has referenced this aspect of Caterpillar's business.[54] The US China Economic and Security Review Commission explained Caterpillar's role in the "Belt and Road" as follows in an annual report to Congress:

> Supplying construction machinery: In 2016, Caterpillar released a white paper on its "vision and commitment for the shared success of [BRI]" in which the company outlined potential areas of cooperation with Chinese companies in BRI countries, including partnering on infrastructure projects and providing project finance. In September 2017 Caterpillar CEO Jim Umpleby said the company "[is] working with Chinese SOEs in 20 [BRI] countries on projects ranging from roads, ports, mines, and oil fields." This includes supplying machinery, training, and maintenance services to China Communications Construction Company for the renovation of the Zhrobin-Bobruisk expressway in Belarus, which was completed in July 2016.

In November 2017, Caterpillar and Chinese SOE China Energy Investment Corporation signed a five-year strategic cooperation framework agreement outlining future agreements for mining equipment sales and rental, technology applications, and product support provided by Caterpillar.

Financing: Caterpillar is providing project finance for Chinese companies to boost BRI sales, according to company executives. The company does not disclose data for such lending.[55]

In other words, one of America's leading industrial companies has provided financing and technological support for Beijing's flagship program for global geopolitical influence, while partnering with China's state-owned enterprises, including China Communications Construction Corporation, a company that built China's military islands in the South China Sea. In marketing materials still available online in 2022, Caterpillar said this about the Belt and Road Initiative:

Capturing Opportunity with the Belt and Road Initiative

Did you know that China plans to build 60 new airports by 2020, India's national railway is laying 9.5 kilometers of tracks every day, and there are about 300 construction projects underway in Africa?

To address this opportunity, the Chinese government launched the Belt & Road Initiative in 2013. It's an ambitious, forward-looking, multi-generational project that will contribute to economic development, grow industrialization and improve living standards throughout multiple nations along its routes.

This initiative is well-suited for Caterpillar, our dealers and our customers now and for many years to come. It includes building roads, highways, overpasses, bridges, dams and other essential infrastructure in Africa, China and the Middle East.

Check out how Caterpillar, our dealers and our customers are already hard at work supporting this initiative.[56]

General Electric, once a backbone company of US industrial power, has also been involved in the "Belt and Road Initiative." As the same report to Congress points out:

> Supplying power equipment: In 2016, GE received $2.3 billion in orders for natural gas turbines and other power equipment from Chinese EPC [engineering, procurement, and construction] firms to install overseas, including in Pakistan, Bangladesh, Kenya, and Laos. In 2014, GE received $400 million in orders from Chinese firms for equipment to install overseas. According to GE China CEO Rachel Duan, "Africa is the market offering the greatest market potential for GE and Chinese EPC firms, followed by the Middle East, South Asia, Southeast Asia, and Latin America."
>
> Financing: In November 2017, GE Energy Financial Services and China's Silk Road Fund signed a cooperation agreement to launch an energy infrastructure investment platform to invest in power grid, renewable energy, and oil and gas infrastructure in BRI countries. Separately, Jay Ireland, CEO of GE Africa, said in 2016 that the company had set up a $1 billion infrastructure fund to help finance projects in Africa. According to Mr. Ireland, one-third of Chinese EPC companies' equipment orders with GE in 2016 were destined for projects in Africa.[57]

The report to Congress also cites Fluor, AECOM, Black & Veatch, Honeywell, Citigroup, and J. P. Morgan's roles in contributing to China's Belt and Road. In other words, leading American companies have wrapped themselves into at least one of China's signature geopolitical initiatives, and some have made it a core platform for their own growth strategies. Inside the China market, Caterpillar's efforts are even larger. Like many multinational corporations, Caterpillar has design, engineering, manufacturing, and research and development facilities, as well as test sites. Here's an example of what their Wuxi research and development center does: "The Caterpillar China R&D Center aims to provide cost-competitive, world-class research and development in products, technologies, engineering services, as well as supply chain management service. It supports Caterpillar's manufacturing facilities and supply base across China, allowing Caterpillar to get closer to customers and take advantage of regional engineering talent to develop leading products."[58] The company's operations, having served the China market for decades now, include the following raft of legal entities in China:

Caterpillar (China) Investment Co., Ltd.
Caterpillar (China) Financial Leasing Co., Ltd.
Caterpillar (Qingzhou) Ltd
Caterpillar Remanufacturing Services (Shanghai) Co., Ltd.
Caterpillar Marine Trading (Shanghai) Co., Ltd.
Caterpillar Marine Trading (Shanghai) Co., Ltd. Pudong Branch
Caterpillar Logistics (Shanghai) Co., Ltd.
Caterpillar (Shanghai) Trading Co., Ltd.
Caterpillar Propulsion Shanghai Co., Ltd
Caterpillar Financial Leasing (Shanghai) Co., Ltd.
CCI Shanghai branch
Caterpillar Remanufacturing Services (Shanghai) Co., Ltd.
Caterpillar Marine Trading (Shanghai) Co., Ltd.
Caterpillar Marine Trading (Shanghai) Co., Ltd. Pudong Branch
Caterpillar Logistics (Shanghai) Co., Ltd.
Caterpillar Propulsion Shanghai Co., Ltd
Caterpillar Financial Leasing (Shanghai) Co., Ltd.
AsiaTrak (Tianjin) Ltd.
Asia Power Systems (Tianjin) Ltd.
Caterpillar Tianjin Ltd.
Caterpillar (Wujiang) Ltd.
Caterpillar (China) Machinery Components Co., Ltd.
Caterpillar R&D Center (China) Co., Ltd.
Perkins Small Engines (Wuxi) Co., Ltd,
Perkins Power Systems Technology (Wuxi) Co., Ltd.
Caterpillar (Xuzhou) Ltd.
Caterpillar Paving Products (Xuzhou) Ltd.[59]

The nature of today's "globally integrated" or "multinational corporation" in China is building China's industrial strength at home and supporting its strategic initiatives abroad. How can companies with this kind of exposure to our primary adversary be expected to take the side of the United States of America in a time of crisis? This position has become the norm for many of America's biggest companies that have substantial China operations.

America's corporations are arguably the most important conduit of capital, technology, and know-how into China. These American entities expose themselves to human rights abuses while supporting the industrial capacity and global strategic programs of the Chinese Communist Party. There's a third and perhaps more dangerous aspect of corporate engagement in China: contributing to the Chinese Communist Party's Civil Military Fusion initiative, designed to incorporate innovation and technology from civilian sectors into Chinese military capabilities. Civil Military Fusion erases the barrier between civilian and military technology and industry. It expands the definition of dual-use systems *to essentially the whole economy.* The Chinese Communist Party has engaged its entire economy and many of its corporations—from technology companies that lead in artificial intelligence to logistics companies that deliver goods by air, road, and rail—in the project of building Chinese military power. While America fails to act in building a New Arsenal of Democracy, China systematically employs its corporations to build an Arsenal of Autocracy.

Here are two examples of Communist Party strategy and action when it comes to the integration of corporate and military power, across high-tech and low-tech industries:

In his discussion of China's 14th Five Year Plan and the MCF [military-civil fusion] strategy, Tan Yungang, a military acquisition expert, urged the formation of "national teams" made up of state-owned defense conglomerates and influential private enterprises in strategic emerging domains. Tan asked, "If Huawei, Tencent, Alibaba, Baidu are deeply integrated with Datang Telecom, Ziguang Group, Tsinghua Tongfang, and Tongxin Software, will Intel, Google, Microsoft, and Apple still be so full of swagger [牛]?"[60]

On October 23 [2019], the PLAAF Logistics Department signed logistics MCF strategic cooperation agreements with five leading logistics and delivery service companies: SF Express Group, China Railway Express Co., Ltd., China Post Express Logistics Co., Ltd., Debon Logistics, JD Logistics. The agreements were said to enable a civil-military integrated systematic, full-organization, full-coverage logistical delivery system, and included an important clause to guarantee contract fulfillment during wartime.[61]

China's railways, transportation companies, and technology companies, among many others, are integrating with the Chinese military.

Let's take a look at the risks that our leading technology companies have created for the United States by operating research and development centers in China and collaborating with China's own technology companies and institutions. In 2018, Tsinghua University in Beijing opened the Tsinghua University Institute for Artificial Intelligence, which "focuses on applied research geared towards the internationalization, intelligentization, and industrialization of the fourth technological revolution," stating that, "Our mission is to fuel the industrial upgrade and propel social advance [sic] with AI technologies. With university-enterprise as double engines for innovation, we aim to make breakthroughs in core AI technologies, develop future industry-leaders, and achieve leapfrog progress with the industry."[62] The institute was announced at the Tsinghua-Google Symposium in Beijing in 2018, with Google's AI chief Jeff Dean joining the Tsinghua University computer science advisory committee.[63] Just weeks prior to this announcement, You Zheng, vice president of Tsinghua University, said this about the importance of artificial intelligence for the Chinese military and Tsinghua's direct relationship with China's Central Military Commission:

In accordance with central requirements, Tsinghua University will closely integrate the national strategy of military-civilian integration and the AI superpower strategy. Tsinghua University was entrusted by the CMC Science and Technology Commission to take responsibility to construct the High-End Laboratory for Military Intelligence (军

事智能高端实验室). With regard to basic theories and core technologies, military intelligence and general AI possess commonalities. Therefore, Tsinghua University regards the construction of the High-End Laboratory for Military Intelligence as the core starting point for serving the AI superpower strategy.

In the process of constructing the High-End Laboratory for Military Intelligence (军事智能高端实验室), Tsinghua University adheres to the concept of gripping with both hands basic research and applied research. Premier Li Keqiang has repeatedly emphasized the importance of basic research. Without basic research acting as a support, it is difficult to sustain the development of high technologies, and it is also difficult to have real competitiveness. Therefore, the consolidation of basic research is a responsibility that colleges and universities should take on in the nation's AI strategy. At the same time, AI development in China has very large dividends in application scenarios, and applied technology research is also very important. Therefore, Tsinghua University insists on basic research as a support in applied technology research in AI talent training and scientific research innovation, with military requirements as a guide, promoting the development of basic AI research.[64]

Tsinghua, the vice president explains, "has a number of AI research bases, including the State Key Laboratory of Intelligent Technology and Systems (智能技术与系统"国家重点实验室) established in 1990 and the Intelligent Microsystems Ministry of Education Key Laboratory of the [sic] (智能微系统教育部重点实验室), and several AI teams." These teams are working directly with China's Central Military Commission, for example, on the "AI Theories and Crux Technologies for Future Human-Machine Cooperative (Combat) Operations" ("面向未来人机协同作战的人工智能理论与关键技术") project with total funding of over 100 million RMB [about $15 million] from the CMC Science and Technology Commission National Defense Frontier Innovation Special Zone (国防前沿创新特区). . . . (They) advanced the achievement of innovative results deep learning adversarial attack and defense (对抗性攻防) theories and algorithms for AI safety/security, winning all three championships in an international competition convened by Google."[65] With regard to the Chinese central government, "It can be said that Tsinghua University possesses a very good foundation and accumulation (of research) in the field of AI, and with regard to serving the AI superpower strategy, is duty bound."[66]

While America's technology companies are often less tied into the China market than our manufacturers and consumer goods companies, efforts to develop and manage a global talent pool have led to American research and development centers in China and Chinese research and development centers in the United States. Here's an example from Microsoft, a company whose own former CEO Steve Ballmer once called out China's intellectual property theft practices—a rare thing for a business leader to do publicly—stating that 90 percent of Chinese companies use Microsoft windows, but only 1 percent have paid for it. "I'm a free trader, by nature. I went to the school of economics—it's the best thing for the world. This one's a tricky issue because it's absolutely clear that the rules don't apply in China, and the US government needs to do something."[67] However, at present writing, four out of six centers in the Microsoft Asia-Pacific Research and Development Group are located in China, working on technologies that are essential to great power competition, including artificial intelligence and big data. Here is Microsoft's own description of its research and development efforts in Asia, including substantial efforts in China:

> Microsoft Asia-Pacific Research and Development Group (Microsoft ARD) serves as one of the core bases for Microsoft global fundamental research, technology incubation, product development, and ecosystem development. It is Microsoft's most comprehensive R&D center outside of the United States, with over 5,000 scientists and engineers in Beijing, Shanghai, Shenzhen, Suzhou, Taipei, and Tokyo. Microsoft ARD is committed to collaborate with local academic organizations and industries to build world-class computer science capacity within the region. It has attracted and cultivated talents that have become an important leading force in the innovation and creation of technologies like artificial intelligence, cloud computing, and big data. . . .

With campuses across the region, our engineers and researchers span Microsoft's major research and engineering divisions, including Microsoft Research (MSR) Asia, Microsoft Software Technology Center (STC) Asia, Microsoft Cloud and AI (C+AI) China, Microsoft Asia Center for Hardware (MACH), and the Strategic Partnership and Service Outsourcing. These groups develop technologies and solutions to address the unique needs of the emerging markets in the region, while moving locally developed innovations to other parts of the world.[68]

The company explains that is has "expanded its business across [China] under its strategy of long-term investment and development. Today, our most complete subsidiary and largest R&D center outside the United States is in China. Microsoft has been working closely with customers and industry partners to realize innovation and both localize and land Microsoft technologies and solutions in China. Microsoft boasts a robust partner ecosystem with 17,000 partners."[69]

What are China's companies doing as America's corporations form partnerships with them—a practice that is often required for market entry into China? China's companies are deepening their own partnerships with the Chinese state, as facilitators and vehicles for its most dangerous practices. Here is what the US State Department said about the broader Chinese technology ecosystem and its role in China's Civil Military Fusion drive:

> [A]cross the malignant ecosystem of China's technologized authoritarianism there is a deep record of cooperation and collaboration between companies such as Huawei, ZTE, Alibaba, Tencent, and Baidu and the state security bureaucracy. . . .
>
> According to a December 2018 article published on the National Military-Civil Fusion Public Platform administered by the Ministry of Industry and Information Technology, products and technologies from Huawei, Tencent, Alibaba, Xiaomi, Lenovo, and other companies have already been used in the research, production, and repair of weapons and equipment for the PLA. These companies have also provided support services for China's military industry in areas related

to electronics, aerospace, shipbuilding, and weapons—all of which, incidentally, are key military-civil fusion target areas when it comes to foreign technology acquisition—to enhance the core competitiveness of China's national defense science and technology sectors.[70]

Human rights groups and professional advisory firms have pointed out the many points of integration between American companies, China's human rights abuses, and the lesser-known problem of Civil Military Fusion.

In the meantime, the Chinese Communist Party's control and influence over its own corporations is becoming tighter and stronger. National teams, industrial parks, innovation clusters, and government guidance funds are all methods of growing and strengthening China's strategic industries as the Communist Party works to execute its long-term goals and build its military, its surveillance state, and its global influence.[71] China's state-owned and state-backed enterprises are the fundamental units of its economic and military grand strategy. China's State-Owned Assets Supervision and Administration Commission, also known as SASAC, consists of companies that are directly controlled by the Communist Party of China in strategic industries including aerospace and defense, automotive, chemicals, construction and engineering, energy, industrials, mining and resources, shipping and shipbuilding, steel and aluminum, technology, and telecommunications. These ninety-seven SASAC "central SOEs" brought in $4.75 trillion in revenue in 2021 according to the Communist Party's State Council.[72] The *China Daily* estimated the total assets of China's SOEs to be $33.78 trillion in 2020.[73]

China's combination of state-owned and state-backed super-companies, the world's largest banks by assets, and a series of mega-mergers in key strategic industries constitute the operational core of Beijing's economic power. Together with macro strategies such as the Belt and Road Initiative, Made in China 2025, Military Modernization, and Civil Military Fusion, these make up the economic and military foundations of China's Vision of Victory. China's merger of China Shipbuilding Industry Corporation and China State Shipbuilding Corporation created the world's largest shipbuilding corporation in 2019, what the *Wall Street Journal* called the creation of a "state-run giant" in "Beijing's latest attempt to supersize state-run businesses for global competition."[74] Beijing's merger of the rare earths assets of three state-owned firms to form China Rare Earth Group is another good example of the operational capabilities of Chinese state-backed capitalism. This merger in an industry that holds the key ingredients to some of the most important twenty-first-century products—including fighter jets, smartphones, and electric vehicles—is an attempt by Beijing to "maintain its dominance in the global supply chain of the strategic metals as tensions deepen with the U.S."[75] The alignment and direction of these firms by the Chinese state and their role in serving the purposes of the Chinese Communist Party's economic grand strategy should be lost on no one. In addition to Communist Party cadres who staff companies and sit on corporate boards, Beijing has officially released its intentions about the increasing penetration of the state into once-private corporations. In "Opinion on Strengthening United Front Work of the Private Economy in the New Era," the General Office of the Central Committee of the Chinese Communist Party outlined the importance of ideology and loyalty to the state within China's private sector. Here is the guidance from the Communist Party:

> Educate and guide private economy actors to arm their minds and guide their practice with Xi Jinping's Thought on Socialism with Chinese Characteristics for a New Era; maintain a high degree of consistency with the Party Central Committee on political positions, political directions, political principles, and political roads; and always be politically sensible. Further strengthen the Party building work of private enterprises and sincerely give full play to the role of Party organizations as battle fortresses and to the vanguard and exemplary role of Party members. Vigorously publicize the Party Central Committee's major policies concerning the development of the private economy, further promote ideological and theoretical innovation, and promptly respond to the ideological concerns of the majority of private economy practitioners. The United Front departments of Party committees at all levels must implement responsibility systems for ideological work in the private economy sector in order to guard the land with responsibility, accountability, and diligence.[76]

The Party must focus on "the main investors and actual controllers of private enterprises, the main shareholding managers of private enterprises, the major individual shareholders of private investment institutions, and the main leaders of social organizations in the industrial and commercial fields, the principals of relevant social service organizations, the principal partners of private intermediaries, Hong Kong and Macao businessmen who invest in mainland China, and representative individual industrial and commercial households."[77]

The Party must focus on "strategic emerging industries, high-tech industries, advanced manufacturing, modern service industries, modern agriculture, and other fields," while working to "cultivate and grow a team of private economy practitioners who unswervingly follow the Party." And finally, the Party must, "Encourage participation in major national strategies: Rely on the United Front to organize the mobilization of private economy practitioners to devote themselves to major national strategies such as the Innovation-Driven Development Strategy," and "Guide private enterprises to actively participate in 'Belt and Road' development [and] consciously safeguard national interests."[78]

In the biggest economic competition in world history, in which the corporation is the main battle unit, is it China or America that is more prepared? American and Allied corporate engagement contributes to the pillars of China's economic and technological ascendancy, even though corporate profits in China are only a small amount of worldwide totals. The US multinational corporation must release itself from hostage status in the China market. US multinationals must be prepared to do battle worldwide against Chinese state-owned and state-backed enterprises, often competing in global markets against their own stolen intellectual property, deployed by Chinese firms that are backed by the Chinese state. When it comes to the two essential pillars of victory in the Economic Arena, Economic Containment of China and Economic Growth for the US and Allied World, our companies will be essential players. We need the full participation of our business and finance leaders. The American and Allied Multinational Corporation versus the Chinese State-Owned and State-Backed Enterprise is the economic battlefield of the future.

PILLAR ONE

The Economic Containment of China

The most important objective in the decade ahead is to transform the contest with China into one we can win. While this contest is unlikely to end in the 2020s, this decade will be decisive, one in which we must make the most important adjustments. We must transform this competition from a contest with *an ascending power* into a contest with *a stagnant one.* At its foundation, the US-China competition will be won or lost in the Economic Arena in a battle for the world economy. The Chinese Communist Party has succeeded at converting China's economic ascendancy into military power, and it plans to continue to do so, to complete "the great rejuvenation of the Chinese nation" by the symbolic year of 2049.[79] We must ensure that this economic ascendancy—brought about through economic engagement with the United States and the Allied World—comes to an end. China, with America's help, has achieved more than enough to provide a good and decent life for its population. China's power need not be exerted any further upon its region, upon the world, or upon the course of history. Given what is widely known about the Chinese Communist Party's objectives and practices, it is not only appropriate but perhaps even humane that American and Allied grand strategy concentrates on putting an end to the economic ascendancy of this neo-totalitarian power and its ambitions to transform the world.

A strategy of economic containment gives us the chance to turn the tide. Historian Michael Mastanduno calls economic containment an effort to "contain the expansion of an adversary's military power by using economic rather than (or in addition to) political and military means."[80] Economic power—and its facilitation of military power and national power as a whole—is one of the main determinants of the outcome of historical contests between major powers. Both the Second World War and the Cold War present clear examples. Economic power will define the US-China competition in the twenty-first century. As Mastanduno explains, "It has long been established that the economic and military capabilities of the modern industrial state are closely related. Both classical liberal and mercantilist thinkers understood that military power rests upon a foundation of economic power both qualitatively and quantitatively."[81] Why then would we continue to *enable* the economic ascendancy of our primary adversary when it has already declared its intentions to become the world's dominant power? We have an excellent alternative. Let's look at what economic containment can do and how we can begin to disable the economic ascendancy of the People's Republic of China.

First, China's global grand strategy is based in large part on economic strategy—achieving an economic ascendancy and position in the world economy that is unrivaled by other major powers. In pursuing a strategy of economic containment, the US and our Allies would be striking at the core of Chinese grand strategy. Sun Tzu himself would commend such an approach. In his words, "The highest form of warfare is to cut down their strategy; the next best is to disrupt their junctions; the next best is to attack their forces; the lowest form is to besiege their cities."[82] We must aim for the centerpiece of China's overall grand strategy—we must strike the trunk of the tree, not its twigs and branches.

Second, the continued rise and progress of China's economy depends on its engagement with the United States and the Allied World. We have a kill switch to the growth of China's economy. Economic containment is a matter of denying China the access and inputs that Beijing requires to continue its intended path toward global economic dominance. It involves constricting the growth and improvement of China's strategic industries and core technologies and reducing its integration, over time, with the major markets and regions of the world. Economic containment involves restricting or withdrawing China's access to technology, capital, and markets that its ascendancy depends on. Right now, we are the ones giving them access to many of these things. We can also take this access away. By simply *not helping China any further*, we change the course of its economic rise. At that point, the troubles of China such as debt and demographic decline begin to take hold. Rather than enabling China to achieve economic breakout capacity, fueled by American and Allied capital, technology, and markets, we can restrict this rise, and watch as the world's largest and grandest authoritarian country falls firmly into what economists call "the middle income trap."[83]

A twenty-first century in which America must contend for global power with a stagnant China is a fundamentally different one than a century in which we must deal worldwide with a rising empire from a position of diminishing resources of our own. To achieve this strategic change, we must embrace some truths that are difficult for many to accept: America's growth and prosperity do not actually depend on China, and neither does global security depend on deep economic relations between China and the United States, or between China and the Allied World. We will turn to American and Allied growth, the second pillar of this economic strategy, soon enough.

Michael Pettis is a leading expert on China's economy. Based at Beijing University's Guanghua School of Management, with a focus on Chinese financial markets, he has an exceptional window into the country. Pettis has consistently warned investors and observers of the Chinese economy about its debt burdens and slowing growth prospects. He has pointed out the colossal borrowing by China's leaders to fuel the country's economic rise. While Pettis' focus is on macroeconomics and financial markets, rather than national security or economic strategy, he has revealed a window of opportunity for economic containment that could alter the course of US-China competition. Here it is in his words:

> Once it is recognized that China's surging debt burden is a function of nonproductive investment, and that this investment must eventually be curtailed, it turns out that there are a limited number of ways the economy can continue growing. Any economy broadly speaking has

only three sources of demand that can drive growth: consumption, investment, and trade surpluses. For that reason, there are basically five paths that China's economy could take going forward:

1. China can stay on its current path and keep letting large amounts of nonproductive investment continue driving the country's debt burden up indefinitely
2. China can reduce the large amount of nonproductive investment on which it relies to drive growth and replace it with productive investment in forms like new technology
3. China can reduce the large amount of nonproductive investment on which it relies to drive growth and replace it with rising consumption
4. China can reduce the large amount of nonproductive investment on which it relies to drive growth and replace it with a growing trade surplus
5. China can reduce the large amount of nonproductive investment on which it relies to drive growth and *replace it with nothing*, in which case growth would necessarily slow sharply.[84]

The identification of these five pathways gives us a targeting window that can bring the growth of the entire Chinese economy—a juggernaut of trade, industrial power, and consumer potential—to a relative standstill. If America and our Allies can take action to erode the Communist Party's credit-fueled spending on China's economic growth—and replace it with nothing—then the ascendancy is largely over. Let's call this the Pettis Window. Targeting this window is not a simple task, and a single course of action will not achieve the result of slowing China down. It will require a comprehensive strategy to surround and contain the myriad global-economic inputs to China's growth. Fortunately, many of these inputs are related to China's economic engagement with the United States and our Allies. The Communist Party is already working to defend the Pettis Window. The Communist Party's focus on global intellectual property theft and industrial espionage is meant to create a path forward through technology-driven growth. Its trading relationships with the United

States, Europe, Japan, and other Organisation for Economic Co-operation and Development (OECD) nations create a pathway for growth through trade, and its Belt and Road Imitative opens new emerging markets to Chinese companies and influence. The Communist Party's attempts to "rebalance" its economy toward growth driven by Chinese consumers is another attempt to continue its economic ascendancy through the expansion of an enormous internal market. However, if these pathways are countered by a robust economic containment strategy—rather than being enabled by American and Allied capital, technology, and markets—then the game changes entirely both for China and for the United States. When debt is the only viable option, the game of real growth is over.

Let's have a closer look at China's economic strategy to see what we are financing, enabling, and developing through US and Allied economic engagement with China.

Like Germany in the 1930s, the Chinese Communist Party has focused on engagement with the world's advanced democracies as a way to source technology and to enable industrial advancement on a massive scale.[85] The Chinese Communist Party's narrative of historical "humiliation" and "rejuvenation" goes farther back than fascist Germany's did—"a century of national humiliation" beginning with the Opium Wars of the 1840s—and its global efforts to obtain industrial and technological advantages dwarf those undertaken by Germany ahead of the Second World War. But Communist China's concept is similar, seeking to obtain every industrial and technological advantage from the world's leading industrialized democracies, the nations who "humiliated" China in the past. US officials have called these industrial espionage efforts "theft on a scale so massive that it represents one of the largest transfers of wealth in human history."[86] The objective for the Chinese Communist Party is not that Western businesses succeed in China in the long run. It is that they provide industrial advancement and technology to China in order to enable its ascendancy. This is one of the real reasons for China's "opening" and engagement with the world. As Xi Jinping explains of China's sprawling and sophisticated technology transfer programs, "[O]nly if the core technology is grasped in our own hands can we then really seize the initiative in competition and development . . . of course, we can't lock ourselves up from the world, we need to proactively develop technology exchanges with the outside, strive to use well the two kinds of science and technology resources—international and domestic."[87]

Analysts with extensive experience in the US intelligence community have categorized China's efforts into three categories: "legal transfers," "illegal transfers," and "extralegal transfers." Legal transfers—technology transfers often done through business and commercial or academic exchange—include China-based foreign subsidiaries, conferences and colloquia, direct technology purchases, enrollments at US universities, foreign-based labs and representative offices, investments and acquisitions of companies, joint research agreements, patent mining and exploitation, PRC-backed venture capital funds, startup competitions, state-backed investments in foreign research, tech exchanges, and trade for tech agreements. Illegal transfers include breach of contract, copyright infringement, computer network exploitation, insider operations, reverse engineering, traditional espionage, violation of NDAs, and willful patent infringement. Extralegal transfers include document acquisition facilities, foreign-based alumni associations, front organizations for PRC offices, national and local PRC ministry offices, overseas scholar returnee facilities, recruiting and brokerage websites, Sino-foreign professional associations, technology transfer centers, transfer incentive programs, and university-linked "innovation" parks.[88]

This system of transfer, theft, espionage, and acquisition has affected many of America's greatest companies (perhaps most of them), from massive, newsworthy breaches to lesser-known examples that have destroyed small and midsized companies altogether. In the words of one former FBI director, "There are only two types of companies: those that have been hacked and those that will be."[89] America's industry-leading companies and the innovation system that created many of our vital advantages in previous geopolitical competitions is on the one hand under illegal siege and on the other essentially for sale as our companies build their businesses in the China market. The consequences of corporate engagement exist today on a larger scale than they did in the decade ahead of the Second World War, and on a scale that would have been impossible in the largely two-bloc Cold War world. It is a source of tremendous advantage to the People's Republic of China.

Just as harmful as China's systematic technology transfer programs is the series of industrial strategies that this system of industrial espionage feeds into, allowing China to dominate foundational industries and position itself to dominate many of the emerging technologies that will define the future. For example, Made in China 2025 envisions Chinese economic dominance in the following strategic industries: new energy vehicles, next-generation information and communication technology, biotechnology, new materials, aerospace, ocean engineering and high-tech ships, railway, robotics, power equipment, and agricultural machinery. In its own words, the strategy sets the following three-step plan to become the world's leading manufacturing and industrial power:

> By 2020, consolidate manufacturing power and increase industrial digitization, mastering core technologies, promoting Chinese multinational companies internationally, all while moving up the value-chain and improving efficiency and quality.
>
> By 2035, China will reach an "intermediate level" among world manufacturing powers, making breakthroughs in major areas and leading innovation where China is most competitive.
>
> By 2049, China will become the leader amongst the world's manufacturing powers, leading innovation and technological development.[90]

These industrial strategies would not be possible without the participation of US and Allied companies in the China market. As a leading analyst of the issue explains:

> As Chinese firms have pushed offshore, the PRC government has leveraged state direction and funding to acquire foreign technology abroad, acquiring advanced capabilities in areas targeted in China's *Made in China 2025* plan—such as aerospace, advanced manufacturing, artificial intelligence (AI), biotechnology, data analytics, new materials, and semiconductors. The imposition of tight market access controls has allowed China to play off global economic competitors by offering preferential market access terms in exchange for technology transfer. They have increased receptivity to China's acquisition bids as foreign firms assess that Chinese ownership is the only pathway to enter a restricted but undeniably important market.[91]

The Communist Party's vision of economic dominance does not end there. Through his "Dual Circulation" strategy, Xi Jinping intends to increase the world's dependence on China while decreasing China's dependence on the world. In Xi's own words:

> We must firmly grasp this strategic basis that is demand expansion, make each link—production, distribution, circulation, and consumption—rely more on the domestic market to achieve a virtuous circle, specify the strategic direction of supply-side structural reform, and promote the achievement of dynamic balance between aggregate supply and demand at higher levels.
>
> In order to safeguard China's industrial security and national security, we must focus on building production chains and supply chains that are independently controllable, secure and reliable, and strive for important products and supply channels to all have at least one alternative source, forming the necessary industrial backup system.
>
> First, we must build on our advantages, solidify and increase the leading international positions of strong industries, and forge some "assassin's mace" technologies. We must sustain and enhance our superiority across the entire production chain in sectors such as high-speed rail, electric power equipment, new energy, and communications equipment, and improve industrial quality; and we must tighten international production chains' dependence on China, forming a powerful countermeasure and deterrent capability against foreigners who would artificially cut off supply [to China].[92]

This vision of economic centrality and supremacy is the foundation of the Chinese Communist Party's grand strategy. This is not merely wishful thinking. In an August 2022 article titled "Pandemic Bolsters China's Role as World's Manufacturer," the *Wall Street Journal* reported on China's increasing share of global exports, noting that, "For all the talk in Western capitals of reducing reliance on Chinese factories, China has in the past two years consolidated its position as the world's dominant manufacturer."[93] China's Belt and Road Initiative, military modernization programs, and vision of industrial supremacy provide the foundations for the Communist Party's ultimate objective. This objective is "The Community of Common Destiny for Mankind," a world with China as the uncontested center, the dominant force in human affairs. However, the Chinese Communist Party can only achieve this objective through our *willful participation.*

BIFURCATION: ECONOMIC CONTAINMENT AND THE GLOBAL ECONOMY

Ending our facilitation of China's economic ascendancy is a matter of restricting technology, capital, and market access from America and the Allied World. If we can reduce or shut down legal, illegal, and extralegal technology transfers in key strategic industries, restrict or eliminate investment and engagement in the strategic industries and emerging technologies that Beijing regards as essential to its rise, and if we can close off market access in the United States, Europe, and Allied Asia for anything other than non-strategic goods, then we will change the game entirely. This will take national will and focus, as well as a complete reevaluation of what American and Allied corporations are legally allowed to do in China. The effect would be to hit the targets within the Pettis Window and close the pathways forward for robust economic growth in China. A natural, technology-based bifurcation in the world economy is already underway, and so is the waning of cheap labor advantages inside China. These two trends will impair China's engagement with the world's democracies—where most of the world's wealth and productivity is concentrated—at both the top and bottom of the value chain. If we reduce and, as needed, eliminate exchange with China in high-tech industries at the top of the value chain and also in low-tech industries at the bottom, then the foundations of China's growth begin to crumble. Rather than the continued siphoning of wealth and technology from the world's advanced democracies, China would then be consigned to economic engagement with Belt and Road regions—the world's emerging markets—where we will have to win another vital aspect of the global competition. If China's high-end and low-end trade with democracies erodes, technology transfer is contained, and investment in strategic industries is restricted, America's toolkit for economic containment can do the remainder of the job.

A bifurcated world is forming through the incompatibility of the world's democracies and technology made in China. As software becomes more important in physical goods, the "Internet of Things" now involves technologies from smart homes to autonomous vehicles. As the "Internet of Things" becomes a part of economic life, there is little chance that the democracies will use China's technology, nor will China use that of the democracies. Mutual distrust means that our industries are in a process of bifurcation and that an integrated world economy will change shape as a result. Already, Beijing has mandated not only the indigenization of key industries and technologies but has also begun a process of removing Western corporations from what it considers certain sensitive technologies and industries. The process, nicknamed in China "De-IOE," or de-IBM, Oracle, and EMC, is an approach to remove Western technology from China's IT infrastructure, and replace it with homegrown Chinese brands.[94] The US has largely won a campaign in America and Allied democracies to remove Huawei, a maker not only of telecommunications and 5G hardware, but also of smart cars, smartphones, and hybrid digital-physical goods.

This bifurcation in telecommunications and IT infrastructure is likely to extend across numerous industries from automotive to consumer goods as digital and physical goods become intertwined. If the democracies come together to block China's corporate competitors—forming a Great Wall strategy against China's technology and industry in the Democratic World—then China's tech giants will expand primarily in the China market and the emerging world. China has begun to export smart cities and surveillance technology built by its domestic "national champions," selling its hardware and software from Africa to Latin America. As these two technological blocs form, it will be essential for democracies to close ranks and fight for commercial and technological integration with the emerging world as well.

This process of bifurcation goes beyond technology, which is the most obvious trend. Manufactured goods and commodities have already been the subject of the US-China trade war, initiated after the Section 301 investigations in 2017 and 2018, and addressed in the 2020 US-China Trade and Economic Agreement. Even this trade deal is one that China has failed to honor, blaming its COVID-19 pandemic for an inability to meet US purchasing requirements.[95] The objective of this "Phase One" deal was to chip away at the massive trade deficit between the US and China through purchasing requirements of US goods and services. However, the US-China trade deal did not solve the problems in the US-China economic relationship, or China's predatory practices. As US trade representative Katherine Tai explained in 2021:

> Even with the phase-one agreement in place, China's government continues to pour billions of dollars into targeted industries and continues to shape its economy to the will of the state, hurting the interests of workers here in the US and around the world.[96]

The US-China trade relationship should be reconsidered from the standpoint of competitive power and capability. Trade that empowers our adversary's strategic objectives or economic efficiency should be discontinued and diversified to other parts of the global economy.

China has demonstrated its willingness to use economic coercion on US Allies, even during the global pandemic. After the Australian government called for an inquiry into the origins of COVID-19, China engaged in economic warfare against Australia, banning or restricting imports of coal, wine, barley, and seafood.[97] The Chinese Communist Party even issued a fourteen-point declaration of Australia's political wrongdoings, which many likened to a call for Australia to behave or become a traditional "vassal state."[98] Additionally, Chinese military scholars and official media called Australia a "target for a nuclear strike" as Australia-UK-US defense ties expanded with the AUKUS Agreement.[99] There should be little expectation at this point that the People's Republic of China will be a responsible member of the international economic community given its long list of actions demonstrating the opposite: the curbing of rare earth elements to Japan during the East China Sea dispute, the halting of trade and tourism to Korea over the deployment of Terminal High Altitude Area Defense systems, the halting of agricultural imports from the Philippines over the South China Sea dispute, and even the nationalization of the factories of American multinational corporations during the COVID-19 pandemic. Let's not forget the threats from official Communist Party media to plunge America into "the mighty sea of coronavirus" by denying us the use of China-made medical equipment.[100]

China has employed economic coercion strategies—the use of economic power to force its political influence—ever since it became a fundamental piece of the global economy. Given its numerous territorial disputes, its history of military conflict with its neighbors, and the Chinese Communist Party's collision course with America and the world—there is no reason to suppose that a global economy with China as a centerpiece or dominant player on which numerous nations depend is a stable structure for the world. US policy should be aimed at making sure that this reality never comes. Economic containment can achieve this goal.

The abusive trading relationship has led to calls to reduce China's leverage. For example, after China's hostage diplomacy involving two Canadian citizens, Michael Kovrig and Michael Spavor, in response to US and Canadian action against Huawei CFO Meng Wanzhou for violation of international sanctions against Iran, a former Canadian ambassador to China offered the following idea for Allied coordination against China's trade malpractices:

> Canada should work with our allies to take [the Australia-US-UK security alliance] one step further and develop criteria that would trigger common responses by the signatory countries, including sanctions on the weaponization of trade. If Australia, Canada, and the US were to agree that if one of the three is subject to sanctions by China, then the two others would agree not to increase their exports to China beyond their historical share of the market there. That would prevent China from playing one country against the other.[101]

In other words, Allies can trade among each other to fill gaps when China bars imports from one as political punishment or economic coercion, and Allies can also refuse to trade with China to fill gaps opened by China's cessation of imports or exports. Some, like myself, have called for an "alliance-based trading system" or a "NATO for trade."[102] The world is already beginning to react to China's actions. The security and strategy reasons for trade diversification and trade substitution are clear—including the ability to withstand China's typical divide and conquer strategies utilized against smaller countries or against coalitions of states throughout the centuries in the classical Chinese art of power.

Doing away with engagement through trade to turn the tide of competition with a nonmarket-economy adversary will offend many proponents of "free trade" economic theory. This theory often holds sway in Western universities, investment banks, and boardrooms. This is not an indictment of these theorists so much as an acknowledgment that in the political economy of today's world—which now includes a neo-totalitarian mercantilist superpower as the center of global manufacturing and supply chains—classical economic theory does us little good when it comes to major power competition. The problem posed by potential dominance of the international power structure by this adversary is outside the bounds of what economic theorists deal with within their theoretical world. It is unfortunate, because many proponents of free trade have also been proponents of the Free World in the past. In the post–Cold War world of globalization, that connection appears to have been lost, though there are exceptions. Here's what the pro–free trade *Financial Times*—which appears to appreciate the nature of the problem—writes of British political economist David Ricardo's classical theory of comparative advantage:

> It's one thing to trade Portuguese wine for English wool. It's another thing to give up your entire industrial base to Asia, and then not be able to put masks on your citizens because the country that supplies 70 percent of your masks, which has an entirely different economic and political model, decides to nationalise its personal protective equipment industry.[103]

The world economy is changing in response to the failure to integrate China *not just economically but politically* with the modern world. The expectations of economic theory and commercial practice must adapt to these realities. As policymakers find their footing on managing a hostile economic superpower, the business and financial world must change its practices as well. In order to achieve a favorable long-term outcome, the economic integration of America and our Allies and partners is necessary. The United States, and North America more broadly, with the combined power of America, Canada, and Mexico, must form the cornerstone of economic power well into the twenty-first century. The Allied powers of Europe, Asia, and also our partner India can grow and trade within an Allied, Free World trading community, whose supply chains are secure, whose innovation and technological advancements are superior, and whose industries are more robust than those of an isolated China. In forming such a community, the economic contest will shift mainly to the emerging world, where China retains much of its influence. This is a better and more advantageous state of affairs than the one we have today, where China has considerable economic influence in the developed world and where "interdependence" leads in fact to considerable Chinese advancements through technology transfer, availability of capital, and access to our enormous markets.

ECONOMIC CONTAINMENT AND TECHNOLOGY

Our adversary is likely to copy and steal from us for as long it is able. We should task numerous agencies with the prevention of legal, illegal, and extralegal transfers in sectors that matter to strategic competition. Even in the Cold War, Soviet technology theft and industrial espionage was a difficult problem to manage. Another approach is to deal with China's transgressions by linking industrial espionage to access to American and Allied markets and capital—and to do this on a scale that we have not yet contemplated. For example, taking what America has been able to do to Huawei—a company with a history of intellectual property theft allegations including from the now destroyed Nortel in Canada and from Cisco in the United States[104]—America and our Allies should apply comprehensive economic sanctions to any Chinese entity that has benefited from stolen or illegally transferred intellectual property originating anywhere inside the Alliance System.

Three denials could be applied: denial of market access in North America, Europe, and Allied Asia, denial of critical technological components such as semiconductors, and denial of access to the global financial system. Such methods would degrade or destroy adversary companies that have benefited from cyber and industrial espionage by ceasing their access to the bulk of the world economy. Even if we cannot stop all or even most instances of intellectual property theft, we can prevent the commercial exploitation of this technology in markets other than China itself or its economic satellite states.

America can create a kind of economic missile defense through numerous tools already available, such as the Committee on Foreign Investment in the United States (CFIUS), the International Emergency Economic Powers Act (IEEPA), and a variety of export controls through the Department of Commerce, in order to prevent the use of our own technology by adversary corporations within the Allied World.[105] The United States has taken such measures on goods purchasing and trade when it comes to human rights abuses in Xinjiang. The same approach can also be applied when it comes to technology theft and transfer.

Here's how import bans work under the Uyghur Forced Labor Prevention Act, where policymakers have connected human rights and trade strategy not only for the United States but for the whole of North America under the US-Mexico-Canada Agreement:

[The Uyghur Forced Labor Prevention Act] directs US Customs and Border Protection, within 180 days, to presume that all goods from China's Xinjiang Uyghur Autonomous Region are made with forced labor and, accordingly, are banned from entry to the US under Section 307 of the Tariff Act of 1930. . . .

The law also directs the Forced Labor Task Force, an interagency body created by the US-Mexico Canada Agreement implementing act, to develop a strategy for supporting enforcement of Section 307 of the Tariff Act of 1930 to prevent the import to the US of goods "manufactured wholly or in part with forced labor in the People's Republic of China"—not just the Xinjiang Region. . . .

The three trade deputies [US, Mexico, Canada] said in a joint statement . . . that they discussed "the importance of full implementation" of USMCA's "prohibition of trade in goods produced through forced labor." They also agreed to "report concrete and measurable outcomes on implementing this key obligation."[106]

A law with a human rights trigger and a broad geographical scope—forced labor atrocities as the trigger and *the whole of China* as a scope—is a pathway to laws that could have a variety of triggers and then industry-wide or technology-wide scopes. For example, in industries such as telecommunications, steel, or solar panels, where intellectual property theft or heavy subsidization from China is widely understood, import bans could be applied to either specific companies, or to an entire industry. Doing so would deny China access to the world's *actual* largest market—the United States of America—while also keeping North America free of problematic goods and services. Applying such initiatives across the entire Alliance System, which represents over half of world GDP and two-thirds of global wealth, would devastate the usefulness of Chinese technology theft in any market outside of China and the world's emerging economies.

Without advanced markets to sell to, the economic proposition of intellectual property theft erodes, as do global market opportunities for China's state-owned and state-backed corporations. To be sure, China would retaliate against our corporations, likely on false charges, but this groundwork is already being prepared. It is up to our companies to fully understand their risks in China and to change their strategies. The "Countering Foreign Sanctions Law," passed in June 2021, for example, allows the seizure of foreign-owned property in China. This law intends to *prevent America's companies from complying with America's own sanctions against China.* Law firm Mayer Brown explains that it applies to "individuals or organizations that have been 'directly or indirectly' involved in the 'formulation, adoption and implementation' of 'discretionary restrictive measures' against Chinese citizens and organizations" as well as their "senior executives or actual controllers." The consequences are that "Targeted Persons can be subject to one or more of the following Countermeasures: 1. Refusal to issue a visa, denial of entry into China, cancellation of a visa or deportation; 2. seizure or freezing of property located within China; 3. ban or restriction on any transaction or cooperation with any organization or individual that is located within China; 4. any other necessary measures."[107]

These measures are underway, as both sides prepare for bifurcation, and each side enacts restrictions and countermeasures utilizing market access as leverage. Access to China's economy is a card that China's rulers have played for centuries. But access to *the world economy* is a card that only America and our Allies can play. We must do so before this advantage is lost for good. If we categorically refuse to grant market access to designated companies and industries, whether Chinese corporations or multinational corporations operating in China, the power of the Allied economic community comes into full force. Blocking China and its economic advantages—a massive labor force and efficient local supply chains—from comprehensive access to this economic community can in turn foster innovation within the Allied industrial base and supply chain system, leveraging the advances that are set to come to fruition in the 2020s and 2030s.

Alongside import bans, Allied coordination on export controls can further change the tide of China's access and utilization of our innovation systems. One of the challenges of the Cold War era, export controls across the Alliance System were employed to limit communist access to Western technology that had military applications. Here, in the words of Michael Mastanduno, is how America and our European Allies came together to work toward the economic containment of the communist bloc in the early Cold War:

> The Western allies formally decided to adopt economic warfare in September 1950. . . . At the September foreign ministers' meetings, Acheson [of America], Bevin of Britain, and Schuman of France agreed that *"in the present world situation,"* the Western allies should employ effective export controls "to limit the short-term striking power of the Soviet bloc, and to retard the development of its war potential in the longer-term." This would entail new restriction of exports "of selected items which are required in key industrial sectors that contribute substantially to war potential."[108]
>
> In addition to items of direct military application, the concept "war potential" covered "industrial sectors that served to support the basic economy of a country and which therefore support either a peacetime or wartime economy."[109]

America has an economic toolkit that can be coordinated across the Alliance System. From historical examples such as the Battle Act of 1951, which coordinated export controls among the Allies, to the International Emergency Economic Powers Act, which allows the president of the United States to take essentially any economic action based on national security concerns, America is more prepared than Beijing for both economic warfare and economic containment. The cost to our companies who have taken risks in the China market is real, but corporate interests and exposure to China is not enough to prevent action that US and Allied security may depend on. China's strategists have already considered the vulnerabilities of American companies in their market. Here is what one Communist Party military theorist had to say at the 2018 Military Industry Ranking Awards Ceremony and Innovation Summit. In addition to advocating that China sink two American aircraft carriers, he highlighted the vulnerabilities of American corporations in the China market, listing agriculture, automotive, and airplanes as three of America's top export sectors to China:

> If America is not in China's developing market, General Motors, Ford, and Chrysler, its three big car companies, will be reduced to second class companies. . . . For every three American Boeing 737s made, one is sent to China. Therefore, we have America's soft ribs in our hands.[110]

Business leaders must assess their risk in China and understand what they are *actually* dealing with in the world's largest authoritarian country. US strategy and policy need not wait for business leaders. Economic containment of China, if implemented as a combined effort across the Alliance System, could hold enormous potential. Conversely, lack of coordination among the Allies presents China with its most desirable position: playing coalitions against each other. If Boeing in America were restricted from selling aircraft or parts to China, the Communist Party would buy from Airbus in Europe, and so on. When efforts to coordinate become squabbles among Alliance partners, the coalition suffers and the adversary gains. Modern historical examples of cooperation abound. They include export controls, Allied institutional coordination, and general and targeted forms of economic and financial warfare that have substantially weakened adversary states and organizations. Throughout the Cold War, for example, the United States, together with Allies in Europe and Asia, maintained an export control regime known as the Coordinating Committee on Multilateral Export Control (CoCom), which was dissolved in 1994. Mastanduno describes it as follows:

The coordination of export controls in CoCom has constituted a regime situated squarely at the intersection of economics and national security; it has represented a collective effort by its members, who are military allies, to regulate their economic competition in order to respond more effectively to what they have perceived as common military threats.[III]

Today, through the Department of Commerce's Entity List, the US government has placed restrictions on dozens of Chinese corporations, from the famous case of Huawei to the lesser-known China Communications Construction Corporation, which, as *China's Vision of Victory* pointed out, was responsible for building China's military islands in the South China Sea. What is needed is a framework for sanctions on Chinese state-owned and state-backed corporations. The US and Allies should apply a tougher version of the "Huawei Template," meaning a comprehensive ban from our markets, our capital, our services, and our technology. These moves will hobble China's companies and relegate them to the China market and to its satellite states, rather than allowing them to "go global" as the Party has directed. Preventing Chinese state-owned and state-backed enterprises from conquering global markets will benefit our corporations. If left unchecked, the expansion of China's companies will be one of the greatest challenges that our businesses will face, especially in the world's emerging markets. If their Chinese corporate competitors are degraded and contained, our own companies will be free to excel in global markets where they are now losing unfair competitions against the Chinese state. Those who say that sector-level containment will only accelerate China's ambitions to indigenize certain industries and technologies may be unaware of the fact that China has had plans to indigenize what it sees as strategic industries and core technologies for decades. What matters is that China will be unlikely to produce or sustain superior companies and technologies without access to the entire global economy, especially without the larger and richer markets of the Allied World.

Economic containment is a two-way street. Beijing is also working to strip foreign technology from its government and state-owned interests. Building upon "de-IOE" initiatives, in Spring 2022 Beijing ordered central government agencies and state-backed corporations to cease using foreign personal computers within a two-year timeframe, in what *Bloomberg* calls "one of Beijing's most aggressive efforts so far to eradicate key overseas technology from within its most sensitive organs."[112] *Bloomberg* reports that this could lead to the replacement of at least fifty million PCs in the central government alone, affecting sales from US hardware leaders like HP and Dell.[113] The *Wall Street Journal* reported on broader efforts toward technology replacement in China years ago through the Communist Party's "AnKe Project," designed to strip American companies from China's strategic industries. As the *Journal* explains: "China has started to cut out American firms elsewhere, too. Beijing's 'AnKe Project' is designed to purge Chinese government agencies, telecommunications companies, and power grids of foreign hardware and software. AnKe is short for 'Anquan Kekao' in Chinese, which means 'secure and controllable.' Under the plan, government and infrastructure operators immediately had to allocate a certain percentage of their procurement to domestic tech providers, starting with 30% in 2019, an additional 50% in 2020, and the remaining 20% in 2021."[114]

Under the Communist Party's vision, Western firms have little future or purpose in the China market other than for technology extraction and improving economic efficiency in sectors where indigenization has yet to be achieved. If Beijing's strategies succeed, it is China's state-owned and state-backed companies that will own the China market and dominate world markets, destroying Western firms with stolen technology and superior state financing. Even as American and Allied multinationals vie for access and expansion in the China market, Beijing plans to reach technological supremacy. In the eyes of the Chinese Communist Party, *technological security* means that the ambitions of US companies in China may amount to very little in the long run. Their work with Chinese companies involved in human rights abuses, Civil Military Fusion initiatives, and strategic industries should be brought to an end and they should refocus their efforts on strengthening American and Allied power as a New Arsenal of Democracy.

ECONOMIC CONTAINMENT AND CAPITAL MARKETS

The third plank in economic containment is to curtail China's access to US and Allied capital markets. It may be the most important. Consider China's role in the world economy, and the fundamental contradiction in the Chinese Communist Party's objective of becoming the world's leading economic power: China seeks to indigenize its industries and technologies, send its state-owned and state-backed corporations overseas to outcompete American multinationals in global markets, and also create a kind of high-tech, innovation-enabled form of industrial autarky, far superior to Russia's attempts to build up "Fortress Economics" ahead of its invasion of Ukraine. However, in Xi Jinping's words at the World Economic Forum in Davos in 2017, China must be able to "swim in the vast ocean of the global market."[115] "Dual Circulation" seeks to reconcile all of this—indigenization at home, with supply chain and market dominance abroad. However, China needs *our capital*—money from New York, London, and other Allied financial centers—to finance these objectives. Routinely feted at the World Economic Forum and other leading venues, Xi Jinping and other Chinese Communist Party officials continue to make a case for China's rise, and our investment and business professionals have been happy to indulge. If this were to stop, then the game changes dramatically for China. Here is what Xi Jinping has said about China's use of the world economy at Davos in 2017:

> There was a time when China also had doubts about economic glo-balization, and was not sure whether it should join the World Trade Organization. But we came to the conclusion that integration into the global economy is a historical trend. To grow its economy, China must have the courage to swim in the vast ocean of the global market. If one is always afraid of bracing the storm and exploring the new world, he will sooner or later get drowned in the ocean. Therefore, China took a brave step to embrace the global market. We have had our fair share of choking in the water and encountered whirlpools and choppy waves, but we have learned how to swim in this process. *It has proved to be a right strategic choice.*[116]

These words may have been music to the ears of the proverbial Davos Man who seeks wealth in China, but what Xi is saying is that access to the world economy enables the Communist Party's path to dominance. Consider the words of Michael Pettis, explaining China's reliance on capital, not labor, for economic growth and power: "It is a mistake to characterize China as an export-driven economy. China is an investment-driven economy." He notes that, "If China's comparative advantage were cheap labor, we would expect its growth to be heavily labor intensive as businesses loaded up on the most efficient input. But China's growth is actually heavily capital intensive. . . . Chinese businesses behave, in other words, not as if labor were the cheapest input they have but rather as if capital were the cheapest input. They are right. Labor may be cheap, but capital is free."[117] Consider these words from congressional testimony by former investment banker Dr. Carl E. Walter on China's access to financing from around the world: "State-owned enterprises have access to all existing channels of finance. They can issue shares domestically and internationally, borrow loans, engage with foreign banks and markets, and so on. They may own controlling interests in trust companies and small banks. Their efforts to raise finances will be actively supported by their state owners—the central or local government. Financing is not an obstacle to their operations."[118]

It is not only China's world-beating export production capabilities that have cemented its place as a cornerstone manufacturing state running massive surpluses with most of the world. It is China's *ability to finance these operations* that creates its strategic power. China's ability to finance these operations would not be possible without access to American and Allied capital markets. China's strategy is to utilize Western technology, capital, and export markets to achieve growth, self-sufficiency, and eventually economic and military dominance. If we have the will, we can stop this process.

The United States must deploy its ultimate economic weapon. Years ago at Oxford, a world-renowned economist told me this: "Americans think that their biggest advantage is nuclear weapons. It is not. Your biggest weapon is the US dollar as the world's reserve currency." The place that can shape the economic life or death of the world's most dangerous regimes is the one that Americans know well from the checks we write at tax season. It may hold the key to our geopolitical future. It is not the Department of Defense that wins an economic contest. It is the Department of the Treasury.[119]

Vladimir Lenin once said that "the capitalists will sell us the rope that we will use to hang them." Listen to certain finance leaders marvel at the "opportunities" in China's rise. Watch not only grand-scale theft, but also willful transfer of American technology. Look back upon the decades-long process of relocating our industrial base to within the national borders of our primary opponent. Who would disagree? But perhaps it is our own form of justice that American capitalism still holds one card that no one else can wield: the global power of the "almighty dollar."

The lifeblood—for now—of the world economy, access to the US dollar has meant health or a crippled existence for many of the world's regimes. Policymakers may tremble at the potential to unleash the power of the dollar in our contest with China. But consider the essence of economic vulnerability and what it means for China. China is an investment-driven economy that deploys massive state financing to send firms like Huawei and CNOOC across the planet in the service of the Chinese Communist Party:

> [T]he most vulnerable target is a state that is both highly dependent on trade with the sanctioning state and is at the same time unable to provide the level of resources demanded by its military sector (or only able to provide these resources if it engages in trade). The least vulnerable target is a state that is largely self-sufficient.[120]

We can see why Beijing is eager to reach self-sufficiency, or what it calls "Dual Circulation." However, Beijing won't reach financial self-sufficiency in this decade. If it does not reach it in the 2020s, it may never reach it at all.

The United States Treasury Department is our break-the-glass strategy in economic warfare or economic containment. Its use on Russia crippled major banks, destabilized the Russian currency, and froze stockpiles of hundreds of billions' worth of US currency reserves that Russia set aside in preparation for its war in Ukraine.[121] US Treasury Department sanctions, together with corporate flight from Russia, arguably thwarted the entire concept of "Fortress Economics," a practice utilized in both Moscow and Beijing. The sanctions on

Russia were punitive, designed to create substantial costs in light of unacceptable actions. The US economic toolkit can also be used to shape capability. Rather than punishing consequences for actions, our tools can do the work of shaping—or ceasing—an adversary's economic rise.

Here is how Juan Zarate, a master practitioner of American sanctions strategy, describes the power of US financial sanctions in *Treasury's War: The Unleashing of a New Era of Financial Warfare*:

> Over the past decade [2000s and early 2010s], the United States has waged a new brand of financial warfare, unprecedented in its reach and effectiveness. This "hidden warfare" has often been underestimated or misunderstood, but it is no longer secret and has since become central to America's national security doctrine. In a series of financial pressure campaigns, the United States has financially squeezed and isolated America's principal enemies of this period—Al Qaeda, North Korea, Iran, Iraq, and Syria. Far from relying solely on the classic sanctions or trade embargoes of old, these campaigns have consisted of a novel set of financial strategies that harness the international financial and commercial systems to ostracize rogue actors and constrict their funding flows, inflicting real pain.
>
> This is warfare defined by the use of financial tools, pressure, and market forces to leverage the banking sector, private-sector interests, and foreign partners in order to isolate rogue actors from the international financial and commercial systems and eliminate their funding sources.[122]

If Treasury's tools are applied to the People's Republic of China, to its state-owned and state-backed corporations, China's economic growth path will be slowed. China's influence throughout the world's most important markets would rapidly wane. While China is already busy building offsets to reliance on the US dollar, through measures such as the globalization of the RMB, the introduction of a new digital currency, and alternative global payments systems, China's companies and banks still rely on the use of the US dollar in order to handle international commerce and trade. Here is what Zarate says about the power of the Office of Foreign Assets Control, a Treasury capability that was applied in the Second World War:

> In World War II, the US government tried to control the assets of German, Italian, and Japanese companies and agents. It managed this with a little office at the Treasury Department known at the time as "The Control." The Control became the US government's primary tool for going after the assets of enemy regimes. In the 1950s, with the Korean War raging, The Control was renamed the Office of Foreign Assets Control [OFAC], and it was used to target Chinese assets."[123]

OFAC's power was in its ability to control access to the US banking system and capital markets, which have been the lifeblood of the global economy for the past hundred years: "What made OFAC so powerful was not so much its ability to freeze assets or transactions as its power to bar designated parties and those associated with them from the U.S. financial system. . . . The OFAC power was an inherently international power because of the importance of the American banking system and capital markets. This power extended beyond US shores thanks to the United States' status as the principal capital and banking market worldwide. If you want to be a serious international institution with the ability to work globally, you have to access New York and the American banking system."[124]

As with other aspects of economic containment, shaping China's access to capital markets is not just a matter of what China has access to; it also has a great deal to do with what America allows its own business and finance leaders to do of their own volition. The US government has placed blanket investment bans on individual Chinese stocks and securities in the aerospace, energy, rail, telecommunications, semiconductor, space, maritime, and technology sectors.[125] The Securities and Exchange Commission has begun the process of potentially delisting Chinese stocks from US exchanges, recognizing the risks presented by opaque financial accounting and Communist Party control of companies. As State Department commentary to the Securities and Exchange Commission explained in 2020:

Many of the PRC's companies on US based exchanges are state-owned enterprises (SOEs), in which either the instrumentalities of the PRC or high-ranking officials of the Chinese Communist Party (CCP) hold significant ownership. It is common and often required that the CCP play a role in management and board oversight, even actively running the companies.[126]

Delisting Chinese equities does not address the entire problem. It is even more significant that Wall Street institutions have crafted numerous investment vehicles that pour American and global capital into China, seeking a return on China's economic growth. For example, the Bloomberg Barclays Global Aggregate Index, as reported in April 2019, included 364 Chinese government bonds, as well as those of the China Development Bank, Agricultural Development Bank of China, and the Export-Import Bank of China, all of which provide financial backing for China's Belt and Road.[127] BlackRock, S&P Global, J. P. Morgan, FTSE, and MSCI have established similar indexes that pour billions into China through passive investment. The inclusion of Chinese equities, including numerous state-owned and state-backed corporations, also creates pressure for individual money managers and institutional investors to invest in Chinese companies in order to compete with those indexes, a measurement of their own performance as managers. As an emerging markets manager told me about Alibaba and Tencent at the start of the 2020s, "I have to be in these stocks. They are a big piece of the MSCI and I have to be able to beat MSCI as an emerging markets manager." Here is what the SEC's Division of Economic and Risk Analysis said about MSCI and other indexes in 2020:

By the end of 2020, we estimate that there will be $38.9 billion of investment in [MSCI] A Shares across the three major equity indexes (Panel A). We also estimate that there will be $15.8 billion of US mutual funds' exposure to the Domestic Bond market via Bloomberg, JP Morgan, and FTSE global market indexes (Panel B). The IMF estimates that the expected inclusion of Chinese domestic securities into major global indexes will generate *up to $450 billion net inflow into the Chinese economy, which equals 3 to 4% of China's GDP*, in the next two years.[128]

We are pouring capital into our primary adversary on such a large scale that the current investment bans barely make a dent. In the early 2020s, it has been commonplace to hear investment professionals state that there should be even more China exposure on global and emerging market indexes, given the size and growth of China's economy. American investment banks are looking to manage China's growing wealth and expand their fee-based services business in China. As a Reagan-era economic warrior said to me about this, "We never had American financiers in the Soviet Union working to improve their economy." We have them in China today, which explains the scale of the problem. If this can be stopped—and America's massive economic toolkit has every means to do it—we will achieve the right strategic ends.

While some have cautioned against the use of the US dollar against the People's Republic of China, as our geopolitical challenges increase, we must remember the true power of the cards we hold, and the potential need to use them before the broader game is lost. Taken as a whole, the application of US economic power against the People's Republic of China is likely to accelerate the bifurcation of the world economy along the lines of technology, trade, and finance, but also to position the United States for a long-term systems competition that we can win. Our adversary, despite its important advantages in industry and trade, is unlikely to match US and Allied capabilities in innovation and productivity. Without full access to our far larger markets, capital, and technology, China is likely to fall short of its ambitions to become the world's largest economy and the centerpiece of global economic and military power. If we are able to accelerate this separation of the Chinese economy from Allied economies, China's real problems—slowing growth, demographic decline, and massive debt—will all assert themselves, placing China in the "middle income trap" and removing the possibility of a world in which it is the dominant geopolitical power.[129]

Such an outcome would still provide a decent livelihood and plenty of the world's most important advancements for the People's Republic of China and its citizens. In that sense, the heartfelt aspirations of many Americans have already been achieved: to lift hundreds of millions of people in China out of poverty through access to our markets, technologies, and industrial advancements. But this need not come at the cost of the long-term destruction of an

American-led world. China's rise has been extraordinary—with many thanks to the largesse of American policymakers and the profit-motive of American businesses. But a contained China, stagnant but large, free to live within the ideologies and practices of its own design, but not to export them nor to impose them upon the world, upon America, nor upon humanity's future, would be a size neither too big, nor too small, but just right. We have everything we need to get there. Such a change means that we must look after ourselves, our future, and that of our Allies and partners around the world. Separation from China is one thing, but most importantly, America must once again become the world's economic cornerstone.

PILLAR TWO

Rebuild America

Creating a new divergence in US and Chinese economic power will require the economic containment of China by the United States and our Allies—the application of sanctions, investment bans, export controls, trade reduction measures, and secure supply chain initiatives. A second pillar is also required: a new pathway for US and Allied prosperity and growth. This means US and Allied victory in a contest for the industries and technologies that will define the twenty-first century, and a vision of the US economy and world economic system in which the US and Allies have far superior economic power. Our advantages in the twenty-first century's key strategic industries must become overwhelming in order to win the overall competition at hand. The United States—like the People's Republic of China—must have a clear vision of what the world could look like in the decades ahead from the point of view of technology, industry, and the economic and military power that this creates.

China's planners have set the course of their nation on a timeframe that tracks two centenaries—the 2021 founding of the Communist Party of China and the 2049 founding of the People's Republic of China, with a 2035 midpoint as a guidepost in between.[130] Their military, industrial, and geographic strategies all track this timeframe, from Made in China 2025 to the Belt and Road Initiative. The Chinese Communist Party has a state-led economy, which is a source of some strengths but also some fundamental weaknesses. The United States should not emulate this model. Rather, we need to enter into a systems competition. China must no longer prey upon US innovation, capital, and technological advantages through "engagement." We must separate our systems to the point that ours can prove its advantages. The importance of long-term strategy and long-term thinking is essential. We, too, must have a vision for 2030, 2040, and 2050.

The US-China competition is a contest for power over time. If the United States is able to secure a lead and build breakaway capacity in terms of economic and technological power while sustaining this lead over the coming decades as new advancements in human progress begin to compound, then we will win the contest for power with China. To do this, we must imagine and realize the technological advancements that exist on the road ahead in the twenty-first century and compound their power at a faster pace than our adversary is able to achieve. These technologies will arrive as a series of inflection points in the industrial and economic potential of humanity, changing the shape and potential of our civilization. Dictatorships like Russia and China have already identified the importance of key technologies and industrial battlegrounds such as space and artificial intelligence and their effect on national power. So have we, but the longer we remain economically integrated and engaged with our adversaries, the longer that our innovations become their advancements, too. To win a battle for the future, we must envision what it looks like and ensure that this future remains American, free, and led by the world's democracies.

What matters here is not the inputs themselves, such as artificial intelligence and quantum computing, but *what these inputs unlock* in our broader industrial, military, and economic potential. Without a comprehensive industrial base that includes fundamental industries such as steel, manufacturing, shipbuilding, and shipping, there is no great advantage that artificial intelligence could bring on its own when our adversaries are poised not only to reap the benefits of advanced technology but also to apply them within a complex and sophisticated industrial base that completes their economic ecosystem. A society that excels at only technology, finance, and services will always rely on other places to have a whole economy. This is untenable in a major power competition. In our case, the atrophy of our own industrial base means nothing short of dependency on our primary adversary, the People's Republic of China. We are primed to lose this competition, whatever our advancements may be, until we rebuild our own industrial base, terminate our reliance on this adversary state, deny this state access to the advancements that we make in America and across the Allied World, and usher in a winnable *systems competition*.

The United States must envision global supply chains, innovation flows, and trading communities that omit the People's Republic of China. We must focus on the fast-tracking of next-generation industries and technologies so that they can ultimately underwrite the economic and military potential of the United States and Allied World. During the Cold War, despite the invention of the internet and the ultimate mass adoption of consumer and enterprise technologies, the technological advancements that took shape during the contest with the Soviet Union were arguably modest in comparison to the gains in productivity and industrial potential that may be unleashed in the next wave of innovation, often called the "fourth Industrial Revolution" or "Industry 4.0." Technologies and systems overhauls including the "Internet of Things," artificial intelligence, quantum computing, and next-generation ICT all have transformative potential for the world's essential industries. The advent of the fourth Industrial Revolution is a fortunate moment in world economic history for US-China competition to begin in full. It presents an opportunity for US-China bifurcation to become a path of acceleration for America and Allied democracies.

While our adversary has been planning to surpass and displace us for decades, we have awakened to this problem recently. If we seek only to regain lost ground, we are likely to fail. If we seek to capture the horizons of the future without securing the foundations of the past, we may also fail. There is no purpose in driving our own car faster when our adversary is sitting beside us in the passenger seat, with total access to anything and everything that we invent and do. We must do two critical things: capture the strategic inflection points on the pathway ahead and build out and revitalize our national and Allied industrial power. In doing so, we can create a second Great Divergence, between the democracies and our authoritarian competitors, allowing us to win the Economic Arena and the US-China contest as a whole. Rebuilding our industrial base is an essential piece. This is our rocket ship. Seizing the technological inflection points of the future is essential; this will be the fuel for our rocket. The interplay of these two elements is the key to the second pillar of the Economic Arena—rebuilding the economic potential of America and the Allied World.

We cannot achieve this without the full participation of our business leaders and private enterprises. Industry leaders and scientists already understand the potential of the economic revolution that may be at hand in the decade ahead, but industry leaders and scientists are not yet thinking in terms of America's existential competition with China. In order for America to prevail, we will need them to buy in. America must make a whole of nation, whole of economy effort to reach the economic horizons of the future. We must maintain and then expand our lead over China through the potential that these horizons create for national productivity and economic power.

THE FOURTH INDUSTRIAL REVOLUTION

We have already entered a period some call "the fourth Industrial Revolution." The founder of the World Economic Forum defines it as "a fusion of technologies across the physical, digital, and biological worlds":

> Consider the unlimited possibilities of having billions of people connected by mobile devices, giving rise to unprecedented processing power, storage capabilities, and knowledge access. Or think about the staggering confluence of emerging technology breakthroughs, covering wide-ranging fields such as artificial intelligence (AI), robotics, the Internet of Things (IoT), autonomous vehicles, 3D printing, nanotechnology, biotechnology, materials science, energy storage, and quantum computing, to name a few. Many of these innovations are in their infancy, but they are already reaching an inflection point in their development as they build on and amplify each other in a fusion of technologies across the physical, digital, and biological worlds.[131]

In the words of the same author, building upon the first Industrial Revolution, which enabled mechanical production in the eighteenth and nineteenth centuries; the second Industrial Revolution, which enabled mass production in the nineteenth and twentieth centuries; and the third Industrial Revolution, defined by computers, "the digital revolution," and the birth of the internet in the twentieth century, the fourth Industrial Revolution will be "characterized by a much more ubiquitous and mobile internet, by smaller and more powerful sensors that have become cheaper, and by artificial intelligence and machine learning." "Smart factories" will be an essential piece of the decades ahead: "By creating 'smart factories,' the Fourth Industrial Revolution creates a world in which virtual and physical systems of manufacturing globally cooperate with each other in a flexible way. This enables the absolute customization of products and creation of new operating models."[132]

Bernard Marr, author of *Tech Trends in Practice*, describes the phenomenon as follows:

> We have never lived in a time of faster and more transformative technological innovation. Incredible technologies like artificial intelligence, blockchains, smart robots, self-driving cars, 3D printing, and advanced genomics . . . have ushered in a new industrial revolution. . . . There are some technologies . . . that are more foundational—like big data, 5G, and artificial intelligence—and then there are others that overlap with or use technologies like big data, 5G, and artificial intelligence—like self-driving cars, chatbots, or computer vision.[133]

Marr includes the following twenty-five technologies and categories in his assessment:

- Artificial Intelligence and Machine Learning
- Internet of Things and the Rise of Smart Devices
- From Wearables to Augmented Humans
- Big Data and Augmented Analytics
- Intelligent Spaces and Smart Places
- Blockchains and Distributed Ledgers
- Cloud and Edge Computing
- Digitally Extended Realities
- Digital Twins

- Natural Language Processing
- Voice Interfaces and Chatbots
- Computer Vision and Facial Recognition
- Robots and Cobots
- Autonomous Vehicles
- 5G and Faster, Smarter Networks
- Genomics and Gene Editing
- Machine Co-Creativity and Augmented Design
- Digital Platforms
- Drones and Unmanned Aerial Vehicles
- Cybersecurity and Cyber Resilience
- Quantum Computing
- Robotic Process Automation
- Mass Personalization and Micro-Moments
- 3D and 4D Printing and Additive Manufacturing
- Nanotechnology and Materials Science[134]

These technologies and this process of economic change have the potential to set the stage for twenty-first-century economic, military, and strategic power. They also create the potential for a second Great Divergence, between the Free World and our authoritarian adversaries. Policymakers have already begun to prioritize these technologies. Beijing's focus on technologies from artificial intelligence to genomics and quantum computing, as well as its technological breakthroughs, is widely known. However, what matters is not only the individual contest and progress for these underlying technologies but the transformation of the economy as a whole, what they all add up to in terms of total economic power and potential. Whichever side can maximize the strategic value of the entire economy will likely have superior resources overall in the twenty-first-century contest for power.

Doing so will require a new American approach to critical technologies and strategic industries, the likes of which is already in the making. As Biden National Economic Council Director Brian Deese explained in June 2021:

It is worth noting at the outset that a national industrial strategy is neither novel or new. In the early nineteenth century, "the American System" described the set of federal policies designed to grow our early nation's nascent infrastructure and industrial base at a time when our nation's economy was driven by agriculture. These policies, including subsidies for transportation and the creation of a national bank grew the US economy in a way that benefited diverse regions of the US. In the twentieth century the federal government again made major strategic investments after World War II, developing emerging technologies and industries such as microelectronics and biotechnology through federal purchasing, public research, and public-private partnerships.[135]

Deese added, "We should be clear-eyed that the idea of an open, free-market global economy ignores the reality that China and other countries are playing by a different set of rules. Strategic public investment to shelter and grow champion industries is a reality of the twenty-first century economy. We cannot ignore or wish this away."[136]

The integration of America's free-market economy with China's state-led predatory economic practices has contributed to deindustrialization in the United States and the enmeshment of leading American corporations into the strategic programs of the Chinese Communist Party. However, if separation takes place, we will be free once again to innovate and build toward our own horizons of economic progress without having our industries, companies, and national future engulfed by the People's Republic of China. The US Congress has already begun to focus on major twenty-first-century industries and technologies. The US CHIPS and Science Act, signed into law in August 2022, is the first major step toward a broad-scale US industrial strategy since the end of the Cold War. Consider the ten industry categories this initiative targets for public support:

- Artificial intelligence, machine learning, and autonomy
- Semiconductors and advanced computer hardware and software
- Quantum information science and technology
- Robotics, automation, advanced manufacturing

- Natural and anthropogenic disaster prevention
- Advanced communications technology and immersive technology
- Biotechnology, medical technology, genomics, and synthetic biology
- Data storage, data management, and cybersecurity
- Advanced energy technologies including batteries and nuclear
- Advanced materials science and related manufacturing technologies[137]

Now let's recall the industries targeted by Made in China 2025, the Chinese Communist Party's flagship industrial policy, which envisions dominance in these sectors:

- Advanced railway and transportation
- New energy and energy-saving vehicles
- High-end computerized machines and robots
- Aerospace
- New materials
- New-generation information technology
- Energy equipment
- Agricultural machinery
- Maritime equipment and high-tech ships
- Biopharma and high-tech medical devices

The overlap between these sectors gives a sense of what is at stake in the eyes of both the American and Chinese governments. However, unlike Beijing, America lacks a clear vision for what the world economy and international system will look like if these economic strategies are successful. This is what America must envision and define: not only a competition for the underlying technologies that are likely to define the twenty-first century by enabling core industries and economic power, but also the entire shape of the world economy, supply chain, and trading system, so that the potential for breakthroughs in underlying technologies and industries becomes an *accelerant* for a kind of American recapturing of the world economy. To do this, we must look at where emerging technologies and strategic industries convene. In these spaces, there is the potential for American innovation, inventiveness, and visionary power. In the words of Dario Gil, Director of Strategic Research at IBM, the economic potential unleashed by new technologies has transformative potential for both US industry and overall national advantage:

> I really believe that the advent of what is going to be possible by using artificial intelligence to allow us to imagine new scenarios like hypothesis generation and this act of creativity to complement what humans can do, coupled with quantum computing, which is going to allow us to solve problems that were unsolvable before, *that powerful combination is going to be the new basis of competitive advantage for our country.* Because with that we will be able to affect the material world. . . . We apply digital for digital very often, the world of websites and so on. Applying now computing to the physical world so that *we can engineer new materials to build new industries,* is such a powerful thought.[138]

Under the Trump administration, the White House released a series of strategy documents on advancements ranging from artificial intelligence, quantum, advanced manufacturing, and 5G that discuss the implications of these technologies for America's industrial potential. However, the United States has not yet articulated a strategy for GDP and productivity growth in the context of a long-term contest with China. America must integrate the sum of these emerging technologies and their implications for US industries into a strategy that applies to the fulcrum of the contest—world economic share—which means a focus on increased productivity, national wealth creation, and GDP growth.

Let's look briefly at the economic history of the twentieth century, in which two of the past three industrial revolutions took place. As economic historian Timothy Taylor explains about the turn of the twentieth century, a time when America was in the process of becoming the leading industrial power: "Compared to today we would think a lot of those people were living in dire poverty." Only 3 percent of homes in America were lit by electricity and over 80 percent were lit by coal, oil, and kerosene. Imagine the world described as follows, which existed a century ago, and you can imagine what another hundred years might bring in terms of new industrial advancements and elevations in the world's standard of living:

> In 1900, maybe a third of the homes in the US have running water. In rural areas almost none of them have running water. Only 15 percent of homes in the country have flush toilets. In fact, half of farm households in rural areas don't even have outhouses. . . . Bodily waste is not being disposed of in that careful a way in 1900, even in an outhouse. Travel around town if you lived in a city was typically walking or horse. Given the bad kinds of roads . . . making three miles an hour, a walking pace, was pretty good.[139]

Electrification in the United States was not an end in itself. The power of this advancement, of this technology, and of others of its time is *what these technologies enabled* in the broader economy, in the broader scope of American standards of living, as well as in industrial and military power. Without electricity, which was not yet in common household use in the early 1900s, there could not have been the enormous success of the Second World War effort in which American factories and mass production overmatched the fascist powers and swept them back in both Europe and Asia. There would not have been the moon landing, computing, the rise of the internet, and now the fourth Industrial Revolution, which itself is just one more milestone in the road of human progress. As Klaus Schwab explains: "The second industrial revolution . . . made mass production possible, fostered by the advent of electricity and the assembly line. The third industrial revolution . . . is usually called the computer or digital revolution because it was catalyzed by the development of semiconductors, mainframe computing (1960s), personal computing (1970s and 1980s), and the internet (1990s)."[140]

Think of artificial intelligence, quantum computing, biotechnology, robotics, and the entire rich menu of new technological inputs as the electricity of the twenty-first century. Just as semiconductors, computing, and the internet were only possible in the later twentieth century through the fundamental advancements and adoption of the early twentieth century, so, too, will the revolutions of the later twenty-first century be made possible by the ones that we invent and adopt today and in the decade ahead. We are building foundations for the whole scope of twenty-first-century economic and military power right here. The future, the next hundred years, is littered with these inflection points and possibilities in the path of human progress. It is up to America to unlock, discover, and compound these advantages until we realize a new and unimagined potential for our country, for our Allies, and for human civilization. These advantages must not be seized and mastered by the states that continue to drag the horrors of human history into the modern era and who fantasize about a future in which they have attained total power and full control. In the words of Winston Churchill, in his speech "Their Finest Hour," "If we fail, then the whole world, including the United States, including all that we have known and cared for, will sink into the abyss of a new Dark Age made more sinister, and perhaps more protracted, by the lights of perverted science."[141]

Because we have fought one Cold War with a communist state whose economic potential was a fraction of our own, we often forget how sophisticated these adversaries were. How fortunate it was that we, not they, captured and utilized the successive turning points in historical progress that have brought about democracy's dominion over recent history. Our adversaries understood these things as well, but they fell behind or failed. Lenin himself, father of the USSR, said: "Communism is the electrification of the whole country and soviet power." He was right about electricity. He was wrong about soviet, meaning communal, power. We must also ensure that the heights that we can reach are places where our adversaries cannot follow. Imagine what kind of world we would have if Hitler, not America, had been first or even second to atomic power.

This is a contest for history, by which I mean, a contest for the future. Our contest with China takes shape within the broader potential of twenty-first-century industrial and technological progress. It is a contest in which every major advancement must be realized and compounded. Our lead, which is presently waning, must accelerate and widen until the unique genius of America and of the free and Allied World creates new possibilities and reaches economic and industrial escape velocity, leaving our adversaries behind in a world of their own that is only a shadow of what the future can actually bring.

America's vision of victory, our unique and full command of the future of human progress, shared with the world's democracies and Allies, but not our opponents, is built upon that most American thing of all: the Next Frontier. America has always been the champion of unimagined things and places. Our inventiveness is our best defense against an enemy that seeks to mobilize multitudes, regiment its force and industry, and marshal it all toward what they call the "bloody battles of our era." China's dictator Xi Jinping states: "Backed by the force of more than 1.3 billion people, we have an infinitely vast stage for our era, a historical heritage of unmatched depth, and incomparable resolve that enable us to forge ahead."[142] In contrast to this "invincible force" with its "infinite stage," America retains advantages that our adversary can never have, but we must unleash them in a systems competition where our innovation finds its own, newly invented means of production and scale, and where the adversary's present industrial capabilities are gradually deprived of innovation. If the innovations of free democracies are taken by autocracies that seek to lay foundations for power that our republics cannot overcome, then we may lose. If our systems separate, if once again as in the whole of the modern era, Democracy versus Autocracy is the nature of the game, we will win.

Once we unlock and apply the new technologies of the twenty-first century, we must apply them to the industries of the future, the points on the horizon that, strung together, are like a star map to an ancient sailor. Compounded and realized, these stars can transform and build upon the world we have today, unlocking newfound wealth and potential, and laying the foundations for a second American and Allied century. Productivity increases can transform our gross domestic product and unlock new horizons for economic growth and national defense. It is productivity that we must work to build at home. In the words of Rob Atkinson, president of the Information Technology & Innovation Foundation:

> The greatest driver of economic progress since the dawn of the industrial revolution has been the development and adoption of technology, especially to either automate work or eliminate the need for it. This will remain just as true in the future. Today, the possibilities are near endless: robots, artificial intelligence (AI) systems, autonomous vehicles (AVs),

and new materials are just a few technologies that promise to boost productivity. By expanding output, this process will lead to increased wages and better jobs. But developing and using technology to boost productivity growth rates will also play a key role in reducing the debt-to-GDP ratio, by increasing both gross domestic product (GDP) and tax revenues.[143]

As Dr. Atkinson and I wrote in 2019, US focus on productivity growth and "moon-shot" innovation initiatives can add $10 trillion to American GDP in the decade ahead.[144] If we do this while closing the doors on China's economy, we will surge ahead and maintain the lead over our opponent in this decisive decade. We need to focus on strategic industries, emerging technologies, and new partnerships between US and Allied governments and our multinational corporations. Just as American companies powered the Second World War effort as our Arsenal of Democracy, public-private partnerships contributed to many of our most important innovations in the Cold War era, from the Space Race to Silicon Valley to the creation of the internet. The American innovation ecosystem includes the role of the federal government for long-term funding toward research and development, basic science, and industry creation. Large corporations enable adoption, utilization, and commercialization at scale. University ecosystems enable advanced research and development. Entrepreneurship in small and early-stage businesses creates speed of innovation and utilization that can outpace larger companies. Our innovation system is likely to present fundamental advantages. If we combine our innovation system with those of other Allied democracies, while blocking China from this system overall, we are likely to maintain technological superiority over the course of the twenty-first century.

The virtuous cycles created by our innovation systems are different from the mechanisms of China's state-led economy, even as it enables entrepreneurship and innovation of its own. Even as Chinese industrial policies create the need to respond with renewed strategies of our own, the best role for the US government in this picture is not like that of the government of an authoritarian command economy. For example, as I once learned in Silicon Valley, nearly 20 percent of US GDP is made up of companies that were initially funded by venture capital. Our adversary may be, to varying degrees, a state-led and often state-controlled economy. Think of US government at its best as the world's largest and most impactful venture capital firm. From the creation of Silicon Valley to the Space Race, when the US government has clear strategic goals, it can aim higher and hold on for longer than any private firm—and it can provide the means for others to invest and build for the long term. A contest between short-term thinking in America and long-term thinking in China is one that we will lose. This is why initiatives like the CHIPS Act of 2022, which garnered support from dozens of American CEOs, are important. Consider this account of the state of US competition against China's dedicated industrial policies in the technology sector, from the President's Council of Advisors on Science and Technology, a group with representatives from the US Fortune 500, US National Laboratories, and leading research universities, written in September 2022: "Today, about 12 percent of semiconductors are manufactured in the United States, continuing a long-term decline from 37 percent in 1990. In 2021, 85 percent of semiconductor fabrication equipment was destined for countries in Asia (28 percent of that going to China), while only 7 percent of fabrication equipment was destined for use in North America. *If the United States does not increase investments in semiconductor manufacturing*, it is estimated that our nation will be on a path to manufacturing less than 10 percent of the world's semiconductors by 2030, while China will be manufacturing nearly 30 percent of the global supply."[145]

From steelmaking to advanced chip fabrication, America cannot afford to lose our strategic industries and let our adversaries dominate the world economy. Public-private cooperation is vital in a time of transformative geopolitical competition. In America, the private sector is our test bed for trial-and-error adoption of new technologies and our free-market system is the forge for innovation. Government backing for the key industries and technologies that will shape the future is essential to engaging the private sector in a geopolitical contest of this scale. The government can provide room for failure and success and hold to a long-term horizon that goes far beyond the quarterly or annual report.

Like the noncommissioned officer corps—which creates a critical advantage in our military operations, by delegating decision-making to battlefield commanders on the ground—our own private sector is likely to act and innovate better than China's state-owned and state-backed opponents. Like our NCOs, they will need some level of support from a US economic strategy that makes clear what is needed in the near- and long-term contest with China. The right combination of government support and public-private partnerships can shape the Economic Arena and provide advantages that companies cannot create alone. Historically, superpower competition has led to economic and innovation breakthroughs including the birth of Silicon Valley. Margaret O'Mara, author of *The Code: Silicon Valley and the Remaking of America*, when asked, "What caused that extraordinary opportunity in Northern California?" said this: "The Cold War. . . . The great growth—not only in military spending on R&D, building up defense, and the nuclear program—but a particularly new thing that the government got in the business of doing during and after World War II: financing basic scientific research and development."[146] Fortunately, the US government's role in research and development has enormous room for growth, which means that new horizons for productivity and gross domestic product await. As Atkinson explains:

[F]ederal government spending on research and development (R&D) has fallen significantly as a share of GDP, and current R&D is not focused on advancing technologies that drive productivity. As such, Congress and the administration need to devote more direct and indirect funding to R&D that is focused on enabling technologies that will boost productivity. In short, it is time to add a new mission for federal R&D: boosting productivity.[147]

If we unlock our wealth advantage—where we, together with our Allies, have over three times China's total national wealth—the scope for successful public-private partnerships in the industries of the future may be virtually unlimited. US government backing can lower the cost of capital for companies and financial institutions to invest in key technologies and strategic industries inside the United States and across the Alliance System. Economic containment measures toward China, together with investment bans, and Wall Street's eventual recognition of the risks in China, can raise the cost of capital in China, creating a virtuous flow of investment leaving China and pouring back into America and the Allied World. The key is a combined maneuver in which we jettison the Communist Party of China as an economic predator while achieving escape velocity for the world's democracies as Allied wealth, investment, and innovation meet the possibilities of the fourth Industrial Revolution. Achieving escape velocity in the 2020s and 2030s means that we will hold a critical advantage, potentially for the remainder of the century, navigating toward a second Great Divergence, this time between China and the Democratic World.

SECURE SUPPLY CHAINS AND A NEW INDUSTRIAL RENAISSANCE

US economic security will require large-scale initiatives that reposition the US at the center of the world economy and siphon economic power and influence away from China. Our battle for the global economy will require us not only to be the leading technological and financial power, but also the leading manufacturing power once again. The shape of the world economy has been badly distorted by China's entry into the World Trade Organization in 2001, and the Chinese Communist Party's use of market distorting initiatives to master key industries and position itself as the world's primary manufacturing base. In a geopolitical competition of these proportions, it will be unsustainable for our primary adversary to also be our main supplier of everything from medical devices to rare earth elements. Additionally, China's massive trade surplus as the world's leading trading nation affords them a supply of capital that can be deployed for many strategic purposes, especially large-scale investment in strategic industries and technological advancements.

Let's look at US manufacturing and the possibility of a North American manufacturing renaissance.[148] In addition to the Trump administration's work to hold China to account as a predatory power in international trade, the Biden administration has begun a comprehensive review of American supply chain security, recognizing the interconnectedness of supply chains, industrial power, and the domestic innovation base. The Biden Executive Order on America's Supply Chains states that:

The United States needs resilient, diverse, and secure supply chains to ensure our economic prosperity and national security. Pandemics and other biological threats, cyber-attacks, climate shocks and extreme weather events, terrorist attacks, geopolitical and economic competition, and other conditions can reduce critical manufacturing capacity and the availability and integrity of critical goods, products, and services. Resilient American supply chains will revitalize and rebuild domestic manufacturing capacity, maintain America's competitive edge in research and development, and create well-paying jobs. They will also support small businesses, promote prosperity, advance the fight against climate change, and encourage economic growth in communities of color and economically distressed areas. More resilient supply chains are secure and diverse—facilitating greater domestic production, a range of supply, built-in redundancies, adequate stockpiles, safe and secure digital networks, and a world-class American manufacturing base and workforce. Moreover, close cooperation on resilient supply chains with allies and partners who share our values will foster collective economic and national security and strengthen the capacity to respond to international disasters and emergencies.[149]

The COVID-19 pandemic exposed massive weaknesses in US supply chains and in our hollowed-out industrial base, a story that has long been known to those who live in or care about the deindustrialized places of America. The shortages that we experienced at the start of the pandemic had everything to do with over-reliance on China. The combination of Chinese Communist Party malpractice and China's outsized role in our medical supply chain was devastating for America and for the world. For example, the Chinese government made massive purchases of lifesaving supplies on world markets while simultaneously feeding disinformation through major international organizations including the World Health Organization about the nature of the pandemic. The Chinese government also nationalized foreign-owned factories in China, including those of American multinational corporations, procuring all masks produced at these facilities in order to meet domestic needs.[150] The US Congressional Research Service explains the problem as follows:

China is a major U.S. and global supplier of medical PPE, medical consumables, and active pharmaceutical ingredients. According to U.S. trade data, in 2019 China supplied over 70% of U.S. imports of textile and face masks, 55% of U.S. imports of protective eyewear, and 55% of U.S. imports of protective garments for surgical and medical use. . . . In January and February 2020, at the height of the COVID-19 outbreak in China, and prior to the emergence of major clusters in the United States, the Chinese government organized a large-scale purchase of PPE for China on the global market, depleting existing supplies in the United States and other countries such as Australia and Canada. In early February 2020, the Chinese government nationalized control of the production and distribution of medical supplies in China, including PPE. China's nationalization efforts . . . may have denied the United States and other countries timely access to critical medical supplies. . . . Multinational manufacturers of PPE, including Minnesota-based 3M and Canadian firm Medicom, informed the media that all masks produced in their facilities in China were procured to meet domestic demand, while China allowed only smaller manufacturers to export PPE, some of which recipient countries, including the United States, found to be unusable.[151]

In the meantime, here is how certain thinkers in the Chinese Communist Party saw the impact of COVID-19 on China's strategy for economic dominance: a cause of economic disruption in Europe and economic decline in America, as well as *ensuring the world's deepening dependence on China* as a manufacturing and industrial base:

Objectively speaking, with the globalization of the epidemic and the general frustration of the global economy, Western countries' reliance on China 's economy and markets will deepen, and the United States' use of the epidemic to accelerate its "decoupling" from China is likely to be counterproductive. . . . Second, China's policy drive for anti-epidemic conversion has fostered strong manufacturing, including of masks, medical devices, and technology systems. All can become new growth points for China's foreign aid and exports, thus providing strong support for the international radiation of China's soft and hard power. Moreover, Europe may fall into an economic downturn under the blow of the epidemic, unprecedented mutual needs and opportunities in China-EU economic cooperation will emerge, and cooperation will deepen, including in 5G industries. These developments will help to break through the US strategic blockade and political threats. Gradual breakthroughs can be made in China-EU economic integration. It [the epidemic] can also promote reconciliation of Russia-Europe relations and the revival of the pan-Asia-Europe continental economic order, all the while structurally reducing dependence on US political and economic forces. The US economy meanwhile will decline.[152]

Manufacturing dependency on an adversary state is among the most foolish outcomes and failed strategies in modern history, and certainly one of the most woeful failures of strategy since the American era began after the Second World War. The United States must make every effort to reduce and, in many cases, terminate this dependency on our primary adversary. Doing so will require every effort to rebuild our manufacturing and industrial capabilities at home, a priority shared by both the Trump and Biden administrations, the two administrations that have been in power since the historic sea change in US strategy toward China. The Trump administration issued many reports related to the subject, for example: *National Strategy for Critical and Emerging Technologies* (October 2020), *Strategy for American Leadership in Advanced Manufacturing* (October 2018), *Recommendations for Strengthening American Leadership in Industries of the Future* (June 2020), *Summary of the 2018 White House Summit on Artificial Intelligence for American Industry* (May 2018), *Charting a Course for Success: America's Strategy for STEM Education* (December 2018), and *National Strategy to Secure 5G* (March 2020). Even ahead of the global pandemic, policymakers could see the problems of interdependency with China and the need for the US to move forward in rebuilding our economic independence and industrial advantages. The Trump administration engaged business leaders from market-leading companies such as Dow, IBM, HP, and Bank of America to combine the knowledge and interests of American industry with the strategic imperatives that face the country.[153] The work of rebuilding the US industrial base has only just begun.

The Biden administration's supply chain review report *Building Resilient Supply Chains, Revitalizing American Manufacturing, and Fostering Broad-Based Growth* (June 2021) may be the most important economic strategy document from the current administration. It recognizes the interplay between supply chains, economic growth, and a domestic manufacturing base, as well as the importance of each of these things to sustaining American leadership in innovation. As the report explains:

> A resilient supply chain is one that recovers quickly from an unexpected event. Our private sector and public policy approach to domestic production, which for years, prioritized efficiency and low costs over security, sustainability, and resilience, has resulted in the supply chain risks identified in this report. That approach has also undermined the prosperity and health of American workers and the ability to manage natural resources domestically and globally. As the Administration sets out on a course to revitalize our manufacturing base and secure global supply chains, rebuilding for resilience at the national level requires a renewed focus on broad-based growth and sustainability.
>
> America's approach to resilient supply chains must build on our nation's greatest strengths—our unrivaled innovation ecosystem, our people, our vast ethnic, racial, and regional diversity, our small and medium-sized businesses, and our strong relationships with allies and partners who share our values.
>
> As multiple reports note, the United States maintains an unparalleled innovation ecosystem with world-class universities, research centers, startups, and incubators, attracting top talent from around the world. The Administration must double-down on our innovation infrastructure, reinvesting in research and development (R&D) and accelerating our ability to move innovations from the lab to the marketplace.[154]

Transformation will abound in the world economy as the US works to enact necessary changes. We must regard our road ahead as a battle for the world economy, one that America must win. There will be great costs, but also great rewards, if we succeed in the Economic Arena. It must be the essential foundation of a true American grand strategy that can succeed against China's bid for long-term global dominance. Additionally, while many falsely regard interdependence as a way to prevent military conflict—two world wars provide a potent counterexample—we must recognize that our peacetime period of economic interdependency is neither novel, nor a guarantee against military conflict. At the turn of the twentieth century, a period of economic globalization took shape that led to a popular belief that warfare among states was too costly to contemplate. Historian Nicholas Lambert describes globalization in those years as follows in *Planning Armageddon: British Economic Warfare and the First World War*:

> Between 1870 and the 1890s the volume of global trade doubled. The increase has been attributed mainly to a spectacular decline in the cost of transporting goods by sea due to advances in marine technologies. Over the next twenty-odd years, freight costs continued to fall; in combination with transformative developments in monetary systems and especially communication technologies, this kindled another doubling of world trade. The result was the emergence of a globally integrated trading system. . . . During this forty-year period, furthermore, Great Britain became ever more dependent upon foreign trade and the maintenance of a thriving global trading system for its national well-being.[155]

Lambert goes on to explain that, "Before the 1880s, few seriously suggested that Britain's growing dependence upon a thriving system of international trade might prove the source of strategic weakness, simply because there was then no other power capable of threatening its international position."[156] America finds itself in a similar situation today. After several decades of rapid globalization and substantial increases in the value of the global goods trade since the end of the Cold War, we find ourselves with massive dependencies that create strategic weaknesses, rather than advantages, not least because it is explicitly clear which nation seeks to take America's position as the lead actor in the world economy. The period of globalization prior to the First World War reminds us that an integrated, interdependent world is not inherently stable. In our case today, the priority must be to reduce or eliminate our dangerous dependencies and open the door for a renaissance in US industrial and economic power, while also preparing for a period of potential economic warfare with China. Given the rising costs of production in China, however, there are opportunities at hand.

China's transformation into "the world's factory" during the post–Cold War era took shape largely because of its ability to succeed in labor-intensive industries, while also moving into capital-intensive industries on the back of this success. Today, through a combination of rising costs in China and geopolitical concerns, the world has already begun to look for alternatives. As economist Gordon H. Hanson explains:

> Over the last 70 years, many of the countries that became export power-houses did so by starting on the ground floor, producing t-shirts, fabric, shoes, children's toys, bicycles, dressers, table lamps, and the like. First Japan, then the East Asian Tigers, and finally China followed this path to achieve high levels of income growth. For the last 30 years, China's presence has complicated life for other countries pursuing a conventional strategy of export-led development. It may have been hard to get ahead via labor-intensive manufacturing if China kept driving down product prices and gobbling up market share. In China's economic shadow, warmth may have been hard to find.
>
> Yet that shadow now appears to be shrinking. As China's labor force becomes more educated, older, and smaller and as rural-to-urban migration decelerates, the country confronts a declining comparative advantage in labor-intensive goods. The diversification and increasing technological sophistication of China's exports—some of which may be due to market forces and some to state intervention—indicated that a shift in global specialization is already well underway.[57]

Hanson sees three possibilities for China, one of which, in this author's view, presents an important opportunity for the United States: "reallocation of labor-intensive export production to other emerging economies, labor-saving technological change in historically labor-heavy industries, and a relocation of manufacturing production within China." Hanson notes that "the first and third appear to be working slowly and the second not at all. Who will fill China's shoes remains something of a puzzle."[158]

The United States and our Allies have an opportunity as China transitions away from labor-intensive manufacturing and into higher-end manufacturing, something that industrialized democracies, including Germany and Japan, already do well. We can use this opportunity to change the shape of the global economy and trading system, working to move manufacturing and supply chains out of China and into third-party countries, and also to focus especially on the middle possibility that Hanson identifies: "the creation of new technology that replaces labor with capital in currently labor-intensive industries." Hanson points out that, while there has been relatively little innovation in this space, "China itself may be partly responsible for the sluggish pace of innovation in these industries. With its earlier large and growing supply of less-educated labor available for export production, the incentive for labor-saving technological change in its initial core industries may have been weak." In other words, the presence of China's massive workforce in the world economy has actually been a drag on industrial innovation, a phenomenon that others have pointed out as well.[159]

As the shape of the world economy changes, and China's labor force becomes less of an essential feature in global production, the US and our Allies may be able to hasten this change in the structure of the world economy with a focus on technological innovation in labor-intensive industries alongside national commitments to build an advanced manufacturing economy. A national manufacturing strategy, and a North American manufacturing renaissance utilizing the comparative advantages of America, Mexico, and Canada, can add a new economic engine for the United States while revitalizing regions that have been devastated by thirty years of globalization. It is something that we simply must do, and that both the Trump and Biden administrations articulate. For example, the Advanced Manufacturing National Program Office released *Manufacturing USA Strategic Plan* in November 2019, which states that its objective is to achieve "US global leadership in advanced manufacturing" through four primary actions:

1. Increase the competitiveness of US manufacturing
2. Facilitate the transition of innovative technologies into scalable, cost-effective, and high-performing domestic manufacturing capabilities
3. Accelerate the development of an advanced manufacturing workforce
4. Support business models that help institutes to become stable and sustainable[160]

This initiative includes a series of US government agency–sponsored institutes across America that focus on essential technologies in advanced manufacturing, including The National Additive Manufacturing Innovation Institute in Youngstown, Ohio; The Next Generation Power Electronics Manufacturing Innovation Institute in Raleigh, North Carolina; the Institute for Advanced Composites Manufacturing Innovation in Knoxville, Tennessee; and the Advanced Robotics for Manufacturing Institute in Pittsburgh, Pennsylvania. In short, the US government is already in the game when it comes to envisioning and enabling a future where manufacturing and industry return to America. Here are some of the other actions in the strategic plan:

Conducting (or funding) precompetitive research and development projects to reduce cost, time, and technical uncertainty related to new manufacturing technologies and to improve existing technologies, processes, and products

Developing and implementing education, training, and workforce recruitment courses, materials, and programs

Developing new technologies, innovative methodologies, and improved practices for integrating and expanding supply chains

Developing and encouraging shared state-of-the-art facilities and infrastructure to reduce the cost and risk of commercializing new technologies and to address relevant manufacturing challenges on a production-level scale[161]

A vision of America returning to industrial eminence has been shared by politicians on both sides of the aisle. For example, in *Entrepreneurial Nation: Why Manufacturing Is Still Key to America's Future*, California Democrat Ro Khanna states that, "[T]he reality is that most international trade is still in goods. . . . We can't balance our books simply by selling more financial instruments, software programs, and Hollywood movies to the world. The money we earn from so-called knowledge work isn't enough to make up for what we spend buying overseas products."[162] The Biden administration has continued the Trump administration's emphasis on manufacturing power, not only in their flagship supply chain review, but by building upon initiatives that go back even further, like the Revitalize American Manufacturing and Innovation Act of 2014, and new direction to the National Science and Technology Council "to develop and to update, in coordination with the National Economic Council, a strategic plan to improve government coordination and to provide long-term guidance for Federal programs and activities in support of United States manufacturing competitiveness, including advanced manufacturing research and development."[163] The Biden administration defines advanced manufacturing as follows: "a family of activities that (1) depend on the use and coordination of information, automation, computation, software, sensing, and networking, and/or (2) make use of cutting-edge materials and emerging capabilities enabled by the physical and biological sciences, for example: nanotechnology, chemistry, and biology. It involves both new ways to manufacture existing products, and the manufacture of new products emerging from new advanced technologies."[164]

In other words, the US government is already moving in this direction, with bipartisan support. What will be necessary is the cooperation of US industry and business leaders to forge a new vision for American prosperity, and to let go of our false hopes about China, its market, and its place in the global economy altogether.

CONCLUSION

T he United States must on the one hand secure our own supply chains, rebuild our industrial base, remain the world's reserve currency and leading financial center, and form an Alliance-based trading system. On the other hand, we will have to do what we can—with our Allies and partners—to erode China's current account surplus, restrict their access to our technology and innovation ecosystem, and restrict access to our capital markets. The first path will enable economic security and prosperity in the United States and within the broader Alliance System, and the latter will begin to cause the economic containment and constriction of the People's Republic of China. A China that is cut back from the developed world's technology, financial markets, and export markets is a China that will cease to grow, will lose leverage over other countries, and that can ultimately be left behind by the course of long-term technological and industrial progress. This will allow the world's democracies to surge forward over time, gradually increasing our lead and enabling a second Great Divergence in history. Coupled with a robust deterrence strategy, an economic divergence is our best hope of reshaping the world economy and winning a contest for overall share of the world economy and overall share of global wealth.

Today's world economy totals $96.1 trillion.[165] China totals 18.4 percent at $17.7 trillion and the US is 23.9 percent at $23 trillion. The US Alliance System as a whole represents over half of the world economy, while the OECD plus India is nearly two-thirds.[166] US economic grand strategy should aim to increase its share of global GDP and global wealth, while setting similar growth goals for our Allies and partners, as well as constricting global GDP and wealth share for adversary states. For example, US share of global GDP has been as high as 50 percent in the aftermath of the Second World War, at the inauguration of the American era, and 40 percent in 1960 with the Cold War well underway.[167] This was due partly to America's large population and industrial strength—a formula China aims to emulate for twenty-first-century global dominance—and partly to the relative weakness of a devastated postwar world.[168] In the twenty-first century, America has generally held about 25 percent of world GDP, enough to be the world's largest economy, market, and a bedrock of the world economy. However, in the absence of robust growth, our share has dwindled. China has contributed the lion's share of global growth during its ascendancy and integration into the world economy since its accession to the WTO. Critically, however, China has not yet surpassed the US economy in total size. In order to ensure that this never happens, America must simultaneously succeed at economic containment of China and robust growth of US share and Alliance System economic integration. For example, if the United States is able to build toward a $30 trillion GDP from $22 trillion today, while holding China to a lower $20 trillion range through the year 2030, we start to create a meaningful divergence in total economic power, building upon the slender advantages we have today. If, by 2040, we can reach a $40–45 trillion GDP while holding China at minimal levels of growth, the gap widens enormously, and so forth through the decades of US-China competition. This increasing US share of global GDP both in absolute and relative terms would set the stage for a global grand strategy defined by possibilities, rather than by constraints, in contrast to what many of our leading strategists contemplate today. It is the only way to turn the game decisively in our favor. In the absence of resources, frugality and agility are virtues; but a better virtue is the ability to create vast resources and become unconstrained.

Our ability to reach these new horizons while holding back an adversary from the same levels of progress is the question on which the future of the Free World fundamentally turns, and this is where victory in the Economic

Arena must aim. Just as many like to say that China is the only country that has risen, fallen, and risen again, America must be the country that has risen, glimpsed decline, and then risen once again. It is the rise of America, not the rise of China, that must define our century and our world ahead. However, organizing such a future will be a matter not only of economic action, but of what would be among the greatest global diplomatic efforts of the modern era, a subject we will turn to next.

PART TWO

THE DIPLOMATIC ARENA

Almost as if according to some natural law, in every century there seems to emerge a country with the power, the will, and the intellectual and moral impetus to shape the entire international system in accordance with its own values.

—Henry Kissinger, *Diplomacy*

OUR GLOBAL CHESSBOARD

The Alliance System and the Emerging World

The question before us is not: Will China rise and shape the twenty-first century? The question is: Will America?

Diplomacy is sometimes misunderstood as the act of talking with other nations—a practice that does not involve military action or the use of force yet is still pursued to attain a country's objectives. As Winston Churchill once said, "meeting jaw to jaw is better than war." But this distinction alone does not capture the scope and purpose of diplomacy. A traditional understanding would see diplomacy as the coordination of all strategy *toward other nation-states*—the overall ways by which a state conducts its international relations.[1] Diplomacy is the design—the architecture of international relations. Diplomacy is more than just a method. In the Diplomatic Arena, economic and military power must meet a vision of *the structure of world order*—how nations and regions fit together and how we can shape and influence an outcome that we desire.

The principal task of American diplomacy in the contest with China will be organizing the world's democracies into a united, superior military and economic coalition that will not only withstand China's aggressive actions, but also surpass China's most ambitious plans. While many analysts and practitioners are focused on China's regional ambitions, prioritizing coalition-building in Asia, or what is now known as the Indo-Pacific region, we must not mistake

China's goals as regional alone. In fact, China's ambitions are global, and its strategic footprint is already global. Moreover, China is in the process of assembling a coalition of its own, one that extends well beyond Asia. While nothing near an Alliance System in the way that we define it, China already possesses a series of strategic partnerships across the globe. Most are economic, but China's engagement with other nations and regions comes in all forms, from investment to military exercises, from influence-buying and elite capture to student exchanges. In short, as *China's Vision of Victory* explains, the Chinese Communist Party has a fully global vision, and massive economic, military, and diplomatic operations to support achieving this vision. Focusing on Asia alone will lead to failure in American strategy.

While our contest with the People's Republic of China may be won or lost in the Economic Arena, the foundation of American power, we must also have a clear vision and purpose for world order. Diplomacy must not be the simple act of negotiation and relationship-building with other nations. We must think of diplomacy as the process of designing a vision and a structure for the international system, one in which America, our Allies, the world's major non-aligned regions, the People's Republic of China, and our other opponents all exist. The challenge posed by China forces us to rescue and rebuild an international order that is in danger of yielding irretrievably to China's growing international power. To do this, we must have a global vision, just as the Chinese Communist Party does in its own intended efforts to seduce, coerce, and ultimately subordinate different nations and regions to its long-term vision of victory. Our vision of world order must never be America alone or America isolated. In fact, that isolation is what our adversaries wish to achieve. Our vision must instead lead America once again to the helm of a great community of nations, one in which democracy and human rights are defended and not in retreat.

In this author's view, to maintain an American-led international order, the core must be made up of the US-led Alliance System and the world's democracies, large and small. These are the fundamental swathes of the world where our economic and military power resides and where our values are expressed and defended. Whether it is our treaty Allies from Europe to Asia, or the world's many democracies in those regions and every other in between, these like-minded nations are the keys to an order that can withstand China's intended rise to preeminence. As I wrote in *China's Vision of Victory*, our second major goal, after remaining the world's leading economic power, must be to unite the world's democracies in common cause to prevail in geopolitical competition with China. The Democratic World presents the foundation for a system that preserves not only our security and prosperity, but the fundamental values for which we stand. The world's democracies *and* America's military Alliance System are the places where the majority of the world's wealth, productivity, and innovation reside. Whichever formulation we choose, whether the Organization for Economic Cooperation and Development (OECD), the North Atlantic Treaty Organization (NATO), or Allied Asia, these communities of democracies together hold the majority of the world's economic power not only in GDP but also in total wealth. The combined economic power of either the world's democracies or America's treaty Allies far outweighs China's own or that of any combination of China and its satellite states. If we can succeed in unifying not only our Allies but also the world's democracies, then the vast majority of global economic power and potential will cohere on one side of this contest against China.

The primary goal of American diplomacy should be consolidating the US Alliance System and by extension much of the Democratic World into an economic community that can develop and apply best practices toward China, Russia, or any other malefactor. In short, we must unite the Alliance System, integrate and align the world's democracies, and reconstruct the Free World. We will need each other for the duration of this contest, united in economic cooperation and security cooperation. Implementing best practices on economic containment, growth, and competition across the Alliance System should become a standard feature of our diplomacy. Bringing non-aligned democracies closer to our side through access to our superior economic community must also be a priority. Strengthening our security cooperation, a path that is already continuously improving and deepening, is another key avenue for a stronger community of Allies and democracies.

The consolidation of the democracies and the Alliance System into a coordinated strategic community led by America must be pillar one of the Diplomatic Arena. As challenging as this might be, pillar two may be even harder: our focus on the nations and regions of the "emerging world." Also known as emerging markets, developing nations, or the developing world, these are the nations and the regions where China is likely to be most successful in its global grand strategy.

If the US Alliance System can come together to reduce or eliminate economic dependency on China, enacting export controls, investment restrictions, import limitations, and other elements of economic containment, then China is likely to build into its intended fallback position on the global chessboard: the emerging markets identified in the Belt and Road Initiative. We have examined the economic strategies that the Communist Party employs, from intellectual property theft to industrial subsidies. Let us be clear about its geographic strategy, expressed most openly in the Belt and Road Initiative—an effort to tie the world's major continents into economic integration and dependency on China. America's global diplomatic strategy must eventually break the Belt and Road, which is the Chinese Communist Party's *second attempt* to establish influence and leadership among the world's emerging nations.[2] From Asia to Africa to Latin America, Mao Zedong sought to open a path for China's influence in a contest with both America and the Soviet Union during the Cold War.[3] At that time, Mao sought to export ideology and violent revolution to the world's new nations from Asia to Africa as European empires rolled back across the earth. In the twenty-first century, the Chinese Communist Party seeks to build influence and economic dependency on China among the world's developing nations under the guise of investment and development. We are likely to see China's attempts to consolidate influence in the world's emerging nations take on an increasingly anti-American, anti-Western, and anti-Indian ideological dimension in the decades ahead, drawing on the original diplomatic strategies of the People's Republic of China.[4] Even as international understanding of the Belt and Road fluctuates with China's changing economy, and even as some determine that its scope is waning, China's companies and capital continue to pour into vital regions and contested nations with the backing and strategic vision of the Chinese Communist Party. This will not change unless the process is derailed and defeated by American and Allied global strategy.

A recent common refrain in Washington acknowledges the extent of China's overseas economic influence: "America cannot be everywhere that China is" or "We can't match China dollar for dollar everywhere in the world." It may be

true that we cannot be everywhere, or that we cannot always match them—
but our Alliance System can. The combination of American economic power
and the combined global reach and pull of all our Allies is more than enough
to present China with economic and diplomatic overmatch in the majority
of the world's vital regions and nation-states. What we will need is a strategy
to create maximal influence and reach with the available resources. If our
resources are consolidated and our efforts are coordinated, they will prove to
be overwhelming.

If we can consolidate our Alliance System, unite the democracies, *and* bring
the world's emerging nations to our side, we will achieve far more than the
economic containment of China and the growth of America and our Allies,
our main objectives in the Economic Arena. We will also achieve diplomatic
rollback of the Chinese Communist Party and the dismantling of its global
grand strategy. This would involve an initial matching or blocking in key states
and regions and then eventually the gradual contraction of Beijing's influence
across the globe. Just as nations from Asia to Africa cast off colonialism in the
twentieth century, in the twenty-first century they must also cast off the dangerous advances of Beijing. But they cannot do this alone. If America and our
Allies ignore their development needs, if the wealthiest regions of the world do
not provide alternatives, then the need for investment and commercial development across the world's emerging regions will remain Beijing's game to win. In
2017, the Asian Development Bank estimated that developing nations in Asia
would require $26 trillion worth of infrastructure investment between 2016 and
2030, including requirements for power, transportation, telecommunications,
and water and sanitation.[5] Beijing has already invested substantially in the
world outside China, approximately $2.2 trillion in investment and construc-
tion between 2005 and 2021.[6] The American Enterprise Institute has cataloged
a total of $189.3 billion in Latin America, $311.8 billion in Sub-Saharan Africa,
$213.9 billion in North Africa and the Middle East, and $644 billion in East
and West Asia including China's investment in Russia.[7]

While the United States has begun to get into the global infrastructure
game with initiatives like the Blue Dot Network and the US International
Development Finance Corporation (DFC), we are not yet responding to the
scale of the challenge. We have not yet heeded the investment needs in global

emerging markets or the coordinated power of Chinese state banks, corporations, and diplomats, which now have enormous experience with combined economic operations in global markets. The United States and our Allies must prepare to marshal much greater quantities of private sector capital toward key emerging markets to compete with China's coordinated efforts. The DFC is a step in the right direction, supporting, in its own words, "private-sector-led investment, offering a robust alternative to [China's] state-directed investment which often leaves countries saddled with debt."[8] However, the key to success is not just methods but quantities of capital. America must fully engage its global investment banks in national interest–related development financing to unlock quantities of capital that can compete worldwide against Beijing. Supported by the US Secretaries of State, Commerce, and Treasury, as well as the head of the US Agency for International Development, the DFC has the potential to become a nexus for whole-of-government–enabled public-private global investment partnerships if it can bring the power of American capital markets to the world's emerging regions. This could involve, for example, a DFC advisory capability from the emerging markets divisions of America's top twenty banks and institutional investment firms by assets under management. As China's predatory lending causes havoc in nations like Sri Lanka, the United States and our Allies can be far better partners, leveraging superior free-market standards and partnering with emerging nations on infrastructure-related concerns such as environmental degradation and climate change.

The Soviet Union was able to contest America globally despite its relative disadvantage in economic power because it offered ideological persuasion and development assistance to decolonizing nations. Our Cold War adversary framed America as one more imperial state like those in Europe against whom emerging nations fought their wars of independence. China today offers investment and one-sided commerce on a much greater scale. In the twentieth century, numerous nations achieved their freedom from colonialism. In the twenty-first century, the nations and regions of the emerging world seek higher standards of living and greater economic development. If America and our Allies can be their better partners, we can win this contest, too. Doing so will require that our economic battle units—our private companies, banks, and multinational corporations—prepare to go head-to-head in global competition with China's state-owned and state-backed enterprises in emerging markets across the world. This global economic battlefront—American and Allied multinational corporations versus Chinese state-owned and state-backed enterprises—will determine much of the strength of our overall diplomatic and economic position. It is here that our economic toolkit and the global playing field of American and Allied diplomacy must converge. Our companies may not be prepared for a looming global contest with China's state-backed corporations, one that is taking shape already because of Beijing's aims. Our companies cannot avoid that contest, even if America were to fail to develop a global grand strategy. However, the combination of private enterprise and the global reach of American diplomacy and security partnerships can invigorate a new alignment of private sector interests and national strategic goals. Public-private partnerships must take on new geographic scope and reinforce the foundations of our global diplomatic architecture. Victory in the Diplomatic Arena rests upon two pillars: unity among the Allies and democracies and a rollback of China in the emerging world.

PILLAR ONE

The US Alliance System vs. China's Anti-Western Coalitions

More dangerous than China's global web of economic and diplomatic relationships is an emerging anti-Western coalition. A joint Russia-China partnership is the bedrock challenge to the United States. A world in which China takes on the US and our Allies alone is a world that would be far easier to handle. A world in which Russia and China mount a joint effort against America in both Asia and Europe is a world that will be challenging indeed. While many doubt the durability of this partnership, harkening back to the short-lived Sino-Soviet alliance in the Cold War, the Russia-China entente has returned and is arguably sturdier now than at any other time in modern history. While Russia and China are clearly the most significant and powerful members of the anti-Western coalition, one must add to this Iran, which challenges America and our Allies in the Middle East and Persian Gulf; North Korea, which can hold our Allies in Asia at risk; and potentially Pakistan as well, whose closeness to China, while it may seem a more distant problem for America, is an existential danger for India, a nation that is likely to become one of our most important partners in dealing with China. Other players exist and will arise, and fence-sitters will abound as well, proving the maxim that "the only thing necessary for the triumph of evil is for good men to do nothing." But the most important actors against America, our Allies, and our friends are the authoritarian regimes in China, Russia, and Iran. Fortunately, this loose coalition need not cohere forever.

Values and ideals are potent forces in forging a coalition. While we will address the power and importance of ideas in full, we should note the essential role that they can play in American diplomacy. There is perhaps no power so great as the power of the American Idea, and the power that this represents to people from every nation who desire to come to America. This idea is an essential aspect to our global reach—not because we have Americans in every nation living and working abroad, but because *our own citizens come from every nation*. This will always be our unique advantage in our message to the world, but we will have to work to reconnect and live up to our ideals and values at home if we are to inspire the many nations of the world. The Chinese Communist Party has already begun to organize a countervailing force in this regard. In a world of Chinese influence defined by dozens of strategic partnerships across the globe, and by a dangerous counter-Western coalition built mainly on military power, there is also a collection of states that is willing to support China's worst atrocities, even in global forums such as the United Nations.

Consider the situation at the United Nations Human Rights Council, where the German ambassador in 2020, on behalf of thirty-nine countries, called on China to "respect human rights, particularly the rights of persons belonging to religious and ethnic minorities, especially in Xinjiang and Tibet." The thirty-eight nations were Albania, Australia, Belgium, Bosnia and Herzegovina, Bulgaria, Canada, Croatia, Denmark, Estonia, Finland, France, Germany, Haiti, Honduras, Iceland, Ireland, Italy, Japan, Latvia, Liechtenstein, Lithuania, Luxembourg, the Republic of the Marshall Islands, Monaco, Nauru, the Kingdom of the Netherlands, New Zealand, North Macedonia, Norway, Palau, Poland, Slovakia, Slovenia, Spain, Sweden, Switzerland, the United Kingdom, and the United States. In other words, primarily democratic nations in Europe and Asia and the Americas. Here are the *forty-four nations* that opposed the statement from the German ambassador, a coalition of China's supporters from across the planet:

Angola, Bahrain, Belarus, Burundi, Cambodia, Cameroon, the Central African Republic, China, Comoros, Congo, Cuba, Dominica,

Egypt, Equatorial Guinea, Eritrea, Gabon, Grenada, Guinea, Guinea Bissau, Iran, Iraq, Kiribati, Laos, Madagascar, Morocco, Mozambique, Myanmar, Nepal, Nicaragua, Pakistan, Palestine, Russia, Saudi Arabia, South Sudan, Sri Lanka, Sudan, Syria, Tanzania, Togo, Uganda, the UAE, Venezuela, Yemen, and Zimbabwe.

China's genocide in Xinjiang is now the subject of enormous public record and testimony and officially designated as such by governments around the world. But the statement of China's supporters, led by Cuba, goes like this: "We commend that the Chinese government pursues the 'people-centered' philosophy in advancing economic and social sustainable [sic] development, eradicating poverty, increasing employment, improving peoples' living standards, and promoting and protecting human rights. . . . [In Xinjiang], people of all ethnic groups enjoy their happy life in a peaceful and stable environment. . . . On Xinjiang related issues it is an imperative to respect the basic facts rather than making unfounded allegations against China and interfere out of political motivations and bias."[9]

We can see that our companies are not alone in their dangerous dance with human rights abuses in China. Dozens of nations from around the world now explicitly endorse Beijing's worst atrocities and methods.

George F. Kennan, perhaps America's greatest twentieth-century diplomatic strategist, "believed that power is the currency of international politics."[10] When confronted with these three layers of the world—China's global web of "strategic partnerships," anti-Western military coalition, and diplomatic supporters of human rights atrocities—our diplomacy must not be solely to argue against these forces. *Our diplomacy must be to build overwhelming power.* We must build our power against coalitions of countervailing states, creating unity among our fellow democracies and like-minded states, and forging a new cohesion in world affairs in which both our ideals and our interests prevail over the will and aims of the People's Republic of China and other dangerous states. Successful American diplomacy will require a Herculean effort to unify and organize an enormous and diverse portion of humanity. It may be the most challenging diplomatic effort in world history. In this contest, our next generation of great diplomats will be formed.

The United States Alliance System took shape in the aftermath of the Second World War, alongside the formation of the Unified Command System, which established a unified command of all US forces worldwide. The evolution of this system comes from a war fought in two theaters: the Atlantic (Europe) and the Pacific (Asia).[11] This war, this combatant system, and this view of the world from across two oceans has defined the American strategic worldview from Kennan to the present day. American strategic thinking often contends that no hegemon should dominate Eurasia, the great "world island" from Europe to Asia, in which the bulk of the world's nations, resources, and conflicts occur. America sits as a kind of continental-sized offshore island, as Britain once did vis-à-vis Europe, able to ensure that a stable balance of power exists—a balance of power that favors the United States and our Allies.

A world in which two primary theaters exist, Europe and Asia, is a world that American strategists have been able to manage for decades from a position of preponderant power. It is also a world that America's enemies, when working together, have tried to exploit. At the inception of the Sino-Soviet Alliance, for example, Joseph Stalin proposed a Soviet focus on Europe and a Chinese focus on Asia. In the words of the Soviet dictator to Liu Shaoqi, China's envoy to Moscow in 1949: "There should be some division of labor between us . . . you may take more responsibility in working in the East . . . and we will take more responsibility in the West . . . this is our unshirkable duty."[12] The following year, Mao would send the Chinese military to fight the United States and United Nations in the Korean War. In the twentieth century, as a nation of greater economic, technological, and industrial strength than both Germany and Japan or both the Soviet Union and China, America's two-theater vision and strategy toward the world's geography made good sense indeed. The results are testimony to its effectiveness: victory in both the Second World War and the Cold War. In Europe, the implementation of the European Recovery Plan in 1948 (better known as the Marshall Plan) and the formation NATO in 1949 set up the architecture for the US presence in Europe and kept the Soviet Union at bay in Europe militarily and economically for the duration of the Cold War.

In Asia, a different kind of system formed, due in large part to the loss of the Chinese Civil War (1945–49) by America's ally, the Republic of China, which then fled to Taiwan in 1949 as power in mainland China was seized by Mao and the Chinese Communist Party. In Europe, the American-led system was a group of Allied states working together within a multilateral system. In Asia, by contrast, the theater of greatest importance today, the American system was one of bilateral alliances, which now needs reform in order to manage the scope of our current contest with China. As historian Victor Cha explains,

> In East Asia the United States cultivated a "hub and spokes" system of discrete, exclusive alliances with the Republic of Korea, the Republic of China [Taiwan], and Japan, a system that was distinct from the multilateral security alliances it preferred in Europe. Bilateralism emerged in East Asia as the dominant security structure because of the "powerplay" rationale behind US postwar planning in the region. "Powerplay" refers to the construction of an asymmetric alliance designed to exert maximum control over the smaller ally's actions. The United States created a series of bilateral alliances in East Asia to contain the Soviet threat, but a congruent rationale was to constrain "rogue allies"—that is, rabidly anticommunist dictators who might start wars for reasons of domestic legitimacy and entrap the United States in an unwanted larger war. . . . The administrations of Harry Truman and Dwight Eisenhower calculated that they could best restrain East Asia's pro-West dictators through tight bilateral alliances rather than through a regionwide multilateral mechanism. East Asia's security bilateralism today is therefore a historical artifact of this choice.[13]

The US Alliance System, along with other Cold War–era architecture, carries with it the genius of an American geopolitical worldview that resulted in relative stability and security for decades among the world's major powers, also known as the Pax Americana or the American Peace. This era is now waning as Russia and China present themselves as committed adversaries. As this era is slipping away, America must do more than increase our economic might, productivity, industry, and technological power. America must update its two-theater general theory of geography—based on our view of two oceans, the Atlantic and Pacific—and we must usher in *a globally coordinated Alliance System.* Our Allies represent the most diverse assembly of nations ever organized in history as partners in power. From Japan to France, from Australia to the Philippines, from Britain to Israel, we have a collection of nations whose engagement with and trust in America is testament to our unique role in the world.

While America has a long history, and current foreign policy, of unavoidably engaging with all manner of societies, from kingdoms, sultanates, and emirates to republics and parliamentary democracies of all kinds and sizes, the ideal type in our global system is the Democratic World, a system that exists, not of our creation, but certainly in our nature. Friends and Allies in the twenty-first century will include countries whose systems are not the same as ours, from the Persian Gulf to Vietnam. We have a beautifully built world of parliaments, republics, and rights-based governments with all the material and moral goods that this entails—from the Americas to the Baltics to the Sea of Japan. This world exists, but it must be unified and led. That is where the hardest, greatest diplomacy of our lifetimes will take place: not toward the persuasion of our enemies, but toward the unification of our friends. Within this picture, we must win a new contest with the world's dictatorships and autocracies, who, invited into the world economic system, have grown rich and hungry, imagining a preeminence of their own. We must overmatch China's dictators, who put forth the idea of "The Community of Common Destiny for All Mankind," a world in which China sits at the center, presiding through coercion, influence, and force over a global set of neo-vassal states.[14]

If the Democratic World, in all its complexity, coheres, then it will constitute the main arena of human progress and the productive core of world affairs. No dictatorship or authoritarian power could successfully challenge the power of the *global* Free World. Such a system is reminiscent of the world that some Americans envisioned in the post–Cold War era, as democracy seemed to be on a course to spread farther across the world. However, these ambitions led to major blunders, both through intervention—the idea that we could impose democracy in Iraq—and through blindness, the idea that democracy or liberalization would take hold in places through economic and diplomatic engagement as we supposed of China. These errors of judgment have contributed in part to a world in which many now believe that democracy itself is in retreat.

What we must do is think of democracy as a defensive, rather than an offensive, position. Democracy is not necessarily a path to impose on other states, but rather a rampart made of nations to be maintained, strengthened, and defended. The existence of a rival system, in which certain nations will inevitably become attachments and dependencies of China, will allow the difference in these systems to become evident over time. While China may build its influence in the world's most vulnerable or undecided places, we, too, will have the ability to pull the swing nations toward our side. We must work to limit China's reach to all places but those that are deliberately abandoned. As our side grows and flourishes in ways that the dictatorships cannot—if their access to the Free World is rolled back and reduced in every way that matters—we may also see some of China's present-day partners swing to our side. Could Russia, a nation with important historical leaders such as Peter the Great who looked to Europe for inspiration, come to our side in the decades ahead as its people come to understand the miserable role they will have in China's "Community of Common Destiny for All Mankind"? What is to say that Iran won't have its own revolution in time and lean toward the West, as it did at times in the twentieth century? Other states in China's orbit now, from Southeast Asia to the Persian Gulf, may be battlegrounds for influence, never wholly owned by our adversaries, but open to the appeals of either side, as in any prior contest of this worldwide scale. We must choose carefully where to prioritize and how to engage. With the combined power of the world's democracies, and the system we can maintain, we will be able to act effectively on a global scale.

Let's view the world through our adversary's eyes—the blueprints of *their* architecture—the plans that we must counter and dismantle. For victory in any major power contest, America must have a clear sense of how the world's geography works, not solely from our own point of view, but from the point of view of our primary adversary. As explained in *China's Vision of Victory*, China's ambitions are global, not regional. The most important expression of Beijing's vision of the world's geography is the Belt and Road Initiative, a vision of an interconnected system in which Asia, Europe, and Africa are bound together though China-built infrastructure, trade links, investment, and influence. Furthermore, China is building a military tasked with defending overseas interests throughout this intercontinental system, a subject that we will revisit in the Military Arena. Beijing envisions an economic conquest of most of the world's continents and the construction of military power and influence that no coalition of nations can challenge. While military power is concentrated on the first and second island chains in the Pacific, China is also working to expand its influence in the Indian Ocean Region, an area through which much of China's resource and goods trade passes. The Indo-Pacific Region, properly understood as the region comprising the Indian Ocean and the Pacific Ocean—and one in which each of these oceans is equally important to our adversary's strategy—is therefore the fulcrum of our geographical contest with China.

While China seeks resource security in the Indian Ocean, which acts as the maritime machinery of the Eurasian-African supercontinental economic system, China also wants to exclude America from this intercontinental system by stripping American power away from the first and second island chains, where an American military presence was earned through an enormous cost of lives in the Second World War. While some military strategists are rightly focused on the island chains as the likely battleground in a potential US-China military conflict, it is vital that our diplomatic strategists work across the global playing field to secure advantages for America and to roll back China's economic and diplomatic influence outside of Asia.[15] Furthermore, the world's democracies will have to work from a globally integrated system in order to reduce or expel Beijing's influence, and to compete to win in the world's contested regions. Economic diplomacy and military diplomacy must combine in order to secure the vital regions of the world.

We need a globally unified strategy, one that includes the Alliance System and the Organization for Economic Cooperation and Development (OECD). The OECD, formed in 1960 by the United States, Canada, and a range of European nations, is now a worldwide economic organization that includes industrialized democracies and is a values-based economic community. In its own words, the OECD is "a like-minded community, committed to the preservation of individual liberty, the values of democracy, the rule of law and the defence of human rights. We believe in open and transparent market economy principles."[16]

Members of this values-based economic community can work together to form a global alternative to the predatory economic practices and geographical ambitions of the Chinese Communist Party. OECD members include Austria, Belgium, Czech Republic, Denmark, Estonia, Finland, France, Germany, Greece, Hungary, Iceland, Ireland, Italy, Latvia, Lithuania, Luxembourg, the Netherlands, Norway, Poland, Portugal, Slovakia, Slovenia, Spain, Sweden, Switzerland, and the United Kingdom in Europe, Israel and Turkey in the Middle East, Australia, Japan, New Zealand, South Korea, and in the Indo-Pacific, and Canada, Chile, Colombia, Costa Rica, Mexico, and the United States in the Americas. This grouping represents the core economic community of the world's democracies.

With our Alliance System and OECD unity in place, we must then attend to the world's emerging regions: the Indo-Pacific, Africa, and Latin America. Finally, we will have to attend to three geopolitical areas that are not altogether defined by the existence of nation-states: the polar regions, the oceans, and space, though much of this is likely to be handled in the Military Arena. In each of these places, we will find ourselves confronted with deep wells of Beijing's influence and capabilities, given the attention that China has given to all these arenas for decades.

The United States must organize its influence and effectiveness outside of the Alliance System by working with major partners that have abundant influence and who generally lean toward America. In Latin America, for example, the direction of Brazil, Argentina, Chile, and Mexico will define much of the region. In Sub-Saharan Africa, Nigeria, Kenya, and South Africa will be essential partners. In Asia, India is already potentially our most important partner outside of our treaty Alliance System. In Southeast Asia, Indonesia is a state that may tip the balance of power for the entire region. In North Africa and the Middle East, Israel, Egypt, and the United Arab Emirates will all be essential partners.

In our two-pronged diplomatic strategy—unification of the world's industrial democracies and a rollback of Beijing's influence throughout the emerging world—America's military Alliances are likely to provide the best starting grounds for consolidation of strategy in Europe, Asia, and the Middle East. While visiting US Indo-Pacific Command in 2019, I remarked to an officer that I was concerned about US global diplomacy in the face of China's long-term strategy. The officer replied that US diplomacy was going brilliantly and that we had been incredibly successful in engaging with our Allies worldwide on current challenges. And from the vantage point of military diplomacy, this observation was correct. Every US ally benefits from American support when it comes to security, which means we have a fundamental advantage when it comes to diplomacy within the Alliance System from Europe to Asia.

The other side of the equation is that, until very recently, most countries from Europe to Asia wanted the United States as a primary security partner, but China as a primary partner for trade. This is a deadly deal not only for America but ultimately for our Allies. There is no way that we can guarantee security across the Alliance System as our adversary grows more powerful through the trade, technology, and capital that we all provide to it. As a friend in Washington once said to me, "America does the dying and China does the buying." This deal among our security partners must end. American military partnership must also include curtailment of engagement with Beijing. What matters now is that, as America reconsiders and reduces our own economic engagement with China, we ask the same of our Allies, developing and applying best practices of economic containment across the Allied sphere.

NATO has already added the China challenge to its remit. Britain, Canada, and the Netherlands have joined military exercises in the Pacific—with the US, Japanese, and New Zealand navies—demonstrating that the Alliance System is gradually becoming more global and that the underlying geography is becoming more interconnected.[17] One adds to this the rise of the Quad, a strategic grouping made up of America, India, Japan, and Australia, and we can see the economic and military geography of the world's democracies beginning to cohere. Many of these countries, on their own, have jettisoned Chinese economic influence or begun to create alternatives to China as an economic partner. India, for example, has banned scores of Chinese technology companies and Japan has begun funding initiatives to move supply chains out of China.[18] Moreover, countries inside and outside the Alliance System have begun to cooperate militarily and economically to balance against China. For example, India and Australia began to hold joint naval exercises in 2015, and India and Japan have begun an investment and infrastructure collaboration in Africa, known as the Asia Africa Growth Corridor, as an alternative to China's Belt and Road offerings.[19] Britain has become more involved in the Indo-Pacific, and so has France, which was one of the first European nations to officially recognize the threat posed by China.[20] The new Australia-UK-US agreement will bring new levels of military integration between two of America's foremost Allies, underpinning not only security architecture, but establishing important new diplomatic avenues that bridge the long-standing divide between European and Asian theater strategies that have existed since the Second World War.

Often, diplomacy is the best avenue for deeper military cooperation. In the contest at hand, our robust and existing military cooperation is likely to be the most durable piece of American global architecture. This is because we did not let our enemies into these institutions, unlike, for example, the World Bank or International Monetary Fund. In today's contest, it is our robust systems for security cooperation that may provide the conduit for comprehensive diplomatic strategy. Our diplomatic strategy must resolve two things above all within the Democratic World: the world's democracies must work and act together to scale back our economic engagement with China and we must replace the economic advantages of China engagement with new initiatives for growth and integration within the Democratic World. Our diplomatic strategy must succeed from the democracies of Europe to those of the Pacific. China will apply many methods to attempt to break our coalitions and stymie our initiatives, and to use the power of its market and its military to ensure that the world continues to engage it on China's terms. Our military Alliances, the fundamental backstop against aggression from Beijing and Moscow, can lead the way in shaping a diplomacy that can stop China's ascendancy. If our Allies can rally and unify, then our contest moves toward the emerging world, the arena where China holds the greatest advantages, and the geopolitical arena where the overall contest is likely to be decided.

PILLAR TWO

China Rollback in the Emerging World

As we head into our global diplomatic contest with China, let us not forget that it was America, not China, that built the institutions of the modern world. From the World Bank and International Monetary Fund to the United Nations itself, it was the United States and our Allies, not the Chinese Communist Party, that set up the architecture of the modern world and the current international system, by building institutions that organized the post–Second World War order and which have aided and assisted every region of the world. While China is content to use this architecture when it serves its interests, the official ideology of the Communist Party is one in which the modern world and its institutions were imposed on China while China existed in a weakened state. This view of history explains why China is essentially in a state of ideological conflict not only with the United States, but implicitly with much of the world. Importantly, in the founding decades of the People's Republic of China, Mao Zedong took on not only the United States and Soviet Union as enemies, but also India in a contest for leadership among the world's decolonizing nations. In short, the period of change in the early Cold War, a time that involved not only US-Soviet confrontation and brinkmanship, but also the decolonization of much of Asia and Africa, has much to teach us about China's strategy and destination today.

China has successfully engaged the world's developed nations on economic terms, running large trade surpluses and obtaining most of the technological and industrial advancements that once created massive differences between the world's democracies and China. China has been just as successful in engaging with the world's emerging nations from Latin America to Africa and Asia. The Chinese Communist Party likely anticipates that developed nations will begin to scale back, or at least question, their economic engagement with China, a process we are already witnessing from Australia to Canada. The Communist Party is far more confident about its ultimate success in the world's emerging regions.[21] While, over the course of the founding decades of the People's Republic of China, the country was in a state of hostility with America's European and Asian Allies and partners, Chinese diplomacy believed that it could outmaneuver both the United States and the Soviet Union in Asia, Africa, and Latin America. To do so, it also had to confront and attack India, a nation with which it had once proclaimed "two thousand years of friendship" in a joint attempt to lead the post-colonial world.

The road ahead will include China's second, not first, attempt to outmaneuver the world's democracies in Asia, Africa, and Latin America. The first time, China's leaders used ideology to appeal to decolonizing nations to use force and violent revolution—China's model—to chart their course as new nations.[22] This time, China will attempt to export its development model, technology, and to a lesser but still important extent its ideological vision in its efforts to rally the developing world.

To understand this approach, one simply has to examine China's geographical strategy. The countries of the Belt and Road Initiative are mostly located in the world's primary emerging regions: Asia, Africa, and Latin America. As the world's industrial democracies gradually come together to counteract Beijing's influence, both political and economic, Beijing will push harder into the world's emerging regions. In this sense, the Belt and Road Initiative exists as an alternative to the Western market economies. As one of the Chinese Communist Party's preferred texts on the Belt and Road explains, "The Belt and Road Initiative will reconstruct the geopolitical and geoeconomic maps of the world, and help Chinese enterprises go global, marking China's transformation from a regional civilization to a global one." This account goes on to define the region as one that "covers 65 countries in Central Asia, ASEAN (the Association of Southeast Asian Nations), South Asia, Central and Eastern Europe, West Asia, and North Africa," an area with 4.4 billion people "and an economic capacity of $21 trillion, accounting for 63 percent and 29 percent of the world's total, respectively."[23] Its geopolitical self-interest is described well in a journal published by the Chinese Academy of Sciences:

> Resources are always scarce; a great nation cannot be stuffed into a narrow space forever. The Eurasian continent is the source where China's national interests are concentrated. It provides a vast stage on which to carry out China's twenty-first century geopolitical strategy. As a result of the interaction of the crystalization of the highest wisdom of the Chinese nation and the conditions of the era, the "One Belt, One Road" strategy [this initiative's original title] has announced to the world that the rise of China has arrived, becoming an important starting point for China to go global.[24]

The continents of the Belt and Road are China's future markets, supply chains, and, as Beijing imagines it, the Chinese Communist Party's twenty-first-century empire. It is a terrible irony that many nations from Africa to Asia, having rid themselves of European imperial powers in the twentieth century, now find themselves as the coveted regions of a new imperialism from Beijing. As with imperialism in the past, Beijing's ambitions cannot move forward without some form of "elite capture," the rallying of elites in foreign countries to their cause. From Sri Lanka to East Africa, China's practices of government-to-government deals and "debt-trap diplomacy" have paved the way for the integration of multiple emerging regions into an economic system that Beijing aims to control. China-funded infrastructure, including strategically located ports, railways, and other infrastructure, have wound up under Beijing's ownership when developing countries can't afford to make debt payments.

Even as protests abound in different countries, China continues to succeed in building infrastructure, granting loans, and exporting technology to these countries. While the Allied World must come together to push Beijing back from our markets, technology, supply chains, and capital resources, we must also push China back from the emerging world. If China succeeds at integrating and dominating the world's emerging regions, the Communist Party would complete a new version of China's Cold War–era strategy: "surrounding the cities with the countryside."[25] This was Mao's global vision of encircling the capitalist democracies with revolutionary movements throughout the developing world. Mao attempted but failed to achieve this vision through ideology and violence, but his successors believe that they can do it through technology, subversion, and economic power. Pushing China back from the developed world is unlikely to succeed in thwarting Beijing's long-term ambitions, if we do not also break Beijing's strategy in the emerging world.[26]

Consolidation efforts among the world's democracies are underway, particularly in the military sphere. While this must ultimately translate into economic initiatives as well—secure supply chains, free trade within the Alliance System, and greater collaboration on innovation—our greatest challenge will be working to win the diplomatic contests that are taking shape in the emerging world. This challenge is important because the United States has not prioritized economic integration and investment at the scale that China has, and it has not engaged our private sector in global strategic initiatives in a way that is already common to China's system of global economic expansion.

Many states in these regions recognize that a future under Beijing's influence is the wrong choice. However, the United States still lacks strategies for diplomatic victories and economic engagement in Africa, Latin America, and much of Asia. Our diplomatic deficit here is partly due to the fact that China's economic profile is much closer to those of many emerging markets than America's. China simply has more business with the emerging world than we do.[27] Why is this? Given China's own development path, goods and services that have been successfully developed in China may be closer to the market realities of many emerging nations. At present, it is China, not America, that is assisting many emerging markets with the second important achievement since national independence in the twentieth century—economic development in the twenty-first century. The US and other developed nations have traditionally pursued an economic aid–based strategy when engaging with emerging markets. By contrast, China uses trade, infrastructure, and investment to lead the way. While much of this is indeed predatory and non-economic by Western standards, China does not need a commercial case in order to make its investments around the world.

As evidenced by ports and infrastructure built by Chinese state-owned enterprises from the Indian Ocean to the East African coast, China creates overseas infrastructure as part of its long-term military and economic strategies, not for the return-on-investment standards that guide the Western private sector. As such, the US and other Allied governments will need to open doors for our private companies in difficult but strategically important markets abroad. US and Allied governments will also need to provide capital assistance and know-how, working together with private companies to make sure that our companies—not China's state-owned and state-backed enterprises—are the most successful in the world's emerging markets. Our corporate battle fleet, supported by the resources of Allied governments, will have to compete and win in markets across the globe. This will also be an essential offset for the private companies in the world's democracies as the China market becomes ever more restrictive and dangerous to operate in.

China's state-owned enterprises have been actively building up their positions in much of the emerging world across the Belt and Road. From physical infrastructure including ports, roads, rail, and power plants to digital technology, telecommunications, and even smart cities, China's companies have been going global with the backing of Beijing, as the vanguard of Chinese economic strategy across the world. Beijing has added many dimensions to the Belt and Road since its inception, from the inclusion of Latin America, the Arctic, and even outer space as elements in which China would like to consolidate its dominance. China's "Digital Silk Road" strategy seeks to add a high-tech, digitally integrated dimension to the physical infrastructure that it has built across the emerging world. Through the "Digital Silk Road," Beijing aims to provide overseas markets for its technology giants in the same way that it has given its banks and infrastructure giants vast regions of the world markets in which to expand their operations. If Beijing succeeds in building not only the physical, but also the digital infrastructure of the world's developing countries, then America will find itself overmatched in the majority of the world's economic and military geography. We must focus on the Indo-Pacific, Africa, and Latin America. In each of these regions, we will have to prioritize engagement with the countries that are large enough to be able to defend their sovereignty, diversify their economic options, and ensure that Beijing does not consolidate overwhelming influence in their region.

The importance of winning over these regions and bringing them to our side is threefold. First, to thwart China's broader strategy of consolidating the world's emerging regions as a counter to the world's industrial democracies. Second, to build a world that can withstand China's challenge to global order. Third, to ultimately achieve containment of Communist China. In order to do so, the United States and our Allies must build superior influence and engagement in these regions. We will have to build superior trade volume, investment, and business engagement in each of these regions, through leveraging the power of the American market and leveraging the pull and capabilities of Allied markets. While each of these regions is important to defend against Beijing's influence, each one is not sufficiently powerful on its own to tip the world's balance of power against China. The world's emerging regions are best understood as requiring a rollback strategy, rather than a balancing coalition of states. Yet, within each region, a balancing strategy can take shape, paving the way for eventual rollback.

Focus must be given to the following elements of China's overseas influence and to dismantling China's geographical strategy:

· Concentrations of economic power: both GDP and national wealth
· Trade saturation: nations with substantial trading relationships with China, especially import dependency
· Investment saturation: nations with substantial Chinese investment or infrastructure
· Nations with important strategic or military geography

America and our Allies must choose "anchor nations" for our engagement in vital parts of the world. There will be nations that loom large within a critical region and whose economic pathways and strategic alignments will determine the path of an entire region. Anchor states within each region can help pull a region toward the Allies or at least check the spread of Beijing's influence. For example, the Indo-Pacific, the swath of geography most central to the contest with China, is the region comprised of both the Indian and Pacific Oceans. Let's take three critical sub-regions: Southeast Asia, where China's investment and trading relations are strongest in the emerging world; the Indian Ocean Region, where Beijing's long-term geographical and strategic interests ultimately must take root to achieve its long-term vision of victory; and the Pacific Island states, where there is important military geography. In Southeast Asia, Indonesia is arguably the most important state. With a population of 277 million, the fourth largest in the world, a gross domestic product of over $1 trillion, and substantial diplomatic and military influence of its own, this non-aligned democracy stands to determine the course of Beijing's long-term influence if it has sufficient access to and engagement with American and Allied economic and military power. In the Indian Ocean Rim, India, a major power and potential cornerstone of American diplomacy in Asia, has influence far beyond the Indian Ocean itself. As the sword astride China's most important sea lines of communication, it is a nation Beijing is busy countering with its own game of encirclement by courting India's neighbors. India is the natural anchor nation in the Indian Ocean Region. By contrast, a smaller state like Sri Lanka, which has come under considerable Chinese influence and whose ports and geographical importance in the region are clear, cannot be underestimated because of its smaller size. The combination of anchor states and vital smaller states must form the framework for American and Allied diplomacy region by region across the world.

Let us look more closely at the world's essential regions. Outside of our Alliance System, they are the Indo-Pacific (Southeast Asia, the Indian Ocean Region, and the Pacific Islands), Africa, and Latin America.

The Chinese Communist Party has strategies for economic, diplomatic, and military engagement with each of these regions. We must also have strategies prepared that bring to bear every aspect of our economic, military, and national power in order to bring a multitude of nations to our side.

THE INDO-PACIFIC

The Indo-Pacific is the fulcrum of the global contest with China. To win in this region, we must understand it as our adversary does, in its global context. We will explore the military geography of this and other regions in the next chapter, but for now, let us look at it in terms of its most important sub-regions and vital nation-states. The Indo-Pacific Region is the region in which the Indian Ocean and Pacific Oceans combine. It is essential to China's global strategy, a place that China seeks to dominate, chiefly through the economic influence and ultimately military potential of the Belt and Road—China's proposed intercontinental system in which Asia, Africa, Europe, and even Latin America would eventually be tied to Beijing as their primary economic partner and eventual military hegemon. Many have viewed the Asia-Pacific, particularly East Asia, Southeast Asia, and the Pacific Island states, as one theater. The use of the Indo-Pacific as a strategic framework in recent years, including the conversion of US Pacific Command to US Indo-Pacific Command in 2018, is a welcome development, placing India and the Indian Ocean within this strategic theater. In addition to understanding this region as the one in which the Indian Ocean and Pacific Oceans converge, it is also helpful to understand it as the region in which both India and China exist—and in which their regional strategic interests overlap. To remind us of how little changes in major power competition, John F. Kennedy said as a senator in the 1950s, "I have spoken here today about India's race with Red China. We want India to win that race. We want India to be a free and thriving leader of a free and thriving Asia."[28] Let us look at three critical pieces that exist largely outside of the US Alliance System: Southeast Asia, the Indian Ocean Region, and the South Pacific Islands, each of which is critical to the future of both Chinese and American power.

Southeast Asia is the single wealthiest sub-region in the world outside of the Middle East, China, and the OECD itself. By total national wealth, it is larger than both Africa and South America.[29] Much as the Soviet Union's control of other states was greatest in the Warsaw Pact nations of Eastern Europe, the worst outcome for this region would be that, by sheer proximity, China would convert the fast-growing region of emerging wealth and potential prosperity into economic satellite states, affixed to China through trade dependence and investment ties. The United States and our Allies must block this outcome through deepening our own economic ties with Southeast Asia. China's trade with this region already far outweighs our own, and even nominal US security partners such as Singapore express the desire to balance their ties between both countries. In the words of Singapore's prime minister in May 2022: "We think that is the better approach, that it is possible for countries to have relations with America, to have relations with China, and to work with both. You may be closer to one than to the other. In the case of Japan, you have the US-Japan security partnership, your defence treaty with the US. We do not have a treaty with the US but we are a major security cooperation partner with the US. At the same time, we have a lot of cooperation with China."[30] However, nearly every state in this region has territorial disputes with and a fundamental distrust of China, because of Beijing's territorial claims in the South China Sea and history of warfare and revolutionary subversion in the region.

Utilizing the three key elements of outbound strategy—American and Allied trade missions, public-private investment and infrastructure coordination, and economic sanctions on Communist Party–backed banks and companies—the United States must bring its economic and diplomatic clout together to block and roll back China in this region. Helping Southeast Asian nations meet their investment and infrastructure needs is a different proposition here than it is in poorer regions of the world. Our private sector must be given every advantage through United States government support, along with coordination with our Asian Allies, particularly Japan, Australia, and South Korea. Indonesia, where the lion's share of sub-regional national wealth and GDP resides, must be our anchor state and priority partner—not only for America but for all our Allies. Coordinating US, Indian, Asian, and European investment and commerce toward Indonesia will demonstrate that the Allied World is a better option for Indonesia's current and future development. Building Indonesia's influence will enable it to push back against Beijing, which already claims parts of Indonesian territory as its own. America's two treaty Allies in the region, Thailand and the Philippines, will also benefit from greater US economic focus in addition to security ties. Laos, Cambodia, and Myanmar are likely to continue to remain under profound Chinese influence. Malaysia may swing toward the Allied World if Beijing's technology and investment initiatives can be countered. The United States must help Southeast Asian nations—as in other parts of the world—to reduce import and export dependency on Beijing, to find alternatives to China's technology exports (from smart cities to IT infrastructure), and to use US and Allied alternatives to Chinese investment. Blocking China's gradual eclipse of these nations is an essential step to preventing Beijing from consolidating its position as the dominant economic partner to the wealthiest part of the developing world, and to a sub-region that is essential to the military geography of Asia.

The Indian Ocean Region is perhaps the world's most significant and most understudied region. The Pacific and Atlantic Oceans connect the Americas to the European-Africa-Asian supercontinental structure, but the Indian Ocean connects Europe, Africa, and Asia to one another. As I have noted, "It is the waterway that makes an Asian trading system possible, and with it the possibility of a world with Asia increasingly at its economic center."[31] It is not hard to understand why the Indian Ocean Region is the geographical fulcrum of China's long-term grand strategy, and one of the two key pieces of the Belt and Road Initiative. Meanwhile, America lacks a bona fide Indian Ocean strategy. Indeed, we lack a widespread understanding of how this region works.

China's sea lines of communication, its essential maritime energy and trading routes, pass through this ocean, linking Middle Eastern energy, African minerals, and European markets back to China. Any form of geopolitical preeminence for China requires economic and military dominance of this region. Similarly, for India—Beijing's geographically gifted main opponent in the Indian Ocean Region—supply chains, energy, and external markets are also linked to this maritime system. To see this region through the eyes of its two principal powers, India and China, we must include not only the parts we call Asia, but also the Middle East and Eastern Africa in the concept of the Indo-Pacific. Beijing's play for economic dominance in Africa is a subject we will turn to. But China's influence among India's neighbors and in the island states of the Indian Ocean, especially Sri Lanka, the Maldives, the Seychelles, and Madagascar, must not be overlooked. It would be wise to regard the Middle East, with its critical maritime choke points in the Strait of Hormuz and Bab al-Mandab, as well as the globally important Suez Canal, as a sub-region inside the Indo-Pacific. China's dependency on Middle Eastern energy drives its strategy here but the United States has far greater experience in the region. Tying our Middle Eastern strategies closer to our broader counter-China strategy in the Indo-Pacific would leverage American experience and institutional knowledge, establish alliances and partnerships, and correctly track with China's views of its own security vulnerabilities and of the weakest points in its overall strategy.

If left unchecked, China's influence in this region in the 2030s could become what it is today in Southeast Asia and the South China Sea: overwhelming trade and investment dependency and a proliferation of military bases that "safeguard the security of China's overseas interests." The United States and the Allied World must counter and roll back China's influence in East Africa, the Middle East, South Asia, and the island states of the Indian Ocean world. Bringing European Allies, especially Britain and France, into this picture recognizes how this region works given its role in connecting Europe to Asia. A coalition led by America, India, Britain, France, Japan, and Australia can work to block and offset Chinese investment, reduce import and export dependencies, and ensure that no small state is ignored or left behind by the combined power of the Allied economies from Europe to Asia. An Indian Ocean Investment Bank, led by this group and joined by emerging nations and small states, can funnel public and private capital into the places that need it most. Greater diplomatic emphasis on forums such as the Indian Ocean Rim Association and prioritizing these groupings in US diplomacy can ensure that we maintain focus on this region, blocking Beijing's longer-term ambitions. Finally, empowering India, a project that America, Europe, Japan, and Australia should take on together, can ensure Kennedy's original insight comes true at last—that India, not China, wins the contest for power in Asia.

China's interest in the South Pacific Islands has long been an essential ingredient in their global grand strategy—not because of the economic potential of these small nations, but because of their importance to the military geography of Asia. As we shall see in the Military Arena, the names of many of these places are familiar to Americans because of their essential role in America's path to victory in the Pacific theater of the Second World War. Japan's military aim, like China's geostrategic aim, was to push America out of the Western Pacific. Control of the Pacific Island states would cut America off from Australia, so that our maritime "highway" from California to Australia would be cut off altogether.[32] While specialists have understood China's interest in these islands for quite some time, China's pact with the Solomon Islands in 2022 and the overture of Communist Party Foreign Minister Wang Yi to Kiribati, Samoa, Fiji, Tonga, Vanuatu, Papua New Guinea, and Timor-Leste show that the aspirations of the Communist Party's long game are becoming actual geostrategic moves.

While these nations other than the Solomon Islands have so far rebuffed China's overtures for security pacts—pacts that would potentially enable Chinese military basing across this southern set of islands—China's overtures will not end with these attempts in 2022.[33] Additionally, these island states remind us of a key lesson that China knows and we do not: in small island states, a small amount of economic influence can go a very long way. This is also a fact of Beijing's economic engagement with small states in the Caribbean Sea, near neighbors to America. And so, the United States must treat this part of the Indo-Pacific's geography as a priority. In addition to bringing these nations into American trade, investment, and economic initiatives and ensuring that there is a standing invitation to this group of leaders and their diplomats in Washington, we must also be willing to use American economic power. Chinese companies and banks that are party to any security pact, ratified, proposed, or otherwise known, should be subject to the force of American and Allied economic retribution. America must never forget the small states of the world. In many regions, their importance is profound, and we ignore them at our peril. Here, our crucial Allies will be Australia, New Zealand, France, Britain, and Japan.

AFRICA

Aside from the Indo-Pacific itself, Africa is probably the most significant continent in China's strategy toward the emerging world. It is both a resource base and a source of future markets and supply chains. China's engagement with the world's second largest continent has surpassed that of the United States and any other country in the Allied World. Without a thorough US strategy toward Africa, any long-term US diplomatic strategy is likely to fail. Even if we consolidate the Alliance System and succeed in holding back China's advances in the Indo-Pacific, should the Chinese Communist Party succeed in consummating its vision of Africa's role in their overall grand strategy, America and the Allied World will find ourselves dealing with a far more economically, militarily, and geographically powerful People's Republic of China. Our adversary's leaders have made no secret about their ambitions for this great continent. While the complexity of Africa's fifty-plus nations may deter coherence in strategy-making for the world's democracies, China works through myriad engagement efforts to pursue influence at both a state-to-state and also whole-of-Africa level.

While China's efforts in Africa are the subject of scrutiny, one recent study stands out in its efforts to showcase Africa's role in the Communist Party's emerging world strategy. Consider this element from French American scholar Nadège Rolland's 2021 report on the subject, which draws on contemporary accounts from Chinese strategists and scholars, one of whom emphasizes exporting elements of China's development model to Africa:

> He Wenping points to two Chinese "innovations" that are worth trans-ferring to African countries. The first is an essential piece of China's eco-nomic model: the combined development of labor-intensive industries, special economic zones (SEZs) and industrial parks, infrastructure con-struction, and human resources training. . . . In addition to Ethiopia, whose Eastern Industrial Zone was originally built by Jiangsu Yongyuan Investment in 2007, five Africa countries (Zambia, Mauritius, Nigeria, Egypt, and Congo) have built large-scale industrial zones in partnership with Chinese companies.[34]

It is easy to see, with projects like this—whether through smart cities that incorporate China's integrated technology stack or entire special eco-nomic zones and industrial parks that tie Africa's development to the coffers of Beijing—that the Chinese Communist Party's investment and development model for the continent will tie it closely, nation by nation and ultimately as a whole, back to the People's Republic of China. As Rolland explains, "While foreign observers are debating whether China is exporting its model overseas, Beijing is evidently striving to encourage African countries to adopt its gov-ernance practices in an effort to make them better client states."[35] Here is one version of the continent's role in China's long-term strategy:

> Among the continent's many desirable assets, Chinese experts focus on Africa as offering a vast pool of labor and potential customers for Chinese companies and products. By 2040, the labor force will come to 1.1 billion, surpassing China and India, and by 2030, 60 percent of

the world's population under 30 will be concentrated on the African continent: "In the next twenty years, the invisible hand of globalization will transfer job opportunities to countries with cost advantages and Africa will replace China as the next world factory in low-end industries," predicts Liu Hongwu. This presents an opportunity for a "win-win" situation: Africa needs to create labor-intensive industries just as China's declining advantages as a low-cost manufacturer are leading the country to look for opportunities to relocate some of its manufacturing capacity: "The only place in the world that can undertake such a large-scale transfer of labor-intensive industries is Africa."[36]

Just as American and Allied neglect of the Indian Ocean Region in the 2020s could become one of China's greatest advantages in the 2030s, neglecting Africa in the decade ahead could ruin any American grand strategy, by missing one of China's essential efforts to broaden its economic reach and project military power outside of Asia. Aspects of China's strategy in Africa directly involve creating new supply chains and labor pools, which China's businesses seek to build and own. A future for Africa as a market, workshop, and economic power base for the People's Republic of China would likely include the erosion of sovereignty and freedom on the continent. To thwart this strategy, the US and Allies must include African nations as an element in our supply chain strategy. As we remove manufacturing capacity from China, looking not only to Southeast Asian nations like Vietnam, partner nations like India, and North American neighbors like Mexico, we must also leapfrog China's long-term supply chain strategies by getting our companies and capital into Africa. As in other regions, anchor states can lead the way. Nigeria, South Africa, and Egypt, the largest nations on the continent by wealth and GDP, can act as cornerstone nations in West, South, and North Africa, respectively. The Ethiopia-Kenya-Tanzania corridor in East Africa presents a substantial opportunity for engagement with nations that form the bulk of East Africa's economic potential. Additionally, countries where wealth and GDP concentrations are relatively high, including Ghana, Cote d'Ivoire, and Senegal in West Africa, and Algeria, Tunisia, and Morocco in North Africa, should be priorities for economic and diplomatic engagement.

The US must engage our European and Asian Allies in these endeavors to provide alternative economic development options and to participate in future market and supply chain development that China's outward-focused enterprises already anticipate. Japan and India have begun collaborative work through their own Asia-Africa Growth Corridor, which can be supported or augmented by other Quad members.[37] Britain's Commonwealth of Nations includes a variety of Anglophone African nations. France's Organisation International de la Francophonie includes many French-speaking nations on the continent. Both of these organizations, if emphasized in British and French diplomacy and supported by Allied economic initiatives, will enable relationship-building that predates China's own initiatives. America and Allied nations must regard Africa as a colossal long-term economic partner. That said, we cannot neglect the nations where China's investment and infrastructure saturation is extreme, presenting Beijing with enormous leverage and future military-basing opportunities. For example, take Namibia, Angola, Mozambique, and Madagascar. As in other regions, Chinese corporations or investment banks that are party to any proposed, ratified, or known security pact should be degraded or destroyed through our total economic toolkit.

Bringing African nations into the wealth and power of the Allied World, and away from the predatory offerings of the Chinese Communist Party, will derail one of the geographical cornerstones of China's long-term strategy. Enabling our companies, banks, and entrepreneurs to succeed and find opportunity in Africa, connecting its major countries closer to our economy, utilizing trade missions, student exchanges, and the long-standing insights of agencies such as USAID and State will be essential to broadening America's connections to the continent. Our ability to achieve this, to lift the tide for other nations without the trade-offs in sovereignty and freedom required by Communist China, is the ultimate test for our diplomacy and power.

LATIN AMERICA

While Asia and Africa have made up the primary geographical areas for China's strategy in the emerging world, trade and investment with Latin America has burgeoned in the twenty-first century. With a diversified trading relationship that includes not only Chinese demand for agricultural goods and minerals, but also Latin American demand for Chinese manufactured goods from textiles to microelectronics, our Western Hemisphere neighbors to the south are in the throes of economic entanglement with China. China's strategists go so far as to include Latin America in the Belt and Road Initiative, demonstrating that the Belt and Road is not only an effort to tie major continents and markets to China, but also an effort to encircle the United States with continental-sized economic dependencies on China in the decades ahead. American diplomacy and economic efforts cannot afford to ignore our own hemispheric neighbors from the Panama Canal to the Drake Passage. While Mexico's future is likely to be deeper integration into the North American cornerstone that must become the bedrock of the world economy, we stand to lose substantially in South America, where major states like Brazil and Argentina are tied ever-more-closely to China, as are smaller resource producers like Chile and Peru. Latin America's own efforts to diversify their economies are likely to be undermined not only in the present but also in the future by import dependency from China. Light and heavy manufacturing in Brazil and other states is jeopardized in the long-run by imports from China, and a second danger is that while China imports a range of commodities, it seeks to embed its own corporations and technology stack—the integrated system built by China's technology companies, known as "national champions," working together from 5G to cloud computing to artificial intelligence and Internet of Things—into Latin American markets in return. Huawei, a company that has been ejected from the United States, Japan, India, Britain, and Canada, continues to thrive in emerging markets, including across Latin America. In Brazil, the company is involved not only in 5G networks, but in smart farming and precision agriculture:

> In Goias state, the government has taken a leading role in the digital transformation of agriculture. FAPEG (State of Goias Research Foundation) is providing agricultural know-how and agricultural applications; Huawei is providing 5G, cloud, and AI solutions; and local telco Claro Brasil is deploying the 5G networks. Cross-industry collaboration will also bring in technologies such as drones and autonomous rovers.[38]

Here is how Huawei executives view their future in the Brazilian market:

Looking ahead, Huawei has great hopes and opportunities for the future in Brazil. First, we will help Brazil to go digital with ICT infrastructure. We can help telecom operators become more efficient and increase ROI. We will do this by helping them deploy all-optical networks across the country. We are building a fully connected, intelligent world based on 4.5G and 5G networks. Second, Huawei focuses on digital technologies like cloud, 5G, big data, and AI. This includes building ICT infrastructure platforms. We will continue to develop open trusted cloud platforms for customers, and build the ecosystem in line with the trends I mentioned earlier. Third, Huawei works closely with local research institutions, universities, and partners in Brazil. The business environment is very important to Huawei. Our ecosystem partners in Brazil across all industries can innovate and grow in the robust business environment that Huawei creates. We hope to establish a system of value creation and sharing *across the entire value chain.*[39]

The entry of companies like Huawei into national information-technology infrastructure allows the rollout of China's entire technology stack into emerging markets—a process of securing Beijing's hold on industries of the future as nations like Brazil continue their development path. The combination of smart cities, Chinese credit and infrastructure building, and the arrival of major Chinese corporations in Latin America presents the same security challenges that have proliferated in Asia and Africa. The United States must push these companies and banks back from Latin America and offer better alternatives to the region's major states. This will involve targeting not only China's technology through export controls and other proven approaches, but also targeting the corporate strategy of the major players. For example, just as US intelligence played a role in alerting the world to Russia's plans in Ukraine, the United States government should consider intelligence sharing on Chinese corporations, their operations, their executives, and their strategic plans with host governments in emerging markets—and also with US and Allied corporate strategy and risk departments. Understanding the full scope of these corporate strategies, their backing from the Chinese state, and their next market moves may prove essential to a larger strategy of rolling China back in emerging markets while also preserving the long-term sovereignty and independence of host governments. As Huawei chairman Howard Liang explained in his speech, "It is my great pleasure to come to Brazil again as Huawei celebrates our first twenty years in this great country. Twenty years ago, Huawei was quick to recognize the enormous potential of Brazil. . . . We have set down roots in Brazil, and we work hard to grow the industry and the ecosystem here. Huawei has worked with telecom operators to connect more than two-thirds of the population of Brazil."[40]

The US and our Allies must work with emerging world governments to uproot Chinese corporations and technology offerings before Beijing's vision of a surveillance-based political future is firmly entrenched through China's technology corporations. It is the next twenty years of the presence of China's companies that may be devastating for Brazil and other nations. Companies such as Alibaba, Baidu, China Mobile, China Telecom, China Unicom, ZTE, Megvii, DJI, Dahua, Bytedance, and Hikvision have proliferated across South America, setting up joint ventures, research labs, data centers, manufacturing facilities, training centers, subsidiaries, and even "smart cities public security projects," according to the Australian Strategic Policy Institute.[41] Companies including Huawei, Hikvision, China Mobile, and China Telecom have already been linked to the Chinese military by the US Department of Defense, and others from this list of companies are already under sanction by the US government for their role in human rights atrocities inside China.[42]

China's technology stack is also paving the way for further integration for its industrial corporations in emerging markets, especially those linked to infrastructure, automotive, and other physical goods, which are increasingly technology enabled through Industry 4.0 innovations. Companies like SANY Group, Weichai Lovol Heavy Industry, Zoomlion, and XCMG continue to build infrastructure. Automakers like BYD are making progress as well, launching the first electric bus corridor in Latin America in Chile in 2021 and exporting vehicles to Brazil, Mexico, Colombia, Uruguay, and other nations.[43] The integration of China's technology stack and its manufactured goods industries is at the heart of China's global markets strategy, presenting problems that our own corporations are not yet prepared to counter. US multinationals are competing head-to-head with China Incorporated in global markets: the combined operation of Chinese technology, capital, and original equipment manufacturers. Without updated strategies and the support of US and Allied governments, our companies may lose this battle for global markets in the decade ahead. Moreover, if the United States is not able to break China's technology stack in our own hemisphere—by degrading or destroying the global reach of these and other Chinese corporations—then geostrategic encirclement by the Belt and Road will be harder to counter in the 2030s.

The United States and other Allied nations must focus on trade missions, replacement of Chinese technology, and supply chain construction that will bring the major states of Latin America closer to our side. Brazil, Argentina, and Chile, as well as our military partner Colombia, must be priorities in American diplomacy and economic engagement. Additionally, curtailing Beijing's influence in the Caribbean should be a security priority, as well as preempting potential military pacts in the Southern Hemisphere.

MAJOR POWERS

India and Russia

Should we complete the difficult task of balancing and rolling back China's influence in Africa, Latin America, and the sub-regions of the Indo-Pacific, the balance of power will turn in our favor, but there is one further element that matters: the importance of two of the world's major powers other than China and the United States. While Europe and Asia can lean toward America building on foundations laid by the Alliance System, India and Russia can tip the world's diplomatic and military balance firmly and irreversibly against Beijing.

There is no perfect sequence to the rebuilding of world order. Each of the world's emerging regions will be a diplomatic and economic battleground. However, if America can unite and consolidate the Alliance System in Europe and Asia, win the battles for engagement and influence in the key emerging regions—the Indo-Pacific, Africa, and Latin America—and bring India and eventually even Russia to our side as major powers, then Beijing will face a world that is deeply resistant to its strategic goals.

India has every great reason to align with the United States and our Allies from Europe to Asia. India's first prime minister, Jawaharlal Nehru, explained during the Cold War in India's first decade of independence, "We want to be friends with the West and friends with the East and friends with everybody." This was an expression of his original vision of India as a meeting place of "East and West."[44] Gandhi's mission of independence and Nehru's mission of non-alignment defined the first two decades of Indian foreign relations in the post–World War II era. However, soon after independence, and despite an attempt to forge a world-leading friendship with the newly formed People's Republic of China in the 1950s, the China-India relationship collapsed, culminating in the China-India Border War of 1962. The Border War was a resounding defeat for India, and a humiliation, not only for a nation that had chosen to limit its military power, but for its belief that nonalignment could create safety in a dangerous world. A decade later, India signed a treaty of friendship and cooperation with the USSR, leading to a deep military and diplomatic relationship, and also, by following the socialist rather than capitalist economic model, to decades of foregone economic potential. It also produced a Russia-India relationship that remains important to this day.

India's outlook on the world has changed dramatically since independence, but these foundations remain essential to an understanding of the country's long-term trajectory. Indian strategic autonomy, a product of its original non-alignment, remains an important pillar in the country's diplomatic outlook, even as the world around India changes. Today, India has become a linchpin of Indo-Pacific security, with robust military relationships with America, Japan, and Australia, as well as with Southeast Asian nations including Vietnam and Indonesia. India's geographic position, as a pointed saber sitting across China's most important sea lines of communication extending from the Persian Gulf to the Chinese mainland, means that the country continues to create anxiety in Beijing. India's geography is one of its greatest advantages. It was vigorously courted by both superpowers during the Cold War and is essential to American strategy and success in the twenty-first century.

From George W. Bush to Barack Obama, from Donald Trump to Joe Biden, every twenty-first-century presidency has understood the importance of India to America's future. Indeed, even our early Cold War presidents, Eisenhower and Kennedy, were fascinated by the country and hoped for deep diplomatic engagement, a hope that did not arrive in their lifetimes. As Kennedy said as a senator in the 1950s, there was a contest "for the economic and political leadership of the East, for the respect of all Asia. . . . We want India to win that race with China."[45]

As its leaders and our leaders have understood, India has always been essential to the destiny of Asia. Today, US-India relations form the bedrock of strategic balancing toward China in Asia. Together with Australia and Japan, a strategic grouping known as the Quad, we are able to field substantial military and geopolitical power. What matters as well is to realize the full potential of India as an economic partner to America and as a major power in its own right. For example, take "Mission 500," an initiative that has long been discussed in Washington and that would increase US-India bilateral trade from roughly $150 billion at the start of the 2020s to $500 billion or more. This should become an absolute priority for American economic diplomacy in the region, enabling a robust US-India economic partnership to form a new center of economic gravity in Asia as an alternative to China.[46] With its potential to form a new supply chain and manufacturing hub, and its long-term strategic alignment with the United States, India should be of great importance to every multinational corporation that wishes to survive the US-China global competition. Businesses whose leaders prioritize China in the 2020s may not be here in the 2030s, but those that prioritize India will be glad that they did so. Quad leaders have already begun to discuss the importance of new supply chains that can be built together; the COVID-19 pandemic has led to vaccine innovation and production cooperation among Quad members; India's place within the world's IT and services supply chain is already established; initiatives proposed by the Indian government on infrastructure and manufacturing deserve the utmost support from the US government and from the Democratic World.

The reality is this: the world's democracies will require Indian participation in order to attain a decisive advantage over our authoritarian adversaries. Together, the democracies form an enormous economic community, possess militaries of unparalleled technological advancement, and an innovation base far superior to our authoritarian rivals. However, in light of China's strategies to integrate the world's developing regions and to bring an anti-American coalition to bear against the US and the Alliance System, we lack a clear path to decisive superiority without another major power in the mix. India is that other major power. Because of India's size, over a billion people, and because of its economic and military potential, the fate of the Free World may depend upon its choices: Will India join America and our Allies, or will India proceed in a dangerous neo-nonalignment, maintaining closeness with Russia? It is up to America and our Allies to empower this nation to the fullest extent that we can, and it is up to India to transcend its diplomatic history and lean wholeheartedly toward the world's democracies. China has been one of India's two primary adversaries (alongside Pakistan) since the Border War of 1962, an event that shook India's worldview and began India's path to significant military power. India is also the first nation in the twenty-first century that China has attacked with lethal military force, killing Indian soldiers on the disputed Himalayan border in the summer of 2020.[47] With extensive military cooperation between India and America already in place, much of the groundwork has already been laid for what could become the most important partnership of the twenty-first century. Annual US-India annual naval exercises, known as Malabar, have expanded to include US Allies Australia and Japan. US-India military relations now include several bedrock agreements: the Logistics Exchange Memorandum of Agreement, Communications, Compatibility and Security Agreement, and the Industrial Security Agreement. US defense sales to India have steadily expanded in recent years, and in 2016 India was designated a Major Defense Partner.[48] Additionally, as Pakistan slides toward the dubious honor of becoming China's first substantial vassal state, where India sits and where its alignment *should be* in the global structure of power is already quite clear. The United States and India—the world's oldest continuous democracy and the world's largest democracy by population—make a natural pair in countering the Chinese Communist Party and its global ambitions. The geopolitics of the twenty-first century may well depend on the success of this partnership. But India must choose America and the Free World, not Moscow and the temptations of the "multipolar world."

One more essential piece remains in the way of a global diplomatic vision for America—and that is Russia, the world's other most consequential major power.

In the aftermath of his invasion of Ukraine in 2022, Vladimir Putin, once thought of by many as a clever strategist, has created a potential geopolitical future for Russia that has not existed in nearly eight hundred years of Russian history. For the first time since the conquest of Russia by the Mongol Empire in the thirteenth century—a conquest that resulted in two hundred years of foreign rule—Russia now faces a future as a subservient state—this time to the People's Republic of China. Neither Napoleon Bonaparte nor Nazi Germany could defeat Russia. Their armies, which had conquered most of Europe, were ultimately destroyed by Russian resistance and the Russian winter as they marched on Moscow in the nineteenth and twentieth centuries, respectively. But with Putin's invasion of Ukraine, and the resistance of the Ukrainian people, Putin has brought about a future for Russia that neither Bonaparte nor Hitler could: subservience to another major power.

The Russia-China entente goes back two decades to the formation of the Shanghai Cooperation Organization in 2001. A departure from the acrimonious Sino-Soviet relationship of the later Cold War, the organization's charter invokes the "historically established ties between [our] peoples," the goal of "further enhancement of comprehensive cooperation," and an international environment of increasing "political multipolarity." While the purpose of this organization remains a matter of debate, the Russia-China entente has flourished in the twenty years since the Russian and Chinese governments came together, along with several former Soviet states to form a new international organization headquartered in Beijing.[49]

What began as a partnership between relative equals in the early 2000s has evolved into one in which China holds vastly more power, not only because of the size of its economy, but because Putin has destroyed Russia's relations with the United States and Europe. Even before the invasion of Ukraine, as the 2020s began, Russia had already become one of America's foremost adversaries, an enemy state that has interfered in US domestic politics, exploited and stoked our national divisions, seized territory in its region in contravention of international law, and conducted substantial cyberattacks on US national infrastructure. The invasion of Ukraine sealed what was already in process in Russia's relations with the Western world. The flight of Western corporations and capital, massive sanctions on Russian banks and companies, the renewed sense of purpose in NATO, and the failures and destruction of much of Russia's military on the battlefields of Ukraine have all put Russia in a position of far greater weakness than it held before the invasion.

The Russia-China relationship, a relationship that collapsed during the Cold War era, and that many analysts and commentators failed to take seriously in part because of this, surged to new heights ahead of the invasion of Ukraine. Known today as a "comprehensive strategic partnership of coordination for a new era," a substantial vision document was unveiled by Xi Jinping and Vladimir Putin on the first day of the Beijing Olympics. It detailed their "no limits" partnership in which "there are no 'forbidden' areas of cooperation."[50] The Russia-China relationship expanded in its complexity and sophistication, including a robust energy trade, frequent military exercises, the use of Chinese technology and engineering capabilities in Russian infrastructure, joint space cooperation agreements, and numerous technical, intelligence, and military exchanges.[51] Putin has made clear his alternate views of history in essays and speeches including "betrayal" by other European powers ahead of the Second World War and Ukraine as a place that Russia must recapture.[52] In this revisionist view of the world, he has aligned himself as a kind of perfect counterpart to the militarist Xi Jinping, who has also told the world of the expansionist aims of the Chinese Communist Party. These two dictators have made clear that they will contest America in both Europe and Asia, just as their predecessors Joseph Stalin and Mao Zedong did during the original Sino-Soviet alliance that preceded the Korean War.

In the 2022 "Joint Statement of the Russian Federation and the People's Republic of China," issued just ahead of the invasion of Ukraine, each side makes clear its support for the other side's geopolitical goals in Europe and Asia, respectively. Regarding the Communist Party's ambitions in Taiwan, Russia pledges this: "The Russian side reaffirms its support for the One-China principle, confirms that Taiwan is an inalienable part of China, and opposes any forms of independence of Taiwan. Russia and China stand against attempts by external forces to undermine security and stability in their common adjacent regions, intend to counter interference by outside forces in the internal affairs of sovereign countries under any pretext, oppose colour revolutions, and will increase cooperation in the aforementioned areas."[53] Regarding NATO and Europe, China pledges its support for Russia's geopolitical position, and Russia pledges support in turn for China's views of the Indo-Pacific:

The sides oppose further enlargement of NATO and call on the North Atlantic Alliance to abandon its ideologized Cold War approaches, to respect the sovereignty, security and interests of other countries, the diversity of their civilization, cultural, and historical backgrounds, and to exercise a fair and objective attitude toward the peaceful development of other States. The sides stand against the formation of closed bloc structures and opposing camps in the Asia-Pacific region and remain highly vigilant about the negative impact of the United States' Indo-Pacific strategy on peace and stability in the region.[54]

In short, Russia and China are as geopolitically aligned as they have been at any time in their respective histories—an alignment brought about by their shared hostility to the United States and the world order that America has built. Even the prior example of the Sino-Soviet Alliance may understate the depth of the current Russia-China entente, given how quickly irreconcilable differences emerged in that period of cooperation between the two communist powers. We must look back even further into Russian and Chinese history to see what a stable Russia-China relationship enables.

Russia-China first contact was made in the Amur River Valley in the 1600s. Two treaties ultimately anchored the relationship as Russian traders expanded eastward, and Qing dynasty armies expanded westward, carrying out a genocide of one million Zunghar Mongols, a steppe people who no longer exist today. As historian Peter Perdue notes, "The Russians took a pragmatic view of frontier expansion: they had moved into Siberia not for glory, but for profit. Territory and imperial honor took second place to promotion of the fur trade. The Qing, for its part, compromised on ritual propriety in order to secure Russian neutrality in the coming conflict with the Zunghars."[55]

It is important to consider, as Perdue does, that the hidden force in the Qing-Russian relationship was the Zunghar Mongols, at whose expense Russian and Chinese relations proceeded with relative ease and consistency. While the Russian desire for trade remained constant, the Zunghar Mongols provided the fulcrum upon which the Qing need for a security alliance rested. Would relations between the two empires have been significantly different without this third force that was eventually slaughtered in the shadow of the imperial peace? It seems necessary to consider the value of a stable border for two empires that are expanding in other directions.[56] Russia and China today, like the Qing and Tsarist emperors in the pre-modern era—and like Stalin and Mao in the 1950s—have determined that they will contest America together, not because they trust one another, but because a stable relationship allows them to push on either front. As an Indian diplomat said to me in New Delhi, "the only reason China can expand to the seas is because they have solved their relationship with Russia."

The popularity of Putin's invasion on the Chinese internet and the Chinese Communist Party's spread of Russian talking points or diplomatic support through every form of global media from Twitter to the *New York Times* are just quotidian realities of the Russia-China "comprehensive strategic partnership of coordination for a new era."[57] Should there be any doubt about the depth of this alignment, consider the joint flight of Russian and Chinese nuclear-capable bombers over the Sea of Japan in May 2022 as leaders from the United States, India, Japan, and Australia met in Tokyo to discuss regional security.[58] Perhaps no clearer picture could be drawn than the joint exercise of Russian and Chinese bombers in the midst of Russia's war on Ukraine. Russian and Chinese military exercises, which have flourished in the past decade, are set to continue by sea, air, and land even as Putin wages war in Europe. In August and September of 2022, Russia and China proceeded with annual Vostok exercises in Russia's far east, which aim, in the words of the Chinese Ministry of Defense, to "enhance the level of strategic collaboration among the participating parties."[59]

For the United States, it must become a strategic priority to undermine this partnership and lay the groundwork for a *second* Russia-China split, along the lines of the original Sino-Soviet split, which changed the Cold War world. Should the United States permit the Russia-China entente to flourish, we are likely to face a military partnership that spans Europe and Asia and the potential for dangerous consequences should a humiliated Russia assist China in a potential invasion of Taiwan or in direct conflict with the United States and our Allies. Despite its growing military, economic, and even ideological depth, today's Russia-China relationship rests on precarious foundations. Above all, like a modern-day Molotov-Ribbontrop Pact, which bound Stalin and the Nazis together in a faux alliance before Hitler launched his offensive eastward into the USSR, a relationship between dictatorships is an inherently unstable thing. Russia and China today are united in their shared animosity toward the United States, the world order dominated by democracies, and in their willingness to confront and probe the limits of American power. One must note that the geopolitical consequences of Russia-China cooperation began in the 2010s, when Russia annexed Crimea (in 2014) and China began construction of its military islands in the South China Sea. Each was probing, as their predecessors Mao and Stalin had, the edges of American power. A Russia-China entente will be a difficult thing to maintain in the long run, provided that American and Allied diplomacy approaches the problem in the right way. China's ability to share the world with the USSR was such a spectacular failure that the two soon became primary enemies, engaged in years of competition and ideological invective and even fought a brief but deadly border war in 1969, paving the way for the US opening to China.[60] Russia-China relations have a long history, and we are likely to see periods of upheaval again. The United States and our Allies must do what we can to prevent this partnership from fusing together along economic and military lines.

As the flight of tens of thousands of Russians to Europe following the 2022 invasion of Ukraine reminds us, there is another side of Russia that does not trust Putinism and its terminal direction for this nation.[61] The responsibility for the collapse of US-Russia relations, even ahead of the invasion of Ukraine, rests with Russia's current leadership, which by most accounts is motivated by a long-standing desire to return Russia to great power status through confrontation with the West. As CIA legend Jack Devine writes in *Spymaster's Prism: The Fight Against Russian Aggression*:

> In 1990 Putin returned to Russia [from his KGB posting in Germany] as the Soviet system and, more important for him, the symbols of Russian greatness crumbled. He has often stated publicly that the collapse of the Soviet Union, and its attendant loss of power, was the greatest tragedy of his generation. Putin's key driving force is to restore "Mother Russia" after the humiliation and disarray that followed the end of the Cold War.[62]

Putinist Russia may even have within it a triumphalist vision in which what happened to the USSR happens to the United States. Former KGB analyst Igor Panarin released a map of America in 1998 predicting the split of America into four sections, "The Californian Republic," "The Central North-American Republic," "Atlantic America," and "The Texas Republic."[63] In a description reminiscent of Philip K. Dick's alternate history classic, *The Man in the High Castle*, Hawaii "will go to either Japan or China," Alaska "will go to Russia," the West Coast "will be part of China or under Chinese influence," and the Atlantic coast "may join the European Union."[64] Fanciful, yes, but when one considers Russia's tactics of attempting to sow discord and chaos in the United States and Europe, while its partners in Beijing attempt to encircle America through an economic and military Belt and Road that includes Europe, Africa, Asia, Latin America, the Arctic, and also sea and space, we can see a glimpse of what geopolitical disaster looks like should the Russia-China entente ever realize its wildest ambitions: an encircled, strangled, and destroyed America, existing for perhaps a moment before the two dictatorships turn upon each another.

It will be up to American diplomats and strategists to disrupt and defeat Putinist aggression while engaging with and learning from the tens of thousands, by some accounts hundreds of thousands, of emigres settling throughout Europe. The people who have fled Putinism and its growing horrors may one day present an alternative path for Russia.[65] As Russia slides further down a path toward becoming a junior partner to a totalitarian China with over ten times Russia's economy, eventually this country's destiny may hinge on whether or not it can turn to the West. While this appears unlikely in the decade ahead, it should remain a long-term objective in American and Allied strategy. Victory in our contest with the People's Republic of China will be far more achievable if we can swing a post-Putin Russia away from China. America may never, even in the decades ahead, have genuinely trusting relations with Russia, but nor should the Russian people ever fully trust the Chinese Communist Party with their future. Laying the groundwork for a second Russia-China split, a twenty-first-century breakup of this entente, may be one of the most important geopolitical objectives in the decades ahead. As one of Russia's leading China specialists said to me at Oxford in 2011, before the total collapse of Russia's relations with the West, "The Chinese tell us to beware of America and NATO, and America tells us to beware of China. And Russia says to both, what can you do for me?"

Putin's actions foreclosed the possibility of Russia as a neutral, self-interested actor well before his 2022 invasion of Ukraine. The right mix of military failure in Ukraine and powerful, unremitting economic sanctions—sanctions not only on Russian entities but also on the Chinese companies that are solidifying the Russia-China economic relationship—may change the course of this nation in the future, and its potential role in our contest with China. Designing Allied economic strike packages to use on China's corporations, which are laying the foundations for Russia-China economic integration, can prevent this relationship from consolidating beyond our control. In addition to technology and telecommunications companies listed in the Economic Arena, China Communications Construction Corporation—which built the military islands in the South China Sea—is planning new infrastructure projects in Russia, and companies like Agricultural Bank of China, China Construction Bank, China Minmentals Corporation, China Mobile, China National Petroleum Corporation, China Railway Construction Corporation, China Railway Engineering Corporation, China State Construction Engineering, Industrial Bank, PowerChina, Sany Heavy Industries, SAIC Motor, Shanghai Fosun Pharmaceutical, and ZTE are still carrying out "business as usual" in Russia, building deep and, if we do not act, potentially permanent bonds between America's two primary adversaries.[66]

CHINA CONTAINED

A Turning Point for the Twenty-First Century

Rebuilding the world will be the greatest task we have seen since the Second World War. It will require enormous imagination, dexterity, and discipline, and we must do it. It must be a world with democracies as the foundation, with the world's emerging regions free to decide their own destinies and ever-more-integrated with the Allied economic community, and with the authoritarian ententes disrupted and no longer joined together in their conflict with the Allied World. Finally, it must provide the groundwork for containing a totalitarian China that is held back behind a Great Wall of Democracies and left behind by the progress of free states.[67]

The older generation among China's people understand that their rulers bring tragedy and devastation through their ambitious plans. Many alive today in China lived through the Cultural Revolution. There are those who experienced the Korean War, the Great Leap Forward, Maoist purges, campaigns, border wars, and diplomatic isolation, and even the massacres in Tiananmen Square. Those memories live on, and we must preserve them outside of China, as China's dictators rewrite their history as a tale of upward glory. It is not America's job to decide or influence the political fate of China. That job is for the Chinese people alone. We must ensure, however, together with our Allies and partners across the world, that China's ambitions do not decide the fate of the world, nor the fate of America. A contained Communist China, living inside a world of its own making, will eventually decide its own fate, but it must do so in isolation. It will be the job of our diplomats to remind China that it was America—our institutions, our capital, our technology, our markets, the world order that we built, and above all our strategy of engagement—that brought China its period of economic prosperity and the end of the poverty and dismay that it had known for much of recent history. However, first we must rebuild the world.

PART THREE

THE MILITARY ARENA

It is startling and fearful to realise that we are no longer safe in our island home.

—Winston Churchill, 1934

A successful US grand strategy depends on a successful defense strategy—because the overarching playbook requires unlimited room for maneuver in economic containment and competition. Containing and impairing an adversary's economy must be backed by enough military power to deter that adversary from going to war. The heart of the China challenge is this: as China grows, its potential to use overwhelming military force also grows. But there's more. A Chinese Communist Party facing collapse or significant internal unrest may lash out militarily to create unity at home or satisfy the nationalism it has stoked for decades. Just as US economic strategy should not aim for collapse within China, but rather for freezing its economic ascendancy and allowing for diplomatic rollback across the major regions of the world, the US military must be strong enough to deter a militarily ambitious Communist China that has made frequent use of force in its history. The essence of US grand strategy must be to decisively win the Economic Arena while also blocking the path for a war initiated by the Chinese Communist Party. China's military investments—the conversion of economic might into military power—have massively altered the military balance in Asia. China's partnerships with Russia and other rogue nations have also revised the global balance of military power. The United States and our Allies must address these changes and apply gains in the Economic Arena to create military superiority at best or military advantage at least over China and its partner states. The wealth and innovative potential of the Alliance System is one avenue for building military advantage. Another is reconstruction of America's innovation-industrial base as initially discussed in the Economic Arena. We will explore these avenues as well as certain critical geographies and military domains.

It must be stated that this book's purpose is to present America with a *peacetime* rather than a *wartime* strategy for global competition with China. The economic, diplomatic, and military dimensions to this strategy seek to create, in the words of Winston Churchill, "peace through preponderance," or as Ronald Reagan phrased it, "peace through strength." While this idea is as old as statecraft itself, it is also in keeping with the American tradition. George Washington stated in his first inaugural address that "To be prepared for war is one of the most effectual means of preserving peace."[1] This tradition has been carried on by both Democrats and Republicans throughout our history. As John F. Kennedy said clearly in the Cold War world: "We prepare for war—in order to deter war. . . . We compare our military strength with the Soviets— not to determine whether we should use it—but to determine whether we can persuade them to use theirs would be futile and disastrous—and to determine whether we can back up our pledges in Berlin, Formosa [Taiwan], and around the world . . . peace, not war, is the objective of our military policy."[2]

Though some may dispute it, the American tradition is not only "peace through strength," but also an emphasis on *peace itself.* Ours is not a nation that usually aims to cast the first blow even when obvious dangers loom. This strategy does not seek the destruction of our opponents, but the defense of our world, our way, and our ideals. Loving friend and fearsome foe, the American approach to the People's Republic of China itself stands among the clearest examples of our generosity in recent history—to enrich and engage a place that harbored dangerous intentions, hoping that this engagement would lead to friendship instead of giving rise to a dangerous challenger. We hoped that our engagement would create a "responsible stakeholder" out of one of the most deadly and dangerous regimes in global history. Having been fooled and having fooled ourselves about those dangerous intentions, we have no choice left but to change our approach to this contender. As we must, we shall build our best defense—and prepare to defend our world and our way—against the People's Republic of China.

We must remember that the global grand strategy of the Chinese Communist Party contains a profound military dimension. Given the Chinese Communist Party's founding philosophy of violence and the imprint of one of history's most prolific mass murderers, Mao Zedong, we should not be surprised by an ongoing genocide, comprehensive military build-up, and regular threats of violence against neighbors large and small. We should also remember that the United States was the original enemy in Chinese Communist Party thinking at the founding of the People's Republic of China. China's leaders continue to view us this way, despite an entire era of US engagement. The Chinese Communist Party fought America in the Korean War that broke out in 1950 almost immediately after the founding of the People's Republic of China in 1949. Communist Party officials have made clear that they expect to fight other wars again in the future.[3] The potential for US-China conflict in the years ahead is an unwelcome surprise for America but also the fulfillment of the original expectations of the Chinese Communist Party. It will be America's job to deter military aggression from China—and we must not underestimate Beijing's willingness and desire to use force. The Korean War, particularly its bloodiest battles against the United States, is the subject of popular propaganda in China at the start of the 2020s, and Xi Jinping's speeches surrounding this event and others remind us that the Communist Party is positioning China for potential conflict with America.[4] Not only does the Korean War give today's Chinese Communist Party a popular anti-American rallying cry, it also enshrines the original antagonisms of the Chinese Communist Party toward the United States.

Mao Zedong, who once envisioned "throwing America out" of the West Pacific, saw Korea as follows: "If the U.S. imperialists win [in Korea] they may get so dizzy with success that they may threaten us. We therefore must come to [North] Korea's aid and intervene in the name of a volunteer army, although we will select the best timing."[5] In the words of historian John Lewis Gaddis:

The technological superiority of the United States, including the atomic bomb, would count for little, [Mao] insisted, when set against his own massive manpower reserves and, even more important, the unshakable *will and determination* of the Chinese people. Unexpected as it had been, the Korean War became, therefore, a challenge and an opportunity. "[A]fter we have consumed hundreds of thousands of American lives in a few years," Mao cheerfully assured Stalin in March 1951, "the Americans [will] be forced to retreat, and the Korean problem will be settled." Or, as he would later put it: "they have many fewer people than we do."[6]

Chinese Communist Party history has it that China won this war against America. The restored importance of the Korean War in today's anti-American propaganda in China should be no great surprise, as the Communist Party makes an effort to tell its people that China is prepared to "fight and win wars" and "fight the bloody battles of our era." The implication is that, as in the early history of the People's Republic of China, America is an opponent that can be beaten. In light of the Communist Party's return under Xi Jinping to the original antagonisms and vilifications of the founding decades of the People's Republic of China, the United States must be prepared not only for China's potential use of force in territorial claims, but also the potential use of force to fulfill its original objectives of overtaking and overpowering America in Asia and beyond. Given the Communist Party's history, ambitions, and ideology, the Communist Party's potential use of military power grows more likely should China grow economically and militarily stronger—which is why economic containment and the reconstruction of peace through strength is an essential path for the United States and our Allies.

America must correct disastrous military imbalances that our leaders have left us with through the China engagement era. Rebuilding our strength may not happen overnight, but this effort must begin with urgency. No better depiction exists than this one from Christian Brose, author of *The Kill Chain: Defending America in the Future of High-Tech Warfare*, describing a conversation with Senator John McCain in the 2010s:

Many of the US ships, submarines, fighter jets, bomber aircraft, additional munitions, and other systems that are needed to fight would not be near the war when it started but would be thousands of miles away in the United States. They would come under immediate attack once they began their multiweek mobilization across the planet. Cyberattacks would grind down the logistical movement of US forces into combat. The defenseless cargo ships and aircraft that would ferry much of that force across the Pacific would be attacked every step of the way. Satellites on which US forces depend for intelligence, communications, and global positioning would be blinded by lasers, shut down by high-energy jammers, or shot out of orbit altogether by antisatellite missiles. The command and control networks that manage the flow of critical information to US forces in combat would be broken apart and shattered by electronic attacks, cyberattacks, and missiles. Many US forces would be rendered deaf, dumb, and blind.

Brose goes on to explain that American bases in Japan and Guam "would be inundated with waves of precise ballistic and cruise missiles," and their defenses "quickly . . . overwhelmed by the sheer volume of weapons coming at them." Chinese hypersonic missiles would glide through our defenses, striking our bases "within minutes of being launched." A kind of high-technology blitzkrieg, China's attacks would pour through American defenses, destroying our positions in the West Pacific: "They would crater runways, blow up operations centers and fuel storage tanks, and render those US forward bases inoperable. If any aircraft did manage to escape the Chinese missiles, it would be forced to relocate to another base in the region, which itself would come under attack. It would look like a US evacuation." In the meantime, the attacks on our naval forces would be breathtaking: "Chinese satellites and radars would be hunting for those [theater-based] aircraft carriers as well as additional carriers meant to provide reinforcement that would begin their long journey across the Pacific Ocean. . . . [T]hose ships would face large salvos of Chinese missiles . . . known in US defense circles as 'carrier killers.'" Again, our carriers and ships would be relatively defenseless against these precision-guided missile barrages which would destroy flight decks, control towers, and aircraft. Finally, direct hits to our aircraft carriers "could be fatal, sending five thousand Americans and a $13 billion ship to the bottom of the ocean—all at the cost to China of around $10 million per missile."[7]

Reviewing the potential for catastrophic defeat, John McCain's words speak to us all: "Future generations of Americans are going to look back at us . . . and they're going to ask how we let this happen, and why we didn't do more about it when we had the chance."[8]

The Brose-McCain scenario of crippling strikes on American positions and forces in the Pacific is one future we could face if we do not prepare. We must also look to the history of the Chinese Communist Party to remind ourselves that this organization uses military force against nations large and small. Additionally, Beijing has demonstrated that its definition of victory is different from ours. For instance, both the Korean War of 1950–53 and the China-Vietnam War of 1979 are portrayed as victories in China, while much of the outside world regards them as costly endeavors resulting in loss or stalemate. Finally, what America and our Allies must understand is that the Chinese military, and the goal of military superiority in Asia and beyond, is not solely for the purpose of pursuing territorial ambitions in Asia—though it certainly may be used for this purpose. The Chinese military is built to advance the mechanisms of the Chinese Communist Party's long-term grand strategy and ideological vision—a new world system with China at its center and the de facto end of an American-led world. The Chinese military is meant to ensure this rise to supremacy and to fulfill the ideological promise of "national rejuvenation"—the restoration of Chinese power from "the century of national humiliation" to the Communist Party's vision of supremacy by 2049. For these reasons Xi Jinping makes use of the rhetoric of violence and militarist power. At the founding of the People's Republic of China, Mao declared that "the Chinese people have stood up" and that "our national defence will be consolidated and no imperialists will ever again be allowed to invade our land."[9]

Xi Jinping, invoking the founding principles of the People's Republic of China, declared on the centenary of the Chinese Communist Party that "[T]he Chinese people will in no way allow any foreigners to come and bully, oppress or enslave us; whoever vainly hopes to do this will bloodily break their heads on a steel Great Wall built of the flesh and blood of 1.4 billion Chinese people."[10] These are not empty words. They are the heart of the Communist Party's ideology of restoration through violence. Mao's diplomats said to their Indian counterparts ahead of the China-India Border War in 1962, "[R]egardless of anything, the liberated, new China cannot permit itself to be pushed back once again to the position of suffering that was the old China."[11] Xi Jinping tells the world his mantra, "preparing to fight the bloody battles of our era," or in his words to former US defense secretary Jim Mattis: "We cannot lose even one inch of the territory left behind by our ancestors."[12] Beijing's calculus for war is different from our own because of its profound roots in the ideas of "the New China" and "national rejuvenation." A conflict over Taiwan or the South China Sea may occur not for the aim of seizing territory, but because its purpose is to demonstrate to the United States and our Allies that China is willing to use force not only to seize territory but also to demonstrate ideological resolve.

How can America and our Allies handle this problem? We did not choose this adversary. We chose to engage and enrich it despite the dangers. We did not choose the unique pathologies that animate its ambitions. However, it is left to us to handle this challenge to the world.

American strategic drift in the post–Cold War era enabled the rise of a hostile foreign power through economic engagement and the failure to prepare for conflict. Addressing the erosion of the military balance and its underlying causes, the economic rise of China, must be done urgently. America must begin its economic containment of China while reinvesting in a military that can maintain deterrence in the Pacific while also refocusing our combatant commands and Alliance System on a global force structure that can deter or obstruct China and Russia on each of the continents in which they can wield disruptive force. Through America's uniting of the Free World and rolling back China in the world's emerging economies, Beijing's economic room for maneuver will be substantially reduced, eventually to the point when China alone presents no transformative possibility for the world economy as a whole. When this is achieved—victory in the Economic Arena, victory in the Diplomatic Arena, and victory through deterrence in the Military Arena—the United States and the world's democracies will regain the upper hand. Communist China will become another failed challenger like Nazi Germany, Imperial Japan, or the

Soviet Union. Whether we can preserve peace through foresight and strategic acumen, or whether Beijing chooses violence in the decade ahead to satisfy its aims, America must be ready to contain this challenger economically and maintain military deterrence long enough that history can do what it is meant to do: leave a weaker rival behind on the road to further progress.

For many Americans who have known the major power peace of the American-led order brought about by the Second World War and by a generation of visionary architects in the Cold War era, the possibility of major power war in the modern world has seemed as remote as it did to those who failed to see the consequences of the rising evils in the 1930s. Putin's invasion of Ukraine has begun to awaken the world to the dangers of dictatorships that believe in the conquest of territory and the resurrection of fallen empires. The invasion of Ukraine resounds across the world far more than the wolfing down of Hong Kong by the Chinese Communist Party. However, dictatorships often find their stride for larger ambitions across the world by working together. It is not only nation-states or once-free cities that show the full extent of the ambitions of these dictatorships—they seek profound changes to the power structure of the world. We must overmatch these places and be poised to foil their designs. In rebuilding, our objective is not to bring war, but to achieve peace through "preponderance"—"peace through strength." As Churchill beseeched his supine nation to *prepare, prepare, prepare,* saying, "you will see that the only choice open is the old grim choice our forebears had to face, namely, whether we shall submit or whether we shall prepare." As Franklin Delano Roosevelt explained of isolationists and others who chose to ignore that era's rising dangers, "Those Americans who believed that we could live under the illusion of isolationism wanted the American eagle to imitate the tactics of the ostrich."[13] We must prepare to defend our world.

MILITARY GEOGRAPHY

China's Path from Regional to Global Power

China's leaders are working to transform the world's geography to their advantage. The United States has had the advantages of being an island continent throughout its history, separated by great distances from the wars and events of Europe, Africa, and Asia. China is at the center of a complex web of nations and geographical challenges. For insecure states like China, security comes through geographical conquest and coercion. Most importantly, China is not, nor can it really be, a self-sufficient nation. As much as its leaders are working to advance their technology and industrial goals, China still relies on the outside world to feed itself, supply its energy, and purchase its manufactured goods. China is building a military designed to "safeguard its overseas interests," and as these "overseas interests" expand, China's military is tasked with new missions to secure the trade and resource acquisition system through integration with the world economy. As we have seen, China is a global superpower with global economic and political interests. While many are concerned about its regional ambitions, we must look at the bigger picture of China's current and future global footprint. Let's look at China's region.

While the United States is situated between two friendly neighbors on its own continent, China's borders are made up of the complex sub-regions of South, Southeast, East, and Central Asia. Most of its population, situated in its "heartland," is locked between several geographically inhospitable features: the

Tibetan Plateau, the Xinjiang and Mongolian deserts, and the Island Chains of the West Pacific. While much of China's military history has been about defending its heartland using these features, today a more expansionist and globally integrated China seeks also to use them as a platform for a broader global military expansion. In the 1940s, Chiang Kai-shek identified six "fortresses" of China's regional military geography that could be used to defend the nation's heartland:

> There are no natural frontiers in the areas of the Yellow, Huai, Yangtze and Han rivers where a strong defense line can be prepared. Therefore [Taiwan], the Pescadores, the Four Northeastern Provinces [Manchuria], Inner and Outer Mongolia, [Xinjiang], and Tibet are each a fortress essential for the nation's defense and security. The separation of any one of these regions from the rest of the country means the disruption of our national defenses.[14]

Much of the Chinese Communist Party's twentieth-century military history, especially its invasion of Tibet (1950), the Korean War (1950–53), its role in Vietnam (1950–75), the China-India Border War (1962), and Mao's initiation of two Taiwan Strait crises (1954–55, 1958), were expressions of modern China's sense of national security and the desire to keep foreign powers away from these "fortresses." China's brief but lethal border conflicts with other states—including India, the Soviet Union, and Vietnam—have also been largely about managing a region where many of China's territorial and political insecurities were unresolved. Today, China's military and security forces retain strict control over Tibet and Xinjiang, where a new genocide against one of China's neighboring peoples is underway, an earlier one having taken place in the steppes during the 1700s.[15] However, Taiwan, while under constant threat, has not yet been absorbed by Beijing. China's territorial disputes continue to exist with India, Japan, Vietnam, Brunei, Malaysia, the Philippines, and Indonesia. In this context, China has built a military that is able to threaten its neighbors and seize territory.

If China can secure military dominance in its region, it opens the world to Chinese power projection from Asia. Taiwan, for example, which Chinese military planners have called the "lock" on the first island chain, today hems China in behind a wall of US and Allied bases and forward positions in Asia.[16] During the Second World War, after the attack on Pearl Harbor, the United States mounted an island-hopping campaign through the Southwest and Central Pacific, paving the way for final strikes on the Japanese mainland.[17] This war, and the postwar Alliance System that was its result, left America in a position of military dominance in Asia. Our grueling fight across the world's largest ocean has positioned us to remain in the region, having forcibly dismantled Japan's "East Asian Co-Prosperity Sphere" and established Alliances with many of the region's nations: Japan, Australia, the Philippines, Thailand, and South Korea. China seeks to reverse this position and to establish its own hegemony over the region. Its leaders since Mao Zedong have envisioned pushing America out of the island chains and breaking up the US Alliance System in Asia. This would free China to use these areas for their own power projection. While the immediate military flashpoints are regional, in Taiwan, the South and East China Seas, and the Himalayas, they are part of an ambitious geographical scope that could place many of the world's important regions under Chinese military and economic dominance.

China's companies have built more than ninety ports in strategic locations from Asia to Africa, and China's military exercises aim to protect key Belt and Road locations.[18] China's military expansion can be thought of in two distinct ways: near seas and homeland operations, and expeditionary forces.[19] In order to bring the military geography and strategic choke points and trade routes of the Indo-Pacific under its control, from the Persian Gulf to the South China Sea, China is building a military designed for both offensive operations in the island chains and expeditionary operations in the Indian Ocean and farther afield. While it lacks the logistical and basing infrastructure the US military maintains, China's port and infrastructure building will enable global operations. In 2022, US AFRICOM Commander General Stephen J. Townsend explained the following regarding China's first overseas military base in Djibouti at the other end of its most important sea lines of communication: "This year, China significantly expanded the capabilities of its Doraleh Naval Base in Djibouti—Beijing's only permanent overseas military base—by adding a large and capable pier while advancing plans to establish a second location along West Africa's Atlantic Coast. By 2030, Chinese military facilities and technical collection sites in Africa will allow Beijing to project power eastward into the Middle East and Indo-Pacific Theaters and west into the Atlantic."[20] News of Communist Party military-basing ambitions and security pacts abounds from Cambodia to the Solomon Islands. The pace of these agreements is likely to increase substantially in the decade ahead should China's economic rise continue. The world has looked on as China has militarized the island fortresses in the South China Sea, built by one of its state-owned enterprises, the China Communications Construction Corporation, adding anti-ship and anti-aircraft missile systems. As US Indo-Pacific commander Admiral John Aquilino explains, "The function of those islands is to expand the offensive capability of the PRC beyond their continental shores. . . . They can fly fighters, bombers, plus all those offensive capabilities of missile systems."[21] With Communist Party–owned infrastructure laid across the world, the Chinese military could install similar anti-access area-denial weapons across its network of ports, and throughout its global shipping fleets and maritime militias.[22]

China has become the world's largest trading nation in goods, having envisioned and planned an intercontinental system in which it would become economically dominant over the nations of Asia, Africa, Oceania, and even Europe. Beijing is now working toward a long-term vision of expeditionary military capabilities in these regions. A 2021 report from the Congressional Research Service describes China's naval build-up as follows: "China's navy is, by far, the largest of any country in East Asia, and within the past few years it has surpassed the U.S. Navy in numbers of battle force ships. . . . The PLAN's overall battle force is expected to grow to 420 ships by 2025 and 460 ships by 2030. Much of this growth will be in major surface combatants."[23] The report explains that "China's naval modernization effort encompasses a wide array of platform and weapon acquisition programs, including anti-ship ballistic missiles (ASBMs), anti-ship cruise missiles (ASCMs), submarines, surface ships, aircraft, unmanned vehicles (UVs), and supporting C4ISR (command and control, communications, computers, intelligence, surveillance, and reconnaissance) systems."[24] Most sources and analysts expect that China's prolific military force building will be directed at Taiwan or the South China Sea. The reality is likely to be that China projects power in any given conflict, not only against US bases in the Pacific, striking American forces in Japan, South Korea,

Guam, and other locations, but also potentially *throughout the entire Belt and Road system* where infrastructure projects and economic dominance give Beijing enormous sway. A conflict with China could become a multi-regional conflict, ranging from Asia to Africa to the Middle East, fought across the world's seas and sea lines of communication. With the potential involvement of Russia, Iran, and Pakistan on China's side, we are talking about a truly global conflict.

As I explained in *China's Vision of Victory*, to prevail in strategic competition with China, the United States must not only remain the world's largest economy and unite the Democratic World, but also maintain military deterrence against both China and Russia, which are military partners. Deterring and outmaneuvering Beijing will have to extend beyond Taiwan, the South and East China Seas, and the Pacific Island chains. The United States, through its global Combatant Command network, will have to anticipate and counter China's expanding global mission, which it is advancing not only through the expansion of its own military, but through the cultivation of client states in Asia, Africa, Europe, and Latin America.

The Cold War had Europe as its primary arena, where NATO and the Warsaw Pact faced each other for decades. However, it was actually a global confrontation, with military and diplomatic theaters all over the planet from Latin America, Asia, Africa, and Southeast Asia, to the polar regions. It was a global Cold War.[25] Our contest with China will be on the same geographical scale. Our underlying strategy must be to prevent the consolidation of Chinese economic expansion around the globe, to roll China back to its region, and impose costly military trade-offs that will force them to focus on Asia alone, abandoning global goals.

Our military strategy must ensure the reconstruction of US and Allied advantage and a return to dominance in the geographical, industrial, and technological domains that matter. This means four military domains especially: maritime, cyber, space, and nuclear. In the maritime domain, the US Alliance System must outpace China's shipbuilding program. This effort will involve sanctioning the Chinese shipbuilding industrial base, Allied coordination on creating comprehensive maritime power, leveraging our subsea advantage with both manned submarines and unmanned underwater vehicles (UUVs), and rebuilding our maritime industrial base. In cyber, the US must harden critical infrastructure because conflict with China and Russia would likely involve cyberwarfare or coercion against civilian, commercial, and industrial infrastructure as well as potential use of cyberwarfare in military operations. Cyber also presents an opportunity for continuous engagement of America's leading technology companies in national security missions. Regarding space and nuclear, we must recognize that building the space economy is one of the key missions of the century, a contest America must win. Commercial space companies working with the United States government can unlock the potential of the Next Frontier. Additionally, given that China's nuclear build-up is designed to support territorial aggression, nuclear deterrence must remain a priority in US defense strategy, both to protect against territorial aggression and against the use of nuclear weapons against the United States or our Allies.

America must find comprehensive advantages within these domains of warfare while rebuilding our economic and industrial power and degrading those of China. We must also aim to maintain deterrence in key flashpoint areas: Taiwan, the South and East China Seas, and the Himalayas. We must anticipate and deter Chinese and Russian actions in other theaters including the Indian Ocean Region, Africa, the Middle East, Europe, the Arctic, and even Latin America. Building and maintaining the right force structure will require disciplined attention to the right missions and platforms, an expanded national security budget, and the full engagement of Allies and partners. The US Joint Force must continue to focus on the Indo-Pacific theater, meaning that operational strategies must be directed at projecting power across a geographical theater that is mostly water and islands.

America's leading military strategists envision defense and deterrence taking place along the two island chains in the Pacific, where many of China's territorial claims are concentrated. This focus is sensible given the likelihood of China's use of force in these areas. The Communist Party has long envisioned stripping these island chains of American power and potentially even using them to keep America out of the Pacific in the long run. While these chains hold back Chinese power today, if they fall into China's hands through force or gradual erosion of US influence, they could be used to keep America out of the Western Pacific. We will have to commence and iterate the Pacific Deterrence

Initiative, an "archipelagic defense" strategy, and a focus on countering Chinese forces in the Indian Ocean Region, South Pacific, and farther afield.

Andrew Krepinevich's "archipelagic defense" is an excellent example of what the geography of a Pacific defense strategy looks like though "deterrence by denial." As he explains, "If Washington wants to change Beijing's calculus, it must deny China the ability to control the air and sea around the first island chain," noting that ground forces will be essential, including the use of artillery for coastal defense, ground forces using mobile launchers and anti-ship cruise missiles, as well as naval mine warfare, all of which "could make large stretches of sea off-limits to the Chinese navy." He explains that "by reducing the demands on US air and naval forces for such missions as air and sea denial, ground forces would enable these air and naval forces to stand in reserve, ready to move quickly to defend a threatened link in the chain."[26]

Krepinevich explains that the United States must: "develop a forward defense-in-depth posture of US and Allied forces along the FIC [first island chain], and between the first and second island chains, as well as with other like-minded states. Given China's A2/AD capabilities, in the event of war, the US military will likely find it prohibitively costly to reinforce its forward-based forces, at least early in the conflict. Therefore, the United States will need to increase its current force levels in the WPTO [West Pacific Theater of Operations] substantially along with their logistics stocks." Japan would assume responsibility for its own defense, and thus for the "Northern Sector" of the first island chain. US forces "should be gradually introduced in forward-deployed rotations to supplement Japan Ground Self-Defense Force units." The US would be responsible for the "Southern Sector" of the first island chain, which would include defense of the Philippines and "covert assistance" to Taiwan. The Philippines, Taiwan, and Vietnam would build resistance forces that can undertake irregular warfare operations against a Chinese force in order to "delay their ability to consolidate gains and expand their A2/AD zones."

The US would also look to Indonesia, South Korea, and Singapore for support: "South Korea has the potential to threaten China's flank along the FIC's northern sector, while Indonesia could further solidify the defense of the southern sector." Furthermore, "Japanese air and naval forces, along with the JGSDF mobile Western Army units, should serve as an operational reserve in the northern sector, while US air and naval forces (including those of the US Marine Corps) function in a similar role along the entire FIC, with priority accorded to the southern sector; specifically, the Philippines and Taiwan, and perhaps Indonesia and Vietnam."

Finally, Australia and India could "provide reserve forces for the southern sector" and draw "substantial Chinese resources away from areas opposite the FIC," respectively. With regard to India, "air and ground forces positioned along that country's common border with China would likely compel a countervailing response from Beijing."[27]

In brief, the defense of the island chains would require a coordinated effort anchored by the United States and Japan, supported by Australia and India, and also involving Taiwan, the Philippines, South Korea, Singapore, and Indonesia. This strategy is a reasonable approach to Beijing's aims within the geography of the Pacific theater. It must be supported by a broader concept for countering China's long-term ambitions. In the eyes of China's twentieth-century leaders, China's traditional strategic "fortresses" include Taiwan and the Pescadores, as well as the Four Northeastern Provinces: Manchuria, Mongolia, Xinjiang, and Tibet. However, the "ceaseless expansion of overseas interests" and the broader geography of China's vision of global economic power must concern us as well. In an effort to explain what the six fortresses of a global China would be, if China's vision of victory were ever to be complete, I laid these out for the US Naval Institute in 2019:

China's fortresses, the strategic grounds of the "Belt and Road," are the following:

First, the West Pacific Island Chains. These are the Pacific gateway to the Eurasian continent. Just as they can be used now to keep America in, they could be used in the future to keep America out.

Second, the Indian Ocean Region. This is the maritime heart of the Eurasian intercontinental system. It connects China to Europe and Africa, and each of these regions to each other. It is the maritime system on which China depends—and in which China remains most vulnerable today.

Third, Australia. Australia remains the continental connector between the Indian Ocean and the whole of the Pacific. In the Second World War, it was a vital foothold that kept America in the Pacific. Encirclement of this giant island from the Indian Ocean to the South Pacific Islands would allow China greater control of the broader Indo-Pacific oceans.

Fourth, Africa. Chinese influence in this great continent is difficult to overstate. It is a vital resource base and the object of decades' worth of Chinese Communist Party political and economic influence. For China to project power here, from interventions in domestic conflicts to basing throughout the continent, would be a cornerstone of power and control, with Atlantic Ocean access on China's terms.

Fifth, Europe. Access to Europe is an integral piece of China's vision—arguably the most important market in the entire "Belt and Road" system. An expanded Chinese military could easily overwhelm any given European power, and China's efforts to build political influence in a host of European nations are clear.

Sixth, the South Pacific. Naval power projection, basing, and political and economic influence throughout the smaller island states of the South Pacific would give China further control of the broader Belt and Road system, and would complicate or deny American approaches to the Eurasian-Africa-Australian supercontinental structure.

This would leave North America, alone, cut off, "thrown out" as Mao said, not only from the "West Pacific countries," but from the larger intercontinental system that China is building, where China's leaders see themselves as sitting ultimately at the center, a global "Middle Kingdom," without rival and without peer.[28]

In the Indian Ocean, in Africa, in Australia, the South Pacific, and in Europe, we will have to maintain decisive military strength to keep America globally dominant, our Allies as the preponderant economic and military force, and our access to the world secure as we roll China back into Asia and secure it once again behind the island chains. This task will require a global vision of American and Allied military power and further integration of Allied defense strategy in Asia and Europe.

Should China's hold over the global economy increase rather than decrease in the decade ahead, we should expect that any potential conflict with Beijing would be global rather than regional. China has the advantage of sustained economic and infrastructure focus along key trade routes and projects that span or abut its Belt and Road regions: Asia, Africa, the Indian Ocean, Europe, and Australia. With military outposts not only in the South China Sea and South Pacific, but also near the Persian Gulf and around the Indian Ocean Rim where US investment and infrastructure may be less extensive, China could rapidly secure advantages and work toward intercontinental power projection well within the 2020s.

As Isaac Kardon of the US Naval War College explains about China's estimated global port and infrastructure system: "Ownership is a major factor in unlocking dual-use potential. Of the ninety-five Chinese-operated/owned ports abroad, central state-owned enterprises (SOEs) have operational roles, ownership stakes, or both in fifty-two of them, and eight involve local SOEs but no central SOEs."[29] Kardon explains that, between China's largest state-owned firms, port holdings in the world's oceans include thirty-one Atlantic Ocean ports, twenty-five Indian Ocean ports, twenty-one Pacific Ocean ports, and sixteen Mediterranean ports. When we examine the picture by continent, the distribution is twenty-two in Europe, twenty in the Middle East and North Africa, eighteen in the Americas, eighteen in South and Southeast Asia, and nine in Sub-Saharan Africa. Furthermore, "Fifty-three of these ports are located proximate to key maritime choke points. Of these, ten are near the English Channel, nine are near the Malacca Strait, nine are near the Strait of Hormuz, six are near the Suez Canal, and four each are near the Panama Canal, the Gibraltar Strait, and the Turkish straits." He notes that "the western Indian Ocean region, or MENA, should be considered the area of greatest concentration—and especially so if we include the seven ports on the eastern Mediterranean, which serve vital roles for traffic moving through the Suez Canal into or out of the Indian Ocean. South and Southeast Asia also host concentrations of Chinese ports at key locations along major sea lines of communication (SLOCs) and proximate to critical choke points."[30]

The intercontinental geography of the Belt and Road system is already being consolidated through dual-use economic/military investment strategies.

While many expect the South China Sea or Taiwan would be the focal point of conflict with China, we must realize that, with the world's largest surface fleet, the world's largest shipping corporations, and the world's largest fishing fleet and maritime militias—which themselves can be transformed into offensive and disruptive maritime capabilities—China has the potential to disrupt global trade and the world's strategic choke points from Europe to Africa to the Pacific. Taiwan may become a focal point, but China's far vaster port and maritime infrastructure, as well as its space capabilities, expanding nuclear arsenal, and cyber capabilities, mean that any conflict would have the potential to become global, and would have to be deterred across multiple domains of warfare.

Unlike the forces that maintained peace in Europe and kept Soviet armies at bay, or the counterinsurgency-focused military of the Middle East and Central Asian campaigns following September 11, the force structure required to defend the Indo-Pacific from Chinese Communist Party aggression must be built on naval and Marine Corps power, with the US Air Force providing cover for sea and land forces, and the US Army drawing upon its Second World War heritage in the Pacific theater.

Given the broader mistakes of offshoring and industrial decline, America no longer has the kind of industrial advantages that enabled victory in prior conflicts. For example, our shipbuilding industrial base has withered, as China becomes the world's ascendant commercial shipping and naval power. As retired US Navy captain Jerry Hendrix explains, "For years there has been a bipartisan consensus that the U.S. Navy should grow to 355 ships from 296. But a larger, more capable Navy needs shipyards to build and maintain the fleet. During World War II, the US had ten large Navy yards with drydocks and repair facilities, as well as more than forty commercial drydocks. Today there are only four industrial Navy yards, in Hawaii, Maine, Virginia and Washington state."[31]

American and Allied shipbuilding will need to prepare to compete against China's potential for massive military production and its peacetime military build-up.[32] We have had a vision of global Allied maritime cooperation in the past—for example in Admiral Mike Mullen's famous "1,000 ship navy" concept from the mid-2000s. Today, we must once again envision Allied cooperation for great power competition. Leveraging the global Allied industrial base, there is no reason for us to fall short, if it proves necessary, of a Thousand Ship Navy for Democracy.[33] With the full strength of our Alliance System, production capability should not be a constraint on strategy. Our armed services recognize the need to focus on the Indo-Pacific theater, and have already identified existing gaps and challenges. As the Marine Corps *Force Design 2030* explains, "We have shortfalls in expeditionary long-range precision fires; medium- to long-range air defense systems; short-range (point defense) air defense systems; high-endurance, long-range unmanned systems with Intelligence, Surveillance, and Reconnaissance (ISR), Electronic Warfare (EW), and lethal strike capabilities; and disruptive and less-lethal capabilities appropriate for countering malign activity."[34] The Marine Corps use of the military geography of Asia is described as follows: "We will equip our Marines with mobile, low-signature sensors and weapons that can provide a landward compliment to Navy capabilities for surface warfare, antisubmarine warfare, air and missile defense, and airborne early warning."[35] We should expect that the US Army will operate along similar lines, providing land-based support within the broad Indo-Pacific theater.

The United States must make full use of its undersea advantage. In America's submarine force we still hold enormous advantages over China. This means that undersea warfare is "a domain which we can own" even in the long term, according to former chief of naval operations Admiral Jonathan Greenert.[36] Our submarine force is the most survivable leg of the US nuclear triad—far more so than the land-based and air-based legs—and is therefore the bedrock of our nuclear deterrent. American advantages in undersea warfare can also give us the upper hand in naval conflict with China. We should concentrate not only on ballistic missile submarines but also on attack submarines—subsea hunter-killers—which can provide an asymmetric advantage in any potential conflict. Our Allies like the United Kingdom also bring advantages to the subsea realm, and understand its advantages clearly. In the words of British defense, "The Ukraine conflict underlines that missile ranges and surveillance systems in space and on aircraft are now such that even surface ships still in harbour can be targeted and destroyed. Submarines can remain undetectable to modern space-based assets and long range missiles and hypersonic [weapons]. Even as capabilities to detect submarines improve, their greater depth, distances and deception plans keep them hidden beyond anything on land, or in the sky or space."[37]

In order to keep pace with China's expanding shipbuilding program, the US will have to revitalize its national shipbuilding industrial base, as mentioned, with a focus on both shipyards and the shipbuilding workforce. The US Navy's current objectives include expanding the development and production of unmanned undersea vehicles (UUVs), such as extra-large UUVs like Boeing's Orca XLUUV—"roughly the size of a subway car."[38] These UUVs could revolutionize mine-laying, reconnaissance, and other critical missions even inside an enemy's anti-access and area-denial envelope while also reducing certain dangers for American sailors. Current naval strategy and procurement emphasizes a "new fleet architecture" with "a smaller proportion of larger ships (such as large-deck aircraft carriers, cruisers, destroyers, large amphibious ships, and large resupply ships); a larger proportion of smaller ships (such as frigates, corvettes, smaller amphibious ships, smaller resupply ships, and perhaps smaller aircraft carriers); and a new third tier of surface vessels about as large as corvettes or large patrol craft that will be either lightly manned, optionally manned, or unmanned, as well as large UUVs."[39]

According to the Congressional Research Service, this new architecture in the maritime domain is both affordable and "operationally necessary, to respond to the improving maritime anti-access/area-denial (A2/AD) capabilities of other countries, particularly China."[40] Take the example of naval unmanned vessels, which may become one of the most interesting areas for naval innovation and advantage:

UVs are one of several new capabilities—along with directed-energy weapons, hypersonic weapons, artificial intelligence, cyber capabilities, and quantum technologies—that the Navy and other US military services are pursuing to meet emerging military challenges, particularly from China. UVs can be equipped with sensors, weapons, or other payloads, and can be operated remotely, semi-autonomously, or (with technological advancements) autonomously. They can be individually less expensive to procure than manned ships and aircraft because their designs do not need to incorporate spaces and support equipment for onboard human operators. UVs can be particularly suitable for long-duration missions that might tax the physical endurance of onboard human operators, or missions that pose a high risk of injury, death, or capture of onboard human operators—so-called "three D" missions, meaning missions that are dull, dirty, or dangerous.[41]

PREPONDERANCE

America, Our Allies, and the Return
to Peace Through Strength

The objective of this book is to help us find a path that enables us to break free of a world defined by constraints and waning advantages. It is far better to find a return to peace through strength than to be forced to make strategy from the position of ever-diminishing advantages. However, the innovation that is likely to take shape as we work to solve problems with limited means may itself become a profound advantage once we are able to unlock larger economic resources in the future. As described in the Economic Arena, we are in a process of bifurcation between China and the United States, which America should shape and encourage, moving the global economy toward a divergence between China and the democracies. As the process of economic and technological bifurcation matures, the United States will also have to identify and seize the lead in the contests that matter to fielding the kind of military power that can prevent a classic dilemma of history: the dictator's gamble on the use of force. Vladimir Putin's gamble on territorial conquest in Ukraine already marks the return of war to Europe, and perhaps most chillingly, the attack by a dictatorship on a democracy not only for the sake of territorial ambitions, but essentially because this state *is* a democracy—because it is choosing its own path. Let us keep in mind that NATO expansion, which both Russia and China jointly oppose, has been *voluntary, not coerced*. The democracies of Europe have sought security against the all-too-real specter of Russian aggression. While one might look at the invasion of Ukraine as a failure of deterrence, its result at present writing has also been the unification of NATO, the Allied coordination of economic warfare, and, thanks to Ukrainian resistance and Allied support, enormous battlefield losses for Russia. China's leaders, whose alignment with Putin remains, must weigh their choices carefully in the Taiwan Strait and other flashpoints. American defense strategy rests principally on deterrence. We should maintain and strengthen this strategy by applying our gains in the Economic Arena to build a twenty-first-century military advantage that can dissuade our adversaries from using force against America, our Allies, and other states and regions.

Considering both real and intended military aggression by the Russian and Chinese dictatorships, we should keep in mind these words by US chairman of the joint chiefs of staff General Mark Milley in 2021 about the broader objectives of US military strength:

> The world order, the so-called liberal world order that was put in place in 1945, that was not designed to prevent Korea or Vietnam or Gulf War I, or terrorism for that matter. It was designed to prevent World War III. It was designed to prevent great power war. And it's been successful, for we're in the 76th year. The two times before, historically, you look at the Treaty of Westphalia, that lasted about 100 years, you look at the Concert of Europe that lasted about 100 years. So we're in the 76th year of this great power peace.[42]

Superior technology, systems, strategies, and the combined mass of Allied power must be used to shore up this world order and to continue the third great major power peace of the past four hundred years. That peace is known as the Pax Americana—the American Peace. Our objective is that this peace should continue. While we can be the cornerstone, the largest portion of military power and combat capability among the Allies, America cannot shoulder this peace alone. As the Diplomatic Arena explains, it is the sheer weight of the Alliance System that can rebuild the superiority of the democracies over the dictatorships of our era. This is true of power in general, and also true of military capability. Consider one period in which major power peace collapsed entirely—the Second World War. The hunger of the dictatorships of the 1930s,

Germany, Japan, and Italy, meant that the twenty-year peacetime period after the First World War, which some called "the war to end all wars," proved nothing more than an interwar period. That is what happens when dictatorships rise on their typical concoction of grievances and opportunism. Our challenge is as follows: that the period of major power peace and prosperity from the end of the Second World War through the fall of the Berlin Wall to the present does not culminate in conflict among the world's major powers. Maintaining this peace isn't possible through appeasement or accommodation of states like Russia and China. Just as the undertakings of the Cold War may not have prevented Korea or Vietnam *but did prevent World War III*, the question becomes how does one hold the ambitions and aggressions of our foremost adversaries at bay? How can we continue our long peace and also secure the frontiers of the Free World?

The preponderance of military power can create a third Great Wall in US and Allied strategy toward China, joining economic containment and diplomatic rollback. If organized globally, the combined power of the world's democracies can ensure the return of our military advantage, through our superior economic and technological power, as well as through our superior numbers. The purpose of such an approach is not to destroy China, but to destroy its ambition to use military power, by demonstrating that wars large or small initiated by Beijing will not succeed.[43] A mere balance of power in Asia is not enough to ensure deterrence. Nor is it sufficient in Europe or potentially in other regions of the world. What is necessary is the decisive superiority of the *combined* military power of the world's democracies. As Winston Churchill explained in 1934 as his nation dithered over the rise of Hitler:

> You have heard the old doctrine of the balance of power. I don't accept it. Anything like a balance of power in Europe will lead to war. Great wars usually come only when both States think they have good hopes of victory. Peace must be founded on preponderance; there is safety in numbers. If there were five or six on each side, there might be a frightful trial of strength, but if there were eight or ten on one side and only one or two upon the other, and if the collective armed forces

on one side were three or four times as large as the other, then there will be no war.[44]

It is this preponderance of power that the Allied World must achieve. Anything short of this will tempt the forces of aggression gathering now. If we fail to move in this direction or if conflict breaks out in Asia before this preponderance of power is achieved, it is likely Beijing can gain from adventurism and aggression. This would be a kind of shock to the Free World as Ukraine has been. We must combine and integrate our military power from the Atlantic to the Pacific to defend against further aggression from Moscow and Beijing. Like the Korean War, which focused minds during the early Cold War, the Russian invasion of Ukraine has awakened the United States and Europe. We must understand that Beijing is building its ability to use its military in its region, too. A US deterrence strategy, if successful, can prevent such dangerous adventurism by China from taking place, but our military advantages must be rebuilt. We can then continue on the long road of deterrence, as we have done throughout the American Peace, allowing other pillars of our grand strategy to slow down these dictatorships while strengthening America and our Allies.

In September 1950, as the Cold War with the Soviet Union had become the guiding principle for US national security and foreign policy, President Truman signed the now-famous Report to the National Security Council—NSC 68. This document was one of America's first attempts at a comprehensive strategy to handle the emerging problem that the Soviet Union posed to American life and to international order.[45] NSC-68 led to an investment in American military power that would set the early foundations for long-term American strategy and comprehensive deterrence over the Soviet Union throughout the second half of the twentieth century. The document defined the purpose of American military power as follows: "For us the role of military power is to serve the national purpose by deterring an attack upon us while we seek by other means to create an environment in which our free society can flourish, and by fighting, if necessary, to defend the integrity and vitality of our free society and to defeat any aggressor."[46] Initiated as a result of the Chinese Communist Party's victory over Chiang Kai-shek's Guomindang in the Chinese Civil War and Stalin's successful test of an atomic bomb, and then implemented as the result of the outbreak of the Korean War, NSC-68 led to massive increases in the US military budget, which would permanently shape the Cold War world, becoming a part of the containment strategy developed by George F. Kennan.[47]

Today, deterring China from the use of its military in the Pacific, particularly under the conditions of economic containment and diplomatic rollback, will be possible only from a position of long-term military superiority. This means causing Beijing to recognize that the use of force can only be self-destructive. Some might point out that, as in the First World War, once war plans have been devised, they are easily put into effect. We must recognize that these war plans *have already been devised by China.* We must ensure that China's military planning never reaches the point where China's leaders have—in their minds—a decisive advantage. Our military competition will evolve over the years and decades ahead and we must work to stay in the lead. If we fail to stay ahead, we may find that the next stage of competition with China *begins* with a military conflict.

We do not have a permanent window for the successful pursuit of a peacetime containment strategy. Just as the trajectory of the multi-decade Cold War was solidified in 1950 by the three-year Korean War, it is possible that if we fail to contain and deter Beijing, China's leaders will solidify a new trajectory by choosing to use their military power. Should this happen, what's most likely to change is the *velocity* but not the *nature* of US-China competition. Should Beijing decide to use its military against Taiwan or elsewhere, an outcome would have to be a massive reduction of trade and termination of investment in China by the United States and Allies as we have seen after Russia's invasion of Ukraine. It is far better to pursue economic containment from a position of necessity and foresight. Failure to slow and stall Beijing's momentum in the Economic Arena *now* grants China an open-ended window to convert increasing economic power into increasing military capabilities.

We can look to the first Cold War to see what one observer has called two chapters that worked toward the preponderance of American power: the first was Truman's NSC-68 as a response to communist aggression in Asia and the second was the Reagan administration's reconstruction of peace through strength for the purpose of ultimate victory in the contest with the Soviet Union.[48] Among the most interesting strategic documents of the Cold War era, the Reagan Administration's National Security Decision Directive on "US Relations with the USSR," or NSDD-75, laid out a series of principles and objectives for US strategy toward the Soviet Union: "external resistance," "internal pressure," and "negotiations," with the following objective: "To contain and over time reverse Soviet expansionism by competing effectively on a sustained basis with the Soviet Union in all international arenas—particularly in the overall military balance and in the geographical regions of priority concern to the United States."[49] Let us turn to Reagan's focus on the military balance. Here is the official overview of the US military strategy that underpinned "peace through strength":

> The US must modernize its military forces—both nuclear and conventional—so that Soviet leaders perceive that the US is determined never to accept a second place or deteriorating military posture. Soviet calculations of possible war outcomes under any contingency must always result in outcomes so unfavorable to the USSR that there would be no incentive for a Soviet leader to initiate an attack. The future strength of US military capabilities must be assured. US military technology advances must be exploited, while controls over transfer of military related/dual-use technology, products, and services must be tightened.[50]

This strategy—which completed the early Cold War grand strategies of Truman, Eisenhower, and Kennedy and led to the peaceful end of both the Cold War and the USSR—makes clear the need for resource mobilization. That mobilization must occur not only in the United States but also with our Allies. Such coordination would establish an intrepid but necessary scope of military capability that could act across "the entire spectrum of potential conflicts":

> The existing and projected gap between finite US resources and the level of capabilities needed to implement US strategy makes it essential that the US: (1) establish firm priorities for the use of limited US resources where they will have the greatest restraining impact on the Soviet Union; and (2) mobilize the resources of Allies and friends which are willing to join the US in containing the expansion of Soviet power.

Underlying the full range of US and Western policies must be a strong military capable of action across the entire spectrum of potential conflicts and guided by a well conceived political and military strategy. The heart of US military strategy is to deter attack by the USSR and its allies against the US, its Allies, or other important countries, and to defeat such an attack should deterrence fail. Although unilateral US efforts must lead the way in rebuilding Western military strength to counter the Soviet threat, the protection of Western interests will require increased US cooperation with Allied and other states and greater utilization of their resources.[51]

While the Reagan administration was well known for driving the Soviet Union into an arms race that broke its economy and concluded the Cold War era, our competition with China is unlikely to drive this adversary to financial ruin on a near-term timeframe, nor should that be our objective. Unlike the Cold War world, which began with two competing economic blocs, we begin in an integrated world that is the result of one of history's greatest periods of peacetime globalization. The path to American victory in this contest is to rebuild the world economy, which China seeks to dominate, so that rather than deeper integration with China, we slice out the Chinese Communist Party from the world's key supply chains, capital markets, technological advancements, and export markets—region by region and sector by sector—until economic containment is complete. Our defense strategy must enable this transformation of the world economy to take shape in America's favor, with an outcome not necessarily of the collapse of China, but rather of a second Great Divergence between the economic and military power of the world's democracies and that of the world's dictatorships.

The lessons from Truman's NSC-68, the Korean War, Reagan's NSDD-75, and the end of the USSR show us how to re-create an overall position of American advantage that secured major power peace for several generations. The position of security through military advantage can grant us freedom to maneuver throughout the Economic and Diplomatic Arenas with unmatched possibilities. In turn, success in the Economic and Diplomatic Arenas will allow us greater scope for investment in peace through strength. Conversely, failing to rectify the military balance will at best lower the costs of the dictator's gamble and at worst create an open field for Russian and Chinese expansionism and aggression.

The reduction in commercial engagement and the termination of investment in China and Russia is already desirable and achievable using America's existing economic toolkit from the International Emergency Economic Powers Act to the Committee on Foreign Investment in the United States. However, we are hampered by American and Allied multinational corporations' willingness to expand their operations in China, even after Beijing's actions in Hong Kong, Xinjiang, and the Himalayas, as well as Chinese Communist Party support for Putin's invasion of Ukraine. Communist Party aggression against Taiwan would have to be a final line, which, if crossed, would likely result in wholesale economic warfare against the People's Republic of China, the destruction of Chinese corporations overseas, the cessation of all nonessential trade, and the seizure of assets by both sides. Chinese military action against Taiwan would be a true "sputnik" moment, not only for the US national security community, but also for the US government as a whole, realizing that deterrence had failed and that we are truly in conflict with China. Any such action would be far from the final chapter in US-China global competition and confrontation. If Beijing were to lose that conflict, they might of course try again, whether soon afterward or well into the future. What would change, however, would be the US government's permission to our private sector to engage with China, especially if US forces were attacked.

The deepest contradiction in Chinese grand strategy is that the Communist Party believes that it can use military power to achieve its ambitions, but it also seeks to maintain economic relations with the outside world, eventually dominating the global economy. Beijing is attempting, as we have seen, to address this contradiction by reducing reliance on the outside world through "Dual Circulation": indigenization of key industries and technologies while also attempting to increase the reliance of other countries on China. Because of this contradiction, an economic containment strategy works in tandem with deterrence through strength. Scaling back technological, commercial, and investment exchange with China will weaken it in the long term—because China depends on the outside world for resources and goods trade—but the prospect of total economic isolation in the near term can also be a deterrent against the use of force in Asia. China will never achieve true autarky, though it may do so in some sectors of its economy. Economic relations with the outside world are the biggest thing that China risks through war in Asia. A wholesale strategy of regional conquest, like Japan's in the Second World War, appears unlikely at present, but the use of military power for "limited" effect in either Asia or other parts of the world—whether territorial conquest or "teaching a lesson" to other states—remains in China's back pocket if we do not have a robust deterrence strategy.

China's leadership today, once holed up in a tumultuous and inward-looking state, have brought their ambitions to a globalized world. In anticipation of the use of force by China, not only in regional flashpoints such as Taiwan, the South and East China Seas, and the Himalayas, but also throughout the Belt and Road regions from Africa to the Middle East, from Southeast Asia to the Pacific Island chains, and even, should their partner states like Russia and Iran become involved, in places as far as Latin America and Europe, we must prepare to defend against these aggressors around the world. A global national security strategy is necessary to manage the ambitions of multiple adversaries, as our existing National Security Strategy is conceived.[52] It is also necessary to handle China's vision of victory on its own. America must strive to achieve superiority in the military domains of the twenty-first century, while also seeking to unlock and master the potential "revolutions in military affairs" and breakthroughs that lie ahead in the path of industrial and technological progress. This is also why our strategy of economic divergence is essential. Owing to our economic integration with China, our gains in critical technologies and industries readily become *their gains as well*. As mentioned before, there is no point in driving faster if our adversary is sitting next to us in the same car.

As Andrew Krepinevich explains of the state of technological competition: "The United States is losing its long-term advantage in a number of key military-related technologies. This is partially unavoidable, as many emerging technologies with the potential to boost military effectiveness, such as AI, big data, directed energy, genetic engineering, additive manufacturing, and robotics are being driven primarily by the commercial sector. . . . [T]hese technologies are available to all who have the means to obtain them."[53] We can see, therefore, the absolutely vital importance of the private sector becoming party to US and Allied grand strategy, and pulling back from China in the strategic industries and emerging technologies that matter, whether by choice or by the prevailing will of US and Allied governments.

China's 2021 test of a hypersonic missile and fractional orbital bombardment system, as well as its expanding nuclear silos in its western regions, demonstrate that the Chinese military is creating what two leading analysts call "stalemate" in the nuclear domain, which would allow them to rely much more aggressively on conventional capabilities and even lean much more heavily into an expanding conflict below the threshold of nuclear war.[54] As I pointed out in *China's Vision of Victory*, Beijing's nuclear weapons capability is, in their minds, a defensive capability, yet one that supports claims to territorial integrity and national sovereignty, both of which require the potential seizure of foreign territory.[55] In other words, China's nuclear arsenal, which is expanding in both size and sophistication, can be used as a deterrent in a conventional war that allows Beijing to seize and hold territory using its conventional forces, while placing the burden of escalation or intervention on the United States. The 2021 US Department of Defense Annual Report to Congress on Military and Security Developments in the People's Republic of China notes that the Chinese military continues to focus on "developing the capabilities to conduct joint long-range precision strikes across domains, increasingly sophisticated space, counterspace, and cyber capabilities, and accelerating the large-scale expansion of its nuclear forces."[56] This report revealed that the Pentagon estimates that China would potentially triple the size of its nuclear arsenal:

> The accelerating pace of the PRC's nuclear expansion may enable the PRC to have up to 700 deliverable nuclear warheads by 2027. The PRC likely intends to have at least 1,000 warheads by 2030, exceeding the pace and size the DoD projected in 2020.[57]

Given these developments, and the overall problem of expansionist, nuclear-armed Russia and China, nuclear weapons and their continuous maintenance and modernization must continue to remain a priority in American defense strategy. We must ensure that whatever direction Russian and Chinese aggression may take, we retain the ability to deter the use of nuclear weapons against ourselves and our Allies. This, alongside a robust new focus on missile defense, will be essential to the strategic environment of the present and the future.[58] The 2022 Nuclear Posture Review continues to emphasize the role of nuclear weapons in US defense:

> Strategic deterrence remains a top priority mission for the Department of Defense (DoD) and the Nation. For the foreseeable future, nuclear weapons will continue to provide unique deterrence effects that no other element of U.S. military power can replace. To deter aggression and preserve our security in the current security environment, we will maintain nuclear forces that are responsive to the threats we face . . . In a dynamic security environment, a safe, secure, and effective nuclear deterrent is foundational to broader U.S. defense strategy and the extended deterrence commitments we have made to allies and partners.[59]

In addition to the dangers of potential nuclear escalation, both China's and Russia's focus on space warfare means that the space domain could come into play early in a conflict. While we will review the constructive potential of space within this chapter, we must note the importance of space defense and space as a warfighting domain, facts absolutely clear to our adversaries in Beijing and Moscow. As a recent Pentagon report explains:

> [The] PRC continues to develop counterspace capabilities—including direct ascent, co-orbital, electronic warfare, and directed energy capabilities—that can contest or deny an adversary's access to and operations in the space domain during a crisis or conflict. The PRC's space enterprise continues to mature rapidly and Beijing has devoted significant resources to growing all aspects of its space program, from military space applications to civil applications such as profit-generating launches, scientific endeavors, and space exploration. . . .[60]
> The PRC continues to strengthen its military space capabilities, despite its public stance against the weaponization of space. The PLA continues to invest in improving its capabilities in space-based

intelligence, surveillance, and reconnaissance (ISR), satellite communication, satellite navigation, and meteorology, as well as human spaceflight and robotic space exploration. . . .

The PLA continues to acquire and develop a range of counterspace capabilities and related technologies, including kinetic-kill missiles, ground-based lasers, and orbiting space robots, as well as expanding space surveillance capabilities, which can monitor objects in space within their field of view and enable counterspace actions. . . .

[PLA] scholars stress the necessity "to cripple or destroy the enemy's information system [which] would drastically degrade the enemy's combat capabilities by making it blind, deaf or paralyzed" suggesting that such systems, as well as navigation and early warning satellites, could be among the targets of attacks designed to "blind and deafen the enemy."[61]

Given these challenges, the creation of the United States Space Force marks the beginning of an important new chapter in US national security. In the words of the Space Capstone Publication *Spacepower: Doctrine for Space Forces*, "The US desires a peaceful, secure, stable, and accessible space domain. Strength and security in space enables freedom of action in other warfighting domains while contributing to international security and stability. The US must adapt its national security space organizations, doctrine, and capabilities to deter and defeat aggression and protect national interests in space."[62] Given the vital role that space will play in the century ahead in providing transformative possibilities for American and Allied prosperity, we must focus on winning a new Space Race—one that can begin to unlock the potential of space and our solar system. Space security will be essential to our progress: "Assuring freedom of operation in space is a fundamental role of the US military, and specifically the United States Space Force."[63]

We must also grapple with the fact that, by today's public accounts, China is moving faster than the United States in its innovation in certain military systems that have the potential to alter the military balance, such as hypersonics. As General John Hyten, former Commander of US Strategic Command and then Vice Chairman of the Joint Chiefs of Staff, explained in 2021 regarding China's hypersonic test, "A test did occur, it is very concerning," adding that,

"What you need to be worried about is that in the last five years, or maybe longer, the United States has done nine hypersonic missile tests, and in the same time the Chinese have done hundreds. Single digits vs hundreds is not a good place."[64] General Hyten explained as well that, "They're going counter-space in a big way, they're deploying weapons in space. They are doing all those things because they saw how the United States has used space for dominant advantage."[65]

To reclaim our military advantages within a fast-paced technological com-petition, a global military geography, and against an adversary who has shown excellence in converting economic power into military gains, many American strategists expect to compete from a position of fundamental disadvantage given China's continuing economic rise. Peace through strength has given way to a related but diminished concept known as "deterrence through denial." The idea is that we can concentrate what limited advantages we retain on the most likely aim of Communist Party aggression, in this case Taiwan, and do what we can to make this an unattainable task for China. This is a commendable strategy in the short term, making the best of a deteriorating position, but it is unsustainable in the long term without a supporting economic strategy. There is likely to be no strategy that allows America to prevail or hold the military bal-ance should China continue its economic ascendancy, ultimately becoming the larger economic power. The pace of change is already so great as China grows that the Chinese military is not only outbuilding us on the seas, but across other key domains as well. In the words of Maj. Gen. Cameron Holt, who leads acquisitions for the US Air Force, China is procuring weapons systems "five to six" times faster than the United States.[66] Economic containment of China along with US and Allied growth becomes an essential strategy. There is likely to be no great strategy that allows America to prevail or hold the military balance for long should China continue its economic ascendancy, ultimately becoming the larger economic power. As Elbridge Colby, lead architect of the Trump administration's National Defense Strategy, explains, "If the United States tried to spend its way to dominance, China could very likely negate such an effort. Moreover, given the enormous demands of attempting to attain dominance against a power like China, the economic costs could be crippling, seriously stressing the US economy, the ultimate source of America's military strength."[67] How can we expect to prevail in a long-term competition if we continue supporting the growth and improvement of the Chinese economy at the expense of our own? Colby and others in US national security have been given the task of having to defend America and our interests while our business and finance sectors enable and enlarge our adversary's economy and by extension its military resources.

To break out of Colby's Dilemma, where America must concentrate limited resources against a growing adversarial power, we must win the Economic Arena. Supremacy in the Economic Arena enables deterrence in the Military Arena, and a successful diplomacy toward unity and engagement with our Allies enables both outcomes. The United States must also have a clear vision for the next horizon in military affairs and industrial power. This means, for example, the implementation of existing plans that can create an advantage for America and an investment in next-generation capabilities that will define the contest with China not only for today, but for decades into the future. For example, as General Hyten says of the vulnerability of US satellite systems to Chinese space weapons, "I wish we'd achieved a resilient space architecture. We talked about it for over a decade, and we designed it for over a decade, the design is out there."[68] Furthermore, as China's military leaders explain their ambitions in space, which go as far as the establishment of moon bases, asteroid mining, and even military dominance in cis-lunar space, the United States must design and execute a comprehensive vision for a space industrial economy and the military power to defend it. US space dominance is essential not only to current terrestrial flashpoints, but also to securing the next horizon of military and economic power and maintaining comprehensive superiority over our adversaries. The United States Space Force has begun to articulate this vision. Together with building an American-led space economy, the Space Force vision must become an absolute national priority.

At present, military space is primarily an arena of reconnaissance and communications. While this is essential to warfare, from GPS to space-based early warning systems that can detect an adversary nuclear launch, what America requires is a long-term vision for space power. In addition to the need to outcompete our adversary in global markets, to secure supply chains, and to build a superior industrial base, it is essential that America, not China, builds the space industrial economy of the future. Our commercial space leaders are already focused on the idea of becoming "a multiplanetary species." Our military must search for a defining advantage in this domain, as well as for superiority within the most important military geographies on Earth. Additionally, we must be fast to apply industrial advances to military power. Working within our Alliance System, we are likely to have a superior military innovation base, and as we solve the challenges of reducing or eliminating our collective dependency on China for an industrial base, we are likely to unlock new technological potential throughout the Alliance System. If this potential can be applied and used in a collective defense system that spans the Atlantic and Pacific, creating an integrated Allied innovation base, we are likely to regain a lead in military innovation. For example, a series of RAND Corporation recommendations to Japan's Ministry of Defense are in fact usable across the Alliance System as a whole, particularly when one considers that between North America, Europe, and Asia, US Allies hold the majority of wealth and private sector capabilities in the industries of the future:

> Japan can leverage commercial interest and investments in key technology areas to aid in their development and operationalization. Emerging space constellations provide valuable services for the commercial market in remote sensing, broadband communications, and environmental monitoring. Likewise, unmanned systems satisfy many commercial needs, such as monitoring undersea infrastructure, reducing personnel requirements for many tasks, and providing services for an aging population. Nanotechnology can be used to contribute to such fields as medicine and construction, advanced telecommunications can improve the speed and reliability of civilian networks, and additive manufacturing is already being used by manufacturers to streamline production. In the information technology domain, AI, big data, and autonomy can help businesses increase their efficiency, capabilities, and profits. . . . In all these cases, technology areas that are the focus of considerable private-sector investment can be harnessed by the MOD.[69]

We must understand, as China already does, how to combine the power of the civilian and military technology-industrial base. The commercial innovation and investment that exists at a vast scale across the Alliance System is likely to be a far superior force for reaching the decisive turning points on the horizon, provided that the Allied World succeeds in denying our adversaries access to these innovations and also finding economies of scale for investment, production, and collective use across the Alliance System. Our superior global innovation base is likely to produce the next revolution not only in industrial potential but also in military affairs. However, we must also have a vision for what this outcome will look like.

A war initiated by Beijing in Asia over territorial aims could expand to intercontinental or global proportions owing to the nature of China's global assets and interests and the nature of the weapons systems available. For example, should it come to horizontal escalation—widening the conflict geographically in order to secure an advantage—as Elbridge Colby explains, "China might, for instance, conduct non-nuclear attacks on the defenders' critical infrastructure or other sensitive targets to inflict pain on what it might judge or hope to be weak-willed populaces in the United States or other coalition countries." Colby compares these attacks to the German bombing of London in the Second World War: "By definition, China's strikes would not be coupled with a plausible way of attacking and subjugating Allied states, which would have already won the local battle. They would thus be cruel but feckless. The German V-1 and V-2 rockets in the Second World War inspired terror among Londoners but did not affect the war's outcome."[70] Furthermore, the distribution and use of China's anti-ship missile capabilities around their network of ports and infrastructure could place Allied fleets and civil shipping at risk from the Atlantic to the Indian Ocean Region.[71] The United States already has options to counter and respond to these potential moves by Beijing, but like China's wars and border conflicts of the twentieth century, we should understand that Beijing's aim is often to make a point to another state, not just to seize territory.

Vertical escalation—using increasingly powerful weapons including the potential use of nuclear weapons—is another important dimension to the problem. As Colby explains, in a Taiwan conflict, "China could also try to use its nuclear weapons to rescue victory from the jaws of defeat."[72] Witnessing Putin's nuclear threats during his invasion of Ukraine, some observe that China could also use nuclear threats to intimidate the West into standing aside as Russia or China carries out a war of conquest.[73] Real deterrence means not only being able to defeat or impose enormous costs on China's conventional forces, but also matching Beijing when it comes to both horizontal and vertical escalation. US defense must be in a position not only to impose enormous costs in a regional conflict but also to maintain deterrence in the global commons. As Chinese nuclear build-up and the Russia-China entente transform the global balance of power, America must maintain its focus on strategic deterrence as well.[74]

Finally, the cyber domain, led by US Cyber Command, presents a vital opportunity for America's private sector technology leaders to enter into deep partnership with US national security in one of our most important missions for our national defense. We have already seen the singular focus of the Chinese Communist Party on industrial espionage and the centrality of this malicious activity to their national economic strategies. We have also recently witnessed Russian attacks in cyberspace not only for the purpose of fanning the flames of national political divisions but also directly targeting US national infrastructure. Securing our civilian infrastructure and national industrial base will be essential to opening a path for progress in an increasingly networked world. While economic bifurcation between China and the democracies is likely to take place, especially in information technology–dependent industries, we must also ensure that our business, government, and civilian infrastructure is hardened and resilient to enemy attacks. Cyber Command's Command Vision explains that, "Military superiority in the air, land, sea, and space domains is critical to our ability to defend our interests and protect our values. Achieving superiority in the physical domains in no small part depends on superiority in cyberspace. Yet we risk ceding cyberspace superiority."[75]

The 2018 *Department of Defense Cyber Strategy* explains one objective of strategic competition in cyberspace as follows: "First, we must ensure the US military's ability to fight and win wars in any domain, including cyberspace. This is a foundational requirement for US national security and a key to ensuring that we deter aggression, including cyber attacks that constitute a use of force, against the United States, our Allies, and our partners. The Department must defend its own networks, systems and information from malicious cyber activity and be prepared to defend, when directed, those networks and systems operated by non-DoD Defense Critical Infrastructure (DCI) and Defense Industrial Base (DIB) entities. We will defend forward to halt or degrade cyberspace operations targeting the Department, and we will collaborate to strengthen the cybersecurity and resilience of DoD, DCI, and DIB networks and systems."[76] In 2018, the White House issued a *National Cyber Strategy*, the first in fifteen years, explaining that "the responsibility to secure the Nation's critical infrastructure and manage its cybersecurity risk is shared by the private sector and Federal Government. In partnership with the private sector, we will collectively use a risk-management approach to mitigating vulnerabilities to raise the base level of cybersecurity across critical infrastructure."[77] The strategy identified seven key areas: national security, energy and power, banking and finance, health and safety, communications, information technology, and transportation.

The exercise of hardening critical infrastructure is a promising arena in which American business and national security leaders can come together out of clear, common interest. Any CEO, board of directors, or group of shareholders should understand that the same country they look to do business with—the People's Republic of China—is engaged in grand-scale industrial espionage and other forms of cyber aggression against our own companies and country. Ensuring deeper public-private partnerships in the cyber domain is not only a necessity for national security, but also an opportunity to further engage our private sector in moving toward the right side of history.

America's major technology companies collaborate extensively with US national security and this relationship must continue to grow as our challenges rise. The market pull of the US government and national security enterprise is evident, for example, in a series of cloud computing contracts awarded or tendered in recent years by the Central Intelligence Agency, National Security Agency, and the US Department of Defense. A Central Intelligence Agency cloud computing contract was awarded to multiple technology leaders in 2020 including Amazon Web Services, IBM Cloud, Microsoft Azure, Google Cloud, and Oracle Cloud, demonstrating the appetite for our leading companies to work closely with essential national security missions and also to publicly embrace their commitment to the United States. Companies like Oracle have their origins working with US national security. Google, which has recently launched Google Public Sector in 2022, stated of its CIA contract award, "We remain committed to serving public sector organizations of all sizes, and this award builds on recent federal momentum for Google Cloud with NOAA, the US Department of Energy, Defense Innovation Unit, US Navy, US Patent and Trademark Office, US Small Business Administration, and more."[78] Despite their continued engagement in the China market, as America's technology giants come to understand the growing risks in China and also the competition that they will face against China's technology giants in key growth markets, it is important to bring them firmly to America's side in the overall competition with China and Russia. New defense technology companies have also emerged whose leaders not only support American national security, but also emphasize their desire to help America win the contest with Russia and China. Brian Schimpf, CEO of Anduril, a defense technology company dedicated to artificial intelligence and autonomy, states that:

> Despite China's and Russia's public rumbling about AI, the United States has a number of advantages over its rivals in the race to develop sophisticated autonomous systems. The seven most valuable technology companies in the world are all American, as are three of the world's five best computer science departments. We have the human capital, the wealth and the scale to develop world-class AI-enabled military technology that will help us make sense of a vaster and more complex battlefield, and act upon it.[79]

Palantir CEO Alex Karp shares his appreciation of the origins of Silicon Valley itself and its relationship with US defense: "[T]he founding spark for Silicon Valley was its embrace of the defense objectives and technological aims of the government whose very existence made its rise possible. The intersection of technical engineering talent, the protection and relative insulation of academia, and the government's aggressive search for truly disruptive technology to advance its defense and intelligence objectives gave rise to the Silicon Valley that we know today." He adds that, "Our expansion as a company over the years was made possible by our work with government agencies in the military and intelligence sectors in the United States, whose leaders took an interest in software and understood its potential to reshape national defense."[80]

America's technology leaders are an essential part of our industrial-innovation base. If we are able to maintain the commitment of our world-leading technology enterprises, harness their potential for innovation, and also rebuild our most important strategic industries, we can regain the American advantage that saw us through the greatest challenges of the past hundred years.

THE DEFENSE INDUSTRIAL BASE

Our Foundations and Our Frontiers

L ike victory in the Economic Arena, victory in the arena of national defense will require the full cooperation of our private sector. Rebuilding the national defense industrial base has become a primary concern among military professionals and citizens who understand the stakes of the contest with China and Russia.[81] That base—which we can also think of as a national defense-industrial-*innovation* base—has been the key to victory not only in military conflicts like the Second World War but also in the most significant peacetime contest in the past century, the Cold War. We must undertake a series of national moon-shot initiatives, rebuild and secure our strategic industries, and ensure that our national and Allied innovation bases are superior to those of our adversaries. It means harnessing the power of the US and Allied private sector and not only building a twenty-first-century national industrial base, but also unlocking new possibilities that can transform our economic and military potential. Both the wartime and peacetime contests of the past hundred years have led to significant technological advancements. The Space Race was one of the greatest examples and so was the birth of Silicon Valley. The history of American innovation is essentially a history of public-private support and partnership. Our innovation clusters that combine entrepreneurship, scholarly research, and strategic government funding have produced many examples of success.

The Information Technology & Innovation Foundation compiled a 2014 report of "22 Examples of Major Technology Advances That Stem from Federal Research Support," noting that "The Second World War institutionalized this important federal role in R&D and resulted in remarkable advances in radar, electronics, jet aircraft and atomic power. The United States has depended on this rich system, supported with federal money, where many of the biggest innovations stem from the work of the community, rather than the lone innovator." The ITIF list includes examples from information technology, energy, health, mathematics, education, transportation, and agriculture. The list features inventions and innovations that have changed American life: the Google Search Engine, brought about by the National Science Foundation and Stanford University's support for Sergey Brin and Larry Page in the 1990s; GPS; ARPANET, which laid the foundations of the internet; smartphone technologies; the Human Genome Project; and magnetic resonance imaging (MRIs).[82] Throughout modern history, our great public corporations have worked with the US government on pressing strategic challenges—and we must now support a renaissance of public-private partnership. Whatever critics may say, the national strategic missions of the United States government have led to enormous progress in technology and innovation. Our contest with China will be a similar moment in which, if we are able to sustain a long-term major power peace, we can make substantial progress in industrial technology and economic growth.

Two important examples are worth examination. The first is a new Space Race and the advent of a genuine space-based economy. Space and national security have gone hand in hand since the Cold War. Today's revolution in private sector spacefaring, in which companies like Elon Musk's SpaceX, Jeff Bezos's Blue Origin, and Richard Branson's Virgin Galactic, as well as lesser known companies like Relativity Space—which uses additive manufacturing to print rockets—is one of the most significant whole-of-industry examples in which government, private sector, national security, and the national science and technology innovation base can coordinate on innovation and industrial potential. Unlocking the next horizon in space defense and space-based resources and economic potential is a likely outcome from a successful contest against China and Russia, the world's two most prominent spacefaring nations other than the United States. The successful development of a space-based economy is likely to create a transformative edge to the US-China economic contest, offering us a new arena in which we can outcompete our adversary and unlock economic potential that goes beyond the earth itself. This is likely to be among the most important features of twenty-first-century history, and therefore a contest that America and our Allies must win. A second example is rare earth and critical minerals supply chains. The essential need for many of these materials—largely found and processed in China—to sustain our way of life and our national defense industrial base creates an urgent national security requirement that goes beyond a typical business case. It is essential that we engage our private sector. Our national security means that these supply chains must be built and secured with a North American or Allied supply chain. As we do this work, we are likely to learn powerful and usable lessons about how national security and the private sector can collaborate to secure America. Like Operation Warp Speed, which brought together a wide range of government agencies in collaboration with leading pharmaceutical companies including Johnson & Johnson and Moderna to develop a COVID-19 vaccine in record time, the efforts that America must undertake in strategic and critical minerals will be vital and must involve public-private partnerships. The space economy presents an example of extraordinary opportunity while critical minerals presents urgent necessity. Each one demonstrates how national security and economic power must be developed together.

RARE EARTHS AND CRITICAL MINERALS

The US Department of Defense has already been tasked with securing rare earth and critical mineral supply chains for the United States. A famous line from Deng Xiaoping goes as follows: "The Middle East has oil. China has rare earths." The Department of Defense notes that when it comes to critical minerals, "Only China has all essential supply chain tiers."[83] Because of their importance in technologies from mobile phones to F-35s, these critical minerals and rare earth elements are as essential to our way of life today as semiconductors. They are also essential to emerging technologies and strategic industries that are now being pioneered. However, decades' worth of globalization have placed these supply chains and stockpiles at risk. Having learned the eye-popping lessons of America's dependency on China for pharmaceuticals and personal protective equipment (PPE) during the COVID-19 pandemic, the 2021 Report of the Defense Critical Supply Chain Task Force from the House Armed Services Committee stated the following:

> Over the past eighteen months of the COVID-19 pandemic, it has become clear that US supply chains have firmly established themselves as an issue of both economic security and national security. Late night calls in search of masks for our nurses, hand sanitizer for our citizens, and microchips for our automakers, laid bare these vulnerabilities in the commercial sector. That searing experience puts new focus on defense supply chains—meaning the international networks that provide the goods and services needed to deliver finished products to the Department of Defense—the defense industrial base, and the ways that our defense supply chains were prepared to respond to supply shocks. The COVID-19 pandemic likewise taught the United States and our allies that adversaries, particularly China, are capable of weaponizing supply chain vulnerabilities to threaten our national security should they choose to. The COVID-19 crisis tested the United States, but our response gave us valuable insights and underscored the imperative to act on them. It is now incumbent on the US Government, in concert with industry and Allied nations, to mitigate critical defense supply chain risks, increase surge capacity, and enhance resilience by increasing the diversity of sources.[84]

The People's Republic of China has already weaponized rare earths exports over territorial disputes with Japan. Let's not forget what China's official government newspapers once said about America at the onset of the Chinese Communist Party's global pandemic:

> Over 90 percent of all pharmaceuticals imported into the US have some connection to China. At this time, if China simply prohibited

the export of these goods to satisfy domestic demand, the US would fall into a long-term coronavirus hell.[85]

It seems wise and reasonable to address other areas of vulnerability, not least of which are the fundamental physical ingredients in much of the technology that constitutes our modern economy and national security infrastructure. America must undertake a journey to secure these resources, first for the sake of the defense industrial base, but also for the sake of the sustainment of our national economy as a whole. The need to secure these supply chains—already an object of enormous study by both the Trump and Biden administrations—must become an initiative of public-private partnership on an enormous scale. The Biden administration's supply chain review listed critical minerals as one of the four main categories in addition to semiconductors, pharmaceuticals, and large capacity batteries. In each case, the need for "reshoring" or "allied-shoring" will be essential. What the necessity of these supply chains also reveals is that certain policy tools can pave the way for a variety of national security and economic security needs in the decade ahead. The Defense Production Act of 1950 (DPA), for example, has been invoked frequently in the context of both pharmaceuticals and critical minerals. The DPA's purpose is as follows: "The security of the United States is dependent on the ability of the domestic industrial base to supply materials and services for the national defense and to prepare for and respond to military conflicts, natural or man-caused disasters, or acts of terrorism within the United States."[86]

The DPA grants presidential authority to mandate the production of any good or service that is deemed necessary to national defense and national security. Like the International Emergency Economic Powers Act (IEEPA), which allows the president to undertake essentially any economic act in the interest of national security—whether that be its invocation in an attempt to force the sale of TikTok to American brands under the Trump administration or the ban on investment in Chinese military-linked corporations under both the Trump and Biden administrations—the DPA grants broad powers to produce what America needs and to turn on the spigot of national industry when it comes to national security needs. The DPA was a bedrock of Operation Warp Speed and has also been invoked by the current White House on a variety of occasions: "We need to leverage the Defense Production Act author-ity in new ways—like investing in advanced pharmaceutical manufacturing technologies."[87] America is finding its footing with a deep war chest worth of legislative and executive power tools, most of which were invented in the economic dimensions of our contests of the past. Critical minerals will be one of our most essential tests because of their importance to our national defense, their neglect during decades' worth of the peacetime globalization of supply chains, and the fact that our primary adversary is the world's most substantial producer and refiner of these materials. The US Geological Survey, under the Department of the Interior, includes the following elements as its "2022 final list of critical minerals":

Aluminum, antimony, arsenic, barite, beryllium, bismuth, cerium, cesium, chromium, cobalt, dysprosium, erbium, europium, fluor-spar, gadolinium, gallium, germanium, graphite, hafnium, holmium, indium, iridium, lanthanum, lithium, lutetium, magnesium, manga-nese, neodymium, nickel, niobium, palladium, platinum, praseodym-ium, rhodium, rubidium, ruthenium, samarium, scandium, tantalum, tellurium, terbium, thulium, tin, titanium, tungsten, vanadium, ytter-bium, yttrium, zinc, and zirconium.[88]

Building and securing a new American and Allied supply chain that guar-antees access to these elements—both in peacetime and potentially in time of conflict—is an urgent exercise. Like initiatives in other key strategic industries, securing our mineral supply chains will benefit from robust public-private partnerships and the unlocking of private American capital to lessen the burden on our public finances. Two approaches, which can be applied to many other critical needs industries, can be employed: first, a three-track approach that includes Manhattan Project, moon-shot, and XPrize incentivization accord-ing to the subsets and sub-missions that will require national effort to achieve supply chain security and access guarantees. Manhattan Project–style initiatives would be secret, strategic, and large-scale, accomplishing important work in areas that need not be revealed to the whole country. Moon-shot initiatives would be public, strategic, and large-scale, enlisting the public imagination in our essential missions but still led by government and industry. XPrize-style initiatives would delegate innovation broadly to qualified competing teams and innovators in search of grassroots breakthroughs that can move a larger mission forward. Public initiatives can be protected by the Huawei template—if and when this technology is stolen or copied by an adversary company or state, the US offensive economic toolkit can be employed to degrade or destroy the perpetrators, either at a company- or industry-wide level. The latter template is likely less essential in the case of critical minerals given that the objective would be to secure our own supply chains, but it may be useful for materials sciences innovations that come as a by-product. Finally, like Operation Warp Speed, which led to the genesis of Allied and Quad-based vaccine supply chains, and manufacturing initiatives once the unique work of American innovation was complete—a critical minerals supply chain must benefit not only America, but the Alliance System as a whole.

From NATO to Allied Asia, as our military systems and operational capabilities continue to align and integrate, we must ensure that the whole Allied defense industrial base is essentially free from bottlenecks and choke points in adversary countries. As with other aspects of this strategic design in each arena, America would remain the cornerstone of Allied military and industrial strength by virtue of its size and for the necessity of leadership and focus in time of crisis, but the Alliance System—with its combined wealth, market power, and innovation capacity—constitutes an economic community that can overwhelm the challenges of limited supply. In the case of physical materials, secure and diversified production bases will be needed, and a vehicle already exists for this among Allies. The National Technology Industrial Base (NTIB) is a means for Allied industrial collaboration that includes stockpiling critical minerals for the defense industrial base. For the purposes of critical minerals, North America (Canada and the United States) as well as Australia are essential players given the rich natural resource bases in each of these countries and the potential to create alternative supply chains if necessary. Other Allies could also be enlisted when it comes to exploration, stockpiling, and other necessities. The US Defense Department's *Strategic and Critical Minerals Review* gives us a sense of what US-Canadian integration looks like, as well as the ability to use the DPA with Allies:

Canada is a member of the National Technology and Industrial Base (NTIB) [along with Australia and the United Kingdom] under 10 U.S.C. 2500. Canadian companies and persons are the only non-U.S. entities and persons who are considered a "domestic source" for the purposes of the DPA (50 U.S.C. 4500 et seq.). Both of these factors reflect the deeply integrated nature of the U.S. and Canadian economies and the very strong security relationship between the United States and Canada. This economic integration leads to Canada being the second-largest import source for those strategic and critical materials for which the United States has net import reliance greater than 50 percent.[89]

One of our most fundamental supply chains—the physical elements that constitute our way of life and military advantages—must be secured. In doing so, we are likely to unlock extraordinary lessons for public-private cooperation, Alliance-based industrial and innovation collaboration, and new mechanisms that can speed up American innovation. This is only one dimension of our industrial requirements—albeit a fundamental one: the elements that we use every day. Our next example is the horizon that may make a transformative difference not only in our contest with China but in the future of humanity.

THE SPACE ECONOMY

Those looking a century into the future are keenly aware of the importance of space. We must ensure that the future of space—one of the primary emerging areas of geopolitical competition—remains in American and Allied hands. Our current-day industrialists have shared their visions of how access to "the last frontier" can transform humanity's potential. From the work of SpaceX and Elon Musk to lower the cost of access to space and ultimately build habitations on Mars to Blue Origin and Jeff Bezos's vision of "millions of people living and working in space for the benefit of Earth," we are entering an era of the ultimate public-private partnership with enormous economic potential and the attendant need for military innovation and protection. Our military and government are aware of the scramble we must make to compete with a

Chinese Communist Party already making progress on the industrial, military, and scientific elements of a long-term grand strategy in space.

Triumph in this frontier, where America has pioneered for decades, may make the difference between success and failure in our long-term contest with China. This is both because of the essential role of space in military power and also because of its capacity to transform the economic potential of human civilization in this century. What is needed for our future should also capture our imaginations as a country. In their masterpiece *Scramble for the Skies,* space analysts Namrata Goswami and Peter Garretson describe the potential for asteroid mining, space industrialization, habitation, and energy, with comparisons to the voyages of Christopher Columbus: "To mine asteroids. To establish Moon bases. To build cities on Mars. To capture the endless green energy of the Sun. To move industry off planet. To look for life on distant icy Moons."[90] The new Space Race taking shape in this decade will set the foundations for the century ahead and it will be essential to victory in our contest with China. China is already an economic superpower here on Earth. While we can counter this as described in the Economic Arena, America will also need to transform its economic potential through the long-term contest for space exploration and economic development.[91] We must take the lead in the "scramble for the stars," because space has the potential to act as a *new geography* in our contest with Russia and China.[92] With asteroids containing *trillions* of dollars' worth of minerals, to the vast energy potential of our solar system, and the habitation potential of asteroid belts and nearby planets, here is a description of the economic potential of space, in the words of Drs. Goswami and Garretson:

> States pay close attention to economic opportunities that do not even amount to a single percent of their GDP. States play hardball over energy resources that are mere years of future domestic supply. But within space lies not a percent, not 10 percent, not 100 percent of a nation's GDP, but many, many times the value of the entire global GDP in resources. Within space is not a small energy source, but sufficient supply of constant solar energy to light a fully developed world six to seven times over. . . . Accessing multitrillion-dollar asteroids or

multitrillion-dollar power markets could accelerate China's rise, prolong U.S. hegemony, or enable a late-blooming India to overtake China.[93]

With a focus on the moon and Mars, and with further advances in essential space technologies, the decade ahead will mark the beginning of a centuries-long quest to develop a space economy that could eventually extend throughout our solar system. This new Space Race will take shape in a period of intensive geopolitical competition unlike any we have seen since the Cold War era. This is one of the truly transformational contests within our broader geopolitical competition with China. If America can prevail, it would shift the overall competition in our favor, enabling America and the Alliance System to add trillions in GDP and solidify the foundations of a second Great Divergence. The contest for the Next Frontier gives the democracies a greater chance in the contest with China and also the hope of victory through peaceful competition.

Buzz Aldrin, one of the first American astronauts to land on the moon during the Cold War Apollo program, explains the potential of a first phase of exploration and industry that we are likely to reach within the next twenty years. Utilizing the cis-lunar space—the area in between the earth and the moon that Chinese Communist Party strategists have already proclaimed they intend to dominate—would allow us to take a step toward permanent habitation on Mars, and toward the genuine beginnings of space-based industry. As Mr. Aldrin says, "By mining fuel from the moon [from lunar ice], we avoid having to launch propellant from Earth into space, and we gain the advantage of being able to refuel in space, thus lowering the cost of space travel altogether. Cis-lunar space is also invaluable for testing exploration modules and other new applications ultimately needed for Mars exploration. From cis-lunar space, we would be able to construct an international lunar base using remotely controlled robots. Once perfected, the same methods could be used to remotely construct, perhaps from Phobos, a moon of Mars, the first base on the red planet." The world-renowned astronaut goes on to explain the importance and purpose of new technologies, all of which are hallmarks of the next industrial revolution, for building the next generation of spacefaring possibilities: "A settlement on Mars can be safe, affordable, and self-sufficient. Achieving self-sufficiency will require a technological toolkit of frontier technologies that includes robotics, machine intelligence, nanotechnology, synthetic biology, and 3D printing. . . . The red planet may well become the proving ground for many new technologies that not only advance Earth's own independence but promote Mars to become the supply source for fuels, oxidizers, life support, spare parts, replacement vehicles, habitats, and other products for enhancing spacefaring beyond low-Earth orbit and beyond Mars itself."[94]

Aldrin's road map to the moon and Mars would allow us to leave Earth's "gravity well"—an essential step in expanding the possibilities of humanity's spacefaring and space-industrial potential.[95] Once we have the ability to manufacture on the moon, likely through 3D printing, the high cost of bringing heavy equipment out of Earth's orbit will have been addressed and we will unlock a new chapter in what humanity can do in space.[96] But this, like other contests, is one America and our Allies must win. Doing so will require full-scale collaboration between our national government, national security community, and our burgeoning space private sector.

Just as we must be unconstrained in the Diplomatic Arena, working to bring unity of purpose to our Alliance System, and to win nations large and small over to our cause, we must utilize the Space Arena to discover the transformative economic and military potential that goes far beyond our decisive decade. America and our Allies cannot win through a focus on Earth alone, nor can we win without inventing and discovering the new domains and arenas that will shape our long-term contest. And so, just as our role on Earth must always be global—a cornerstone of prosperity and power—our role in space and among the stars must also seek unlimited potential. To do this both on Earth and in space, we must always lead, and never work alone.

If we fail to win in the Next Frontier, we would cede not only the world we know today, but the world of tomorrow to our adversaries. China and Russia understand the importance of space. Unlike our original Cold War adversary in the first Space Race, the Chinese Communist Party looks at space as an economic frontier, a path to a future that would preserve the "infinite" ascendency of the People's Republic of China and complete "the great rejuvenation of the Chinese nation." Chinese space strategists have already compared the moon and Mars to islands that China has claimed or militarized in the East and South China Seas. Should China, not America, achieve the rewards of space exploration and economic development, this would mean the irreversible destruction of the American era.

Take the following analogy to heart.

Among the dangerous strategic ideas that I have encountered is the idea that the United States could succeed through retreat to "Fortress America," allowing China and Russia to compete with other powers in Eurasia and Africa while the United States, supported by abundant agricultural and energy production, could take care of itself and not engage. The temptation of isolationism, which has stalked the American mind throughout our history, was largely put to rest by the Second World War and by the worldbuilding period that followed when a great generation established enduring architecture for global security and prosperity. But there is another lesson that we must take from the idea of Fortress America. Much American strategic thinking already has the character of the "offshore balancer" role that Great Britain played in Europe. America will not allow a hegemon to rise in Europe or Asia, and we have conducted strategy accordingly for several generations. Britain, similarly, could not allow a single power to dominate continental Europe, and so it played a balancing role among the European powers. But when that hegemon did rise, when Hitler's Germany conquered the whole of Europe, it was soon Britain's skies and cities that darkened with fascist offensive operations from the conquered continent. Churchill said this:

> We shall go on to the end. We shall fight in France, we shall fight on the seas and oceans, we shall fight with growing confidence and growing strength in the air, we shall defend our Island, whatever the cost may be, we shall fight on the beaches, we shall fight on the landing grounds, we shall fight in the fields and in the streets, we shall fight in the hills; we shall never surrender. *And even if, which I do not for a moment believe, this Island or a large part of it were subjugated and starving, then our Empire beyond the seas, armed and guarded by the British Fleet, would carry on the struggle, until, in God's good time, the New World, with all its power and might, steps forth to the rescue and the liberation of the old.*[97]

Churchill's England, offshore balancer to a Europe that was ultimately over-run, could be an appealing example to an America that has tired of its global commitments and responsibilities. However, the United States—and herein lies the entire conundrum that we face in our contest with China—has been the place in modern history that has rescued other nations. In time of peril, who could rescue America? There will be no rescue unless our Alliance System holds strong and unless we are able to defend ourselves. Fortress America is no winning strategy. We must not only work together with the democracies across the geography of Earth, but we must unlock the new geographies of space, which will themselves have transformative effects. Our spirit of exploration and our cooperative relationship with many nations of the world are the keys to a secure and prosperous future. Just as Britain in its "darkest hour" could withstand siege and appeal to a world beyond Europe, America and our Allies must begin the hard work of building our security not only here on Earth but also across the Next Frontier. This is where *the geopolitics of this decade and the geopolitics of this century converge*. Britain may have been a balancer in Europe, but access to the world's oceans and to like-minded states that would ultimately come to its side was Britain's salvation in the Second World War. In the century ahead, space will become to us like our seas and oceans. Victory in the contest for space will become the essential work of this generation and the ones that come after it.[98]

PART FOUR

THE ARENA OF IDEAS

America is an idea. . . . That's how we see you around the world, as one of the greatest ideas in human history.

—Bono

Be the America that Hong Kong thinks you are.

—Twitter

t is not enough for America to have an economic grand strategy. It is not enough for us to have a global diplomatic strategy. And it is not enough for us to return to deterrence by way of peace through strength. While each of these is fundamentally doable, they cannot be done unless we attend to one of our most important tasks of all. We will never succeed within these strategic arenas as a divided nation. Unifying our nation around shared principles is perhaps our greatest challenge. Once, in China, I was told that dynasties fall when there is a threat from outside and a threat from inside—when these two threats come at once. My time in China taught me the enormous scale of what America will face in international affairs. My time in America has shown me that, despite our enormous potential, we live today as a wounded nation. Every scrap of wisdom we've inherited from the Founding Fathers to the American Civil War reminds us of one thing, and that is this: Divided We Fall. United We Stand.

We can have confidence in our ability to design and execute a global grand strategy. We have done this in the past, from the wartime global strategy of the Second World War to the discipline, the genius, and the simplicity of containment that won the Cold War. We must recognize that our ability to focus on the world's essential problems is linked to our ability to live together in peace and dignity. So it will be in today's great contest, which will test every feature of American strength, every aspect of American creativity and brilliance, and every ounce of American will and determination. We understand that in times of external peril, such as the two world wars in the twentieth century, we came together and acted with enormity on the world stage, delivering multiple continents from unmitigated acts of aggression and horror. In the Cold War, we had sufficient national consensus that enabled us to design and execute a multi-decade, multi-generational grand strategy, passing it on and evolving it across the aisle and throughout the country, working together in the Truman-Eisenhower-Kennedy continuum and ultimately through Reagan-Bush, who peacefully concluded the Cold War era. No one can say that the twentieth century was a time of perfect union inside America—far from it—but today's divisions among us trouble everyone whom I meet or know, including those who lived through prior periods that tested global peace.

We are all aware of these divisions.

Any American grand strategy requires us to come together and heal our differences as best we can, or if we cannot heal them, to find civility with one another and work from common ground. Our adversaries understand the power of division, that they can rend apart any chance of success against them in geopolitical confrontation. Our opponents exploit this feature of twenty-first-century American life in ways that we will soon address. How, in this state of division and strife, can we proceed to work against a threat that we have only begun to comprehend? We must appreciate that not only our success but also our survival depends on our ability to coexist with one another and to work together on a contest that matters to the destiny of us all.

While the Arena of Ideas is itself a form of warfare—information warfare is how it's known—the Arena of Ideas is also the realm of the mind and spirit where our concept of who we are is formed and known. It is different from the Economic Arena, which creates the potential for power. It is different from the

Diplomatic Arena, which is how we deal globally with other nation-states. It is different from the Military Arena, which, if all else fails, can stop dangerous actors from executing unchecked plans. The Arena of Ideas contains the reasons why we are what we are and the reasons why we must do what we must. It also creates the spirit that enables us to continue through the hardest trials. For America, perhaps more than any other nation, it is also an arena in which we have tremendous strength. What is unique about this country is not its wealth, its military power, or its global diplomatic reach. History has other examples of all those things. What is unique is that this place is founded on the most powerful ideals in human history. Every great American leader has understood the importance of this: that our ideals, the American Idea, the American Experiment, must survive and must continue. That is the inheritance of our generation and of every generation of Americans. It is our job to ensure not only that this place continues but that it continues to have great power in this world.

America's example resounds across the globe, often for good and sometimes for ill. How we treat each other—and our own ability to understand what we can represent to the world—I believe, is an essential foundation for any contest on which our future depends. Additionally, it is the power and goodness of our values that makes American leadership worth having in the world. Our Founders called the American Revolution "the Cause."[1] Our Cause has become the cause of many other nations: liberty, human rights, the rule of law, and democracy or self-government. We must remind ourselves what this means and why it is worth applying ourselves as a nation to its success and its survival. Our values are universal, and our values are widely adopted. It is not only America, but the Free World that is part of who we are, as we are part of it. It is not only the Free World, but the countless nations, peoples, and individuals that aspire to ever greater freedom, who also share the spirit of the purpose of this nation. That is why, for America, it is a boundless world—not just in simple terms of commerce, defense, and interest but because of our promise to humanity. In this regard, ours is "the indispensable nation."

What we have ahead of us, *should we prevail in this contest*, is an extraordinary horizon. America must succeed not just for the sake of stopping the malicious deeds and dangerous intentions of China and Russia. There will be many vital partners, but America, the place made of every nation, must lead this effort and must be the cornerstone. We must also choose to carry the American Experiment forward for the sake of our own bright future and that of many others. America sits today at the head of the most diverse and fascinating group of Allies ever assembled, and still the most globally interconnected stage the world has yet seen. We are poised to lead transformative advancements in technology, industry, and prosperity, and to begin to build a world not only made of the earth we know but the beginning of possibilities in space. The tools and pathways of human progress will unfold before us. The question that America must resolve is whether they are in the hands of authoritarian and totalitarian states or in the hands of our democracies. Why must we do it? Why must we do the work to prevail in these arenas? In all of history's most decisive contests, the question of what regime, what system, what place holds these keys to the next advancements and transformations for humanity is the most important question. In the words of Vladimir Putin to students in Russia, "Whoever becomes the leader in AI will rule the world."[2] In the words of China's military strategists, "outer space and cyber space have become the new commanding heights in strategic competition among all parties."[3] Do we wish for the Kremlin or Beijing to prevail in the tools and arenas that will shape this century? What these places are is on display for all the world to see. From the killing fields of Ukraine to the brutalities that ended liberty in Hong Kong, to the technology-fueled genocide taking shape in Xinjiang, the difference between these systems is something that we must once again understand.

Let us take the long view for a moment, for it is the view that can teach us the most. In 1950, Paul Nitze authored one of America's most significant strategic programs, NSC-68. Reflecting on the decades that preceded America's new approach to the Cold War world, he wrote the following assessment of history and power:

Within the past thirty-five years the world has experienced two global wars of tremendous violence. *It has witnessed two revolutions—the Russian and the Chinese—of extreme scope and intensity.* It has also seen the collapse of five empires—the Ottoman, the Austro-Hungarian, German, Italian, and Japanese—and the drastic decline of two major imperial systems, the British and the French. During the span of one generation, the international distribution of power has been fundamentally altered.[4]

The challenge we face today—and perhaps the greatest argument for those who contend that we are now entering a second Cold War—is not the result of global wars, nor of the collapse or decline of empires or imperial systems. It is the fact that these two states, China and Russia, with roots in revolutions and systems that are antithetical to our own, continue to make their way through the twenty-first century, seeking ever greater power. These actors who defined the first Cold War, are strengthened by their transformation from one form of totalitarianism to another. America must be prepared to continue the work of preventing these states from tearing down the horizons of human freedom and the promise of the twenty-first century.

A British diplomat once spoke to me of the Arab Spring, the revolutions that shook the Middle East in the 2010s, calling it "the greatest enlargement of human freedom" since the fall of the Berlin Wall. While the diplomat was not wholly right about the events in question, the phrase he used was one I will always remember. He was right about what happened at the end of the Cold War: the borders of free and rights-based societies had expanded. Many expected this to continue until the whole world rang with the advance of democracy and freedom. If nations as diverse as Britain, Japan, Korea, France, the Philippines, and Israel could be both democracies and American Allies, then why not the world? If places as varied as Brazil, Indonesia, and Bulgaria can thrive and grow as democracies, then why not all? A moment of triumph after a hard Cold War gave birth to a feeling of unending possibilities. Yet, this exuberance proved wrong. The bountiful American vision was shared at the time by people with many different political points of view. But it failed to understand the return and revenge of China and Russia, and what their revolutions and their visions of the future meant for them. These two states, each with historical roots in an age of empires, suppression, and expansion, were ultimately determined not to succumb, as they saw it, to the dangers of democracy or of American and Allied influence. Our contest and confrontation with these two powers defines the road ahead. What we must remember is that these two states—because of their authoritarian form and also their individual concepts of national destiny—fear not only American power but also the American and democratic ideals. Understanding their fear of our values and ideals is fundamental to our success.

China and Russia rely on the suppression of information, political indoctrination, brutal forms of internal control, and the justification of external aggression for the sake of deeper ideological pathologies. They do these things not only for the sake of national interests but also for the preservation of their dictatorial systems and the pursuit of their unique ideas of national destiny. The military and, essentially, imperial ambitions of both Russia and China are intimately tied to ideas that exist at the core of these two dictatorships. They have weaponized their ideas in ways that have a subtle but profound effect across the world. Let's examine several of them and also what, in the eyes of their leaders, they seek to fight against—which is what we represent, not only because of our economic, military, and diplomatic power, but because of the nature of our democratic, rights-based system.

The Chinese Communist Party's infamous Document Nine, "Communiqué on the Current State of the Ideological Sphere," explains: "Cohesion among our nation's people has become stronger and our confidence in our path, our theory, and our system has become more resolute. Mainstream ideology is becoming healthier and more vigorous. . . . The ideological foundation of our united struggle is unceasingly solidifying." The document notes "a complicated, intense struggle" in the ideological domain. The following "false trends, positions, and activities" are the key ideas to be fought against:

1. Promoting Western Constitutional Democracy: An attempt to undermine the current leadership and the socialism with Chinese characteristics system of governance.
2. Promoting "universal values" in an attempt to weaken the theoretical foundations of the Party's leadership.
3. Promoting civil society in an attempt to dismantle the ruling party's social foundation.
4. Promoting Neoliberalism, attempting to change China's Basic Economic System.

5. Promoting the West's idea of journalism, challenging China's principle that the media and publishing system should be subject to Party discipline.
6. Promoting historical nihilism, trying to undermine the history of the CCP and of New China.
7. Questioning Reform and Opening and the socialist nature of socialism with Chinese characteristics.[5]

For the Chinese Communist Party, the ideological sphere has always been a battle arena, at home, and increasingly abroad. As China's totalitarian vision, expressed in the twenty-first century as "social management,"[6] expands in sophistication, increases in pace and urgency alongside Beijing's confrontation with the world, and grows in its reach to many of the world's contested places, we cannot underestimate the Communist Party's experience in this arena. America and our Allies must return to the game of ideological competition.

Russian information operations are even more notorious and widely known to the American and international public: whether it is attempts to sow discord within our own society, or in the most potent traditions of the USSR, to destroy the meaning of truth both inside and outside of Russia, we live in an information battlespace in which this state is an experienced and innovative practitioner. As Russian novelist and émigré to America Elena Gorokhova wrote of the Soviet Union: "The rules are simple: they lie to us, we know they're lying, they know we know they're lying, but they keep lying to us, and we keep pretending to believe them."[7] But the lies that flourish in these dictatorships have deadly consequences for the world. Here is a recent statement from a Russian prisoner of war in Ukraine about the alternate universe that Russia has become under Vladimir Putin:

They are constantly brainwashed. They get this unilateral information that Ukraine is seized by fascists. Maybe I really deserved to learn this lesson, oh Lord, so I could finally see and try to tell those who are in Russia. Maybe they do not realize what is going on here.[8]

It is clear that the pathologies of an authoritarian nation—what takes place inside—become the foundations for the most consequential acts of aggression abroad. The "brainwashing" this captured Russian soldier speaks of in a society dominated by state television and media laid the foundations for the invasion of Ukraine and for crimes against humanity. When Chinese official media recycles Kremlin talking points on the invasion of Ukraine—ranging from Russian massacres being "staged" to NATO expansion as a *casus belli*—we see that our enemies work together intently in the domain of information and ideas. The Chinese Communist Party is more subtle and, in many ways, a more effective practitioner of information warfare than its counterparts in the Kremlin. Focused on elite capture, corporate coercion, and painting an image of China's unstoppable rise, Beijing set the stage for resounding economic and commercial success despite genocide, military build-up, and crimes against humanity. Anti-American rhetoric is a mainstay of Chinese diplomacy under Xi Jinping, and Putin's aggression in Ukraine has become a catalyst for Russia-China information warfare alignment. Our adversaries deny genocide and justify crimes against humanity, including through American social media channels like Twitter. America has gone from a position as victor against the tyrannies of the past hundred years to a position of disadvantage in the twenty-first century, despite the power of the American Idea. Let us remind ourselves of what America is and what it means. Let us mobilize the power of our values and our ideals.

THE AMERICAN IDEA
AND THE AMERICAN DREAM

ontemplating the range of what must be done to defend against and
to dismantle China's vision of victory, the need for economic containment, the task of uniting the world's democracies and emerging
nations in a necessary cause, and the need to prepare, prepare, prepare, as
Churchill said, against our adversary's growing military strength, it is natural
to ask why should we do this work? Why *must* we do this work? Why should
America take on this job, these responsibilities? What is it about our way of
life, our country, our world, that is worth such effort? How can we have the
confidence to carry out decades' worth of effort and action to secure a world
that is safe not only for our values and our prosperity, but also for the many
nations and peoples that share our way, our values, and our ideals?

We must remember where we came from. We must remember who we are.

This book contends that the world will turn, the future will hinge, the fate
of us all will rest upon whether or not America will act according to its true
and rightful place within the world. We must remind ourselves of the power
and importance of the American Idea, of our commitment to the defense
of human freedom and to our values around the world. The American Idea
is simple. America is a nation built upon the *values* of liberty and justice.
We must regard these values with thoughtful minds. We must find clarity in

these words. Here is an expression of these values from the Declaration of Independence:

> We hold these Truths to be self-evident, that all Men are created equal, that they are endowed by their Creator with certain unalienable Rights, that among these are Life, Liberty and the Pursuit of Happiness—That to secure these Rights, Governments are instituted among Men, deriving their just Powers from the Consent of the Governed.

The American Revolution was an unprecedented compact between the citizen and the state: that we, the people of this country, hold as individuals natural rights, in contrast to a historical world of tyranny, oppression, emperors, and kings. The founding purpose of our nation was to secure and guarantee those rights. One may say that we know this, it's taught in school, why review it here? However, our true power is in our fundamentals, and we will soon see the global scope of the American Idea. Consider another expression, fashioned two hundred years ago, our Bill of Rights, the rights of every American. While our realities may fall short, our ideas and beliefs are clear at their foundations:

> Amendment I: Congress shall make no law respecting an establishment of religion, or prohibiting the free exercise thereof; or abridging the freedom of speech, or of the press; or the right of the people peaceably to assemble, and to petition the Government for a redress of grievances.
>
> Amendment II: A well regulated Militia, being necessary to the security of a free State, the right of the people to keep and bear Arms, shall not be infringed.
>
> Amendment III: No Soldier shall, in time of peace be quartered in any house, without the consent of the Owner, nor in time of war, but in a manner to be prescribed by law.
>
> Amendment IV: The right of the people to be secure in their persons, houses, papers, and effects, against unreasonable searches and seizures, shall not be violated, and no Warrants shall issue, but upon probable cause, supported by Oath or affirmation, and particularly

describing the place to be searched, and the persons or things to be seized.

Amendment V: No person shall be held to answer for a capital, or otherwise infamous crime, unless on a presentment or indictment of a Grand Jury, except in cases arising in the land or naval forces, or in the Militia, when in actual service in time of War or public danger; nor shall any person be subject for the same offence to be twice put in jeopardy of life or limb; nor shall be compelled in any criminal case to be a witness against himself, nor be deprived of life, liberty, or property, without due process of law; nor shall private property be taken for public use, without just compensation.

Amendment VI: In all criminal prosecutions, the accused shall enjoy the right to a speedy and public trial, by an impartial jury of the State and district wherein the crime shall have been committed, which district shall have been previously ascertained by law, and to be informed of the nature and cause of the accusation; to be confronted with the witnesses against him; to have compulsory process for obtaining witnesses in his favor, and to have the Assistance of Counsel for his defense.

Amendment VII: In Suits at common law, where the value in controversy shall exceed twenty dollars, the right of trial by jury shall be preserved, and no fact tried by a jury, shall be otherwise re-examined in any Court of the United States, than according to the rules of the common law.

Amendment VIII: Excessive bail shall not be required, nor excessive fines imposed, nor cruel and unusual punishments inflicted.

Amendment IX: The enumeration in the Constitution, of certain rights, shall not be construed to deny or disparage others retained by the people.

Amendment X: The powers not delegated to the United States by the Constitution, nor prohibited by it to the States, are reserved to the States respectively, or to the people.

Imperfect as we are, as difficult as our history has been, and as hard as our challenges remain, our ideas, our rights, our liberties are designed around the sanctity of the human being. Our nation is nothing more and nothing less than an experiment in the dignity of humankind and the possibilities created by human freedom. Our American Experiment and our design suppose that the individual has such value and such potential that the individual citizen can be trusted with the governance of the entire nation. America is built not only from great faith in humanity's potential, but also with a disciplined governing structure that can function and endure.

Every great American leader has understood the power of these ideas: liberty, equality, and justice. Every great American leader has understood that the American Idea and the American Experiment must survive. Here is how Abraham Lincoln described the purpose of this nation, and the need for its survival:

> Four score and seven years ago our fathers brought forth on this continent, a new nation, conceived in Liberty, and dedicated to the proposition that all men are created equal.[9]

In his time of Civil War, Lincoln spoke that "We here highly resolve that these dead shall not have died in vain—that this nation, under God, shall have a new birth of freedom—and that government of the people, by the people, for the people, shall not perish from the earth."

These ideas, of liberty, equality, and justice, and the structure of our democracy—government of the people, by the people, and for the people—have been so fragile at times that our leaders fought for their existence and for their survival. These ideas have spread and prospered across the world, shared by other republics and democracies. China's founding leaders once declared that theirs was a continuous revolution—the need for constant struggle and purges was at the core of the Communist Party's authoritarian dream. In a far different way, ours is a continuous revolution, too. America fights to live up to its original promise. The story of our journey as a nation—the founding of this nation, the eventual progress on emancipation, women's suffrage, civil rights—is the process of reaching higher and farther toward the American Idea that has been with us from the start. That process is *our* ongoing revolution—that we continue to fight for what rights and liberties mean both in spirit and in practice.

Those who worked to establish the United States of America understood what these ideas mean. Those who fought for its survival understood what these ideas mean. Those who took us farther on this path understood what these ideas mean. Consider Martin Luther King Jr. who wrote and spoke repeatedly of the American Dream, who hailed "the architects of our republic" and "the magnificent words of the Constitution and the Declaration of Independence" and "the promissory note" of "the unalienable rights of life, liberty and the pursuit of happiness." The Reverend Dr. King said:

> So even though we face the difficulties of today and tomorrow, I still have a dream. It is a dream deeply rooted in the American dream. I have a dream that one day this nation will rise up and live out the true meaning of its creed: We hold these truths to be self-evident, that all men are created equal.[10]

America's greatest leaders *worked and gave their lives to raise us up to this great standard*, not to bring us down to further strife and pain. Those who fought hardest for equality worked *from* the American Idea and *toward* the American Dream. Consider Langston Hughes:

> Let America be the dream the dreamers dreamed—
> Let it be that great strong land of love
> Where never kings connive nor tyrants scheme
> That any man be crushed by one above.[11]

Our Constitution and Bill of Rights are expressions of the fundamental differences between our society and those of our historic adversaries, from Nazi Germany and the Soviet Union to twenty-first-century China and Russia. They are also the result of thousands of years of historical effort along the path of human freedom. From Ancient Greece, the Magna Carta, the European Enlightenment, and above all, the American Revolution and our own history of advancing and defending human freedom, both within our country and around the world. To be sure, there remains enormous work to be done but this reason is as good as any reason that the American Experiment must be defended and preserved. It is not only from comparison of our own potential perfect form that we should draw our most important lessons—as Langston Hughes wrote, "I say it plain, America never was America to me, and yet I swear this oath—America will be!" We are a country that carries within us the next horizons of humankind, a country of great impatience to do the right thing, find the right path, and to realize what we can be. It is this place where an individual from any place can come and find their potential. This is the essence of the American Dream. It is the promise of America that exists not only here, but for the world. Our ideas are our greatest standard.

Another of our greatest powers is that anyone, from anywhere, can come and be American. I have personally encountered the power of this on continents across the world. Our universal values, our history of immigration, the potency of the American Dream—that one may come to our shores, to this continent, and build for themselves a life of greater opportunity, and to join in the work of this great nation. This, too, is an indelible piece of who we are: a land of refuge and also of prosperity and opportunity for the people of every place and every nation. As Emma Lazarus wrote of Lady Liberty in Manhattan:

> Not like the brazen giant of Greek fame,
> With conquering limbs astride from land to land
> Here at our sea-washed, sunset gates shall stand
> A mighty woman with a torch, whose flame
> Is the imprisoned lightning, and her name
> Mother of Exiles. From her beacon-hand
> Glows world-wide welcome; her mild eyes command
> The air-bridged harbor that twin cities frame.
> "Keep, ancient lands, your storied pomp!" cries she
> With silent lips. "Give me your tired, your poor,
> Your huddled masses yearning to breathe free,
> The wretched refuse of your teeming shore.
> Send these, the homeless, tempest-tost to me,
> I lift my lamp beside the golden door!"

We have not lived up to all of this. We have not reached the heights imagined by Jefferson, Lazarus, and King. But we do know what the goals sound like, what they look like, and what they mean. The unique privilege of Americans today is that we are one more generation that can advance the cause and defend the spirit and existence of this nation. That heritage, that possibility, is something we live with every day. Every generation of Americans has reflected on the unique purpose of this nation. While we can lose sight of who we are, in our words and history, it is clear: *we do know our ideals* and who we want and need to be.

The American Experiment, the American Idea is a process of becoming. It is one that was clearly conceived at the beginning and has been advanced and defended for nearly 250 years. The American Idea builds upon a heritage of philosophical and political aspiration that has existed for hundreds and even thousands of years. Our efforts as a nation are part of the history of an idea essential to humanity: the existence of human freedom and the progress of human freedom. Our history is an essential chapter in the story of democracy. Ours is a Revolution because it established among the community of nations the basic principles of rights and freedom and wrote them into governance and law. These principles are the heritage of Ancient Greece, the Enlightenment, the Magna Carta and other representations and milestones on the path of human freedom that were well understood by America's Founders. They inspired other documents such as the Declaration of the Rights of Man and the Universal Declaration of Human Rights. It was a revolution that brought these principles into the modern world and out of an age of empires. It is an experiment because it has been tested time and time again, whether or not a nation so founded will survive.

THE FREE WORLD
AND ITS DEFENSE

The American Idea extends worldwide—not only because ours are universal, humanitarian values, but also because of a global system, an architecture, that derives from these same values of democracy, rights, and freedom, an architecture established by Americans and by other democracies. This system of interlocking Allied democracies that spans the world from the Atlantic to the Pacific was once known as the Free World. It exists because it has fought together, worked together, and even governed together, led and backed by the economic and military power of the United States of America. Once again, the Free World must be the bedrock of our diplomatic, economic, and military power, and the founding architecture of the international system that guarantees our security and prosperity and sustains our aspirations and our values. Constitutional democracies and republics number in the dozens around the world, in varying degrees of progress and imperfection. What we have in common are the values of liberty, human rights, self-government, the rule of law, the consent of the governed, and of free economies, free inquiry, and free enterprise. We must again understand here at home—United We Stand, Divided We Fall. *This applies as well to the world's democracies and free nations.* America's Founders signed our "Unanimous Declaration" as follows: "We mutually pledge to each other our Lives, our Fortunes, and our sacred Honor." So it must be with our Alliance System.

As Benjamin Franklin stated in his famous image of a snake cut into thirteen pieces, "Join, or Die." We have grown used to thinking of a democracy as a divided place. A place that has a hard time getting things done. And as Churchill once said of allies, the only thing worse than fighting with them is fighting without them. Like our values and ideals, the structure of the global system of democracies, built upon shared values and aspirations, provides the best defense for each of us, and the best defense for all. This is something that great American leaders also understood.

As someone who has traveled widely in the world, I can attest to the fact that our global architecture is also an expression of the American Idea and the American Dream—liberty for ourselves, and also for the broad community of nations that shares our ideals and our values, what has historically been called the Free World. This Free World is again under threat because of China and Russia. Should its bulwarks be broken, we shall be forced to learn again the terrible lessons that gave rise to our global defenses and to the global community of Allies and Democracies—that the events outside America invariably come to strike us here at home. We are now a global superpower. We must remain a global superpower. The American Idea and the American Dream sought to turn historical realities on their head and replace them with the values of individual liberty and possibility as expressed in the Declaration of Independence, the Constitution, and the Bill of Rights. The Free World is an expression of the progress of these values and ideas not only here at home, but also in many other nations.

John F. Kennedy prepared these words but never spoke them in Dallas:

> We in this country, in this generation, are—by destiny rather than choice—the watchmen on the walls of world freedom. We ask, therefore, that we may be worthy of our power and responsibility, that we may exercise our strength with wisdom and restraint, and that we may achieve in our time and for all time the ancient vision of "peace on earth, good will toward men." That must always be our goal, and the righteousness of our cause must always underlie our strength. For as was written long ago: "except the Lord keep the city, the watchmen waketh but in vain."[12]

Like our idea at home, our idea abroad is also clear: we are the watchers on the walls of freedom, the guarantors of progress for all mankind when it falls into jeopardy or is threatened by horrific forces. Just as there are walls that keep certain dangers out, when tyranny takes over in parts of the world that may seem far away, that tyranny often builds its walls to keep people in. As Ronald Reagan stated at the Brandenburg Gate in Berlin: "As long as this gate is closed, as long as this scar of a wall is permitted to stand, it is not the German question alone that remains open, but the question of freedom for all mankind."[13]

Our generation cannot fail in our turn to persist at the work at hand: to strive to fulfill the purpose of this Idea and defend its safety and ensure its prosperity in the world. The great journey that we are on is a journey that is worth making. The country that we have is a country worth defending. The duty that we have to the Free and Democratic World—those who, like our own Founders said, will either hang together or will hang separately—is a duty of enormous honor and purpose. It is a duty we are fortunate to have, and one that reflects our true and best ideals. Make no mistake: our adversaries fear our ideals. Tyranny fears liberty and chooses to fight it, just as liberty must defend against tyranny in order to continue in this world. Our mission and our duty are not to impose our ideals by force, but to defend the walls and ramparts of the world's free nations. Our efforts must prevent these ideals from being rolled back and our progress dashed from Europe to Asia across the earth.

America represents the possibility of justice, and the possibility of liberty. These are possibilities for which our opponents do not strive, but which they crush out. As Dr. King spoke of the promise of America: "If I lived in China or even Russia, or any totalitarian country, maybe I could understand some of these illegal injunctions. Maybe I could understand the denial of certain basic First Amendment privileges, because they hadn't committed themselves to that over there."[14] America contains this promise. America is this promise. Whatever our divisions, we know who we are. We know what we are. We know that we must build, defend, and advance this country's promise and its idea. This is why we cannot fail in the trials that rise and cause danger to us and to the world.

Dangerous forces have begun to climb and break apart the Walls of Freedom. In Ukraine, Russian forces shell apartment blocks, massacre civilians, and execute prisoners for the sake of imperial ambitions. In Taiwan, China's forces threaten to "prepare for war," practice blockades, and fire missiles over these free people. The Free World is made not only of the world's democracies—but also of those who are threatened or persecuted by our adversaries both inside and outside their borders. Tens of thousands of Russian emigres have filled the cities of free Europe, fleeing Putin's destruction of all rights and freedoms. Uyghurs, Tibetans, Hong Kongers, and mainland Chinese have fled to the world's free states and made their homes and refuge here. Those who live with tyranny understand it best. Alexander Solzhenitsyn illuminated the horrors of the Soviet gulags for all the world, as no one in the world's free nations could possibly do. Artists like Ai Weiwei, activists like Nobel laureate Liu Xiaobo and the blind lawyer Chen Guangcheng, as well as countless people, unknown to the outside world, who exist under the repression of Moscow and Beijing, have fought for the values that we share. They, too, are citizens and members of the Free World.

We must never forget when the Goddess of Democracy was carried through the streets of Tiananmen Square—the Statue of Liberty, made by Chinese students in 1989, before Chairman Deng Xiaoping sent in the Communist Party's tanks. We must never forget the Hong Kong youth of our present day who waved American flags in crowds before the crushing of this city. We must never forget the Uyghurs in China's concentration camps, where Communist Party officials have said, "You can't uproot all the weeds hidden among the crops in the field one by one. You need to spray chemicals to kill them all. Reeducating these people is like spraying chemicals on the crops. That is why it is a general reeducation, not limited to a few people."[15] We must never forget the Tibetans who have lost their place in this world to the Chinese Communist Party's decades-long programs of brutality and control. The Dalai Lama has said of us, it is America, not China, where the Dharma continues to be taught.

In our darkest moments, we can find what is needed if we remind ourselves of our idea and of our history as a defender of the Free and Democratic World. As Ukraine burns and Taiwan lives under the shadow of ever-growing danger, we must arm ourselves and also those who live according to the democratic way. Here is what Franklin Delano Roosevelt said as war raged across Europe and Asia:

Let us say to the democracies: "We Americans are vitally concerned in your defense of freedom. We are putting forth our energies, our resources and our organizing powers to give you the strength to regain and maintain a free world. We shall send you, in ever-increasing numbers, ships, planes, tanks, guns. This is our purpose and our pledge."[16]

The Cause of Freedom is not new. It is as old as history itself. We and our Allies are its force today. We and those who fight off this world's aggressors. The world has watched the Ukrainian Resistance—which has been by all accounts a marvelous thing. I think of the words of Winston Churchill, who said, of another country resisting the Russian Army many decades ago, "Finland—superb, nay, sublime—in the jaws of peril—Finland shows what free men can do. The service rendered by Finland to mankind is magnificent."

Now, Ukraine sacrifices for all of us. For all of us the world over who know the difference between the forces of authoritarian malice, and those of democracy, rights, and freedom. Ukraine is not alone. In Hong Kong, in Xinjiang, in other theaters and trampled places in what is already a global confrontation against breakers of human beings in both Moscow and Beijing, we can see what kind of forces are rising.

The Ukrainians fight not only for their own homes but also for the cause of freedom and sovereignty. We will see the price of that fight as it unfolds. This is a moment and a resistance that portends other things to come. Ukraine fights for all of us.

As has been said in history, "Ich Bin Ein Berliner," "Russian warship, go f— yourself," and, "Ukraine, superb, nay, sublime in the jaws of peril, Ukraine shows what free men can do. The service rendered by Ukraine to mankind is magnificent."

In Taiwan, where Beijing pledges conquest and "reeducation" in the image of its concentration camps in Xinjiang, where China's leaders plan to bring war to the Pacific, we must also prepare, prepare, prepare. We were the Arsenal of Democracy. We have been the Watchers on the Walls of Freedom. America is not America unless it stands with those who stand for freedom and with those who suffer under these regimes. That is the meaning of "our sea-washed, sunset gates" and our "lamp beside the golden door." That is the meaning of America. The pathways of freedom are long and hard. The arc of history, with work, may bend toward justice. We must remember who we are.

OUR ADVERSARIES
AND THEIR METHODS

What does it mean to defend democracy? What does it mean to destroy it? Remember the Chinese students in Tiananmen Square who carried their handmade Statue of Liberty and called her the Goddess of Democracy. Here is what happened in Tiananmen Square at the hands of the Chinese Communist Party, as reported in a newly declassified British diplomatic cable:

Fact . . . [The soldiers of 27 Army] were kept without news for ten days and told they were to take part in an exercise. A TV film would be made of the exercise which pleased them. They were informed of martial law on May 20. For the first 4 days after arrival they were driven around Beijing city to familiarise them with the area. 27 Army are at full strength with their own tanks and APCs and a full outfit of ammunition, tear gas and flamethrowers. Other armies are only at 1 division strength. The leadership keeps 27 Army on the move so that it can attack from a different direction each time.

Fact . . . 27 Army APCs opened fire on the crowd (both civilians and soldiers) before running over them in their APCs.

Fact . . . Students and residents understood they were given one hour to leave square but after five minutes APCs attacked. Students linked arms but were mown down including soldiers. APCs then ran over bodies time and time again to make "pie" and remains collected by bulldozer. Remains incinerated and then hosed down drains.

Fact . . . Minimum estimate of civilian dead 10,000.[17]

The memory of this massacre in the heart of Beijing has been removed from China's national life by the Chinese Communist Party. To a certain extent, it has been removed from ours as well: even after the massacre in Tiananmen Square, America allowed for Most Favored Nation status with China in US-China trade, and the economic relationship that has transformed the international balance of power against the United States in the twenty-first century began in earnest. While many in America believed that China would eventually liberalize because of economic engagement, we are now relearning the lessons that Paul Nitze and others in the Cold War era knew quite well.[18] We must remember that the Chinese Communist Party and the People's Republic of China emerged from a Revolution that has been in conflict with the United States and with our system of values and government from its beginning.

What is the purpose of China's Revolution? The most succinct and truthful explanations that I am aware of come from two eminent Cold War historians, Chen Jian and Qiang Zhai, who describe the founding vision of Mao Zedong and other members of the Chinese Communist Party. In the words of Chen Jian: "Mao's revolution never took as its ultimate goal the Communist seizure of power in China; rather, as the chairman repeatedly made clear, his revolution aimed at transforming China's state, population, and society, and simultaneously reasserting China's central position in the world."[19] In the words of Qiang Zhai: "When he devoted his life to revolution, Mao aimed at transforming not only the old China but also the old world order. . . . Just as the old international order had helped cause China's suffering and humiliation, so too would the creation of a new order contribute to the rebirth of a strong and prosperous China.[20]

Xi Jinping, like other Communist Party leaders before him, participates in the Revolution of the Chinese Communist Party, with the aim of returning

China to "center stage" and preeminence in world affairs. Today's Communist Party envisions three turning points, in 2021, 2035, and 2049, at the end of which "the great rejuvenation of the Chinese nation" will be complete. And so, this Revolution continues, seeking in the coming decades China's restoration, the return of China's "central position in the world," and by extension, the transformation of the American-led world order. This Revolution continues today as the Chinese Communist Party has amassed enormous global power. Its conflict with the United States has been there from its inception. The Korean War, as discussed, was the Chinese Communist Party's first attempt to confront the United States in Asia. Document Nine explains in lucid terms the hostility to the principles and ideals of democracy and individual liberties. Tiananmen Square gives just one example of the methods of the Chinese Communist Party when it comes to the challenge to their power in the name of greater rights and freedoms. How else does the Chinese Communist Party enforce its will against challenges internal and external? Let us look inside China's concentration camps. This is not the China of the past, of 1949, or 1989, but the China of the present, of 2022. Here are two stories from Xinjiang's high-tech camp system:

> If anyone moved, their motion was automatically detected. "When they made any gesture, the camera captured that. For example, if anyone talks to others, even in the middle of the night, the guards would yell at them over the intercom," she remembered. What was even more startling was the way "the police could click on that person's face to make it bigger on the screen." They could pull up the detainee's name and number in an instant. You could also use the system to search for particular detainees or groups. "For example, if you want to check the number 10 cell, you just click 10," she said.
>
> What Qelbinar saw was the command center of a "smart camp" system—a facility that the tech firm Dahua says is supported by technologies such as "computer vision systems, big data analytics and cloud computing." According to the manual approved by Zhu Hailun, the camps were to "perfect peripheral isolation, internal separation, protective defenses, safe passageways, and other facilities and

equipment, and ensure that security instruments, security equipment, video surveillance, one-button alarms, and other such devices are in place and functioning." This "smart" camp scheme resonates with regional Party Secretary Chen Quanguo's vision that the camps should "teach like a school, be managed like the military, and be defended like a prison."[21]

This is life in the twenty-first century for those in Xinjiang, a region the size of Alaska. China's companies—including Tencent, Alibaba, Megvii, and iFlytek—have all participated in the technology of China's twenty-first-century oppression, according to researchers and investigators around the world.[22] As of the present writing, anyone can invest money in the technology behind these concentration camps on global markets. The company referred to in the account above is Zhejiang Dahua Technology Ltd., which is available for investment at present writing through Blackrock's iShares MSCI China-A ETF as well as Blackrock's iShares MSCI Emerging Markets ETF.[23] Both the US Federal Communications Commission and the US Department of Commerce have issued warnings or taken action against this company. However, it is still included in publicly traded funds.

What does the Communist Party's vision mean, to be taught like a school, managed like the military, and defended like a prison? Here is another story from the camps:

[T]he detainees were forced by the automated surveillance system and the guards who monitored it to sit absolutely still for most hours of the day—a form of physical torment that prevented them from relaxing and over time began to wreak havoc on their bodies. "They sat between these beds on plastic stools, reciting the rules. You had to recite, whether you knew Chinese or not. And because the people had to sit there for such long hours, there were many people whose intestines 'fell down.'" Baimurat recalled, regarding the Qitai camp where many detainees suffered from rectal prolapses. "When they had such problems, they were finally allowed to see a doctor." Continuing, he describes how detainees would be hooded, shackled, and escorted by police armed with automatic weapons to the hospital. . . ."[24]

For the first six months, the detainees did not leave the cell except for weekly showers. "We just sat there and watched Xi Jinping tours," Adibek said. "We watched several hours on the weekend, always about how prosperous China is."[25]

The methods of Communist Parties, from the Soviet Union until today's Chinese Communist Party, which aspires to dominance in the global international system, have remained consistent with a view of the human being as subordinated to the ambitions of the state and ruling dictators. Testimonies from Xinjiang's genocide and atrocities have spread as survivors of the concentration camps of the Chinese Communist Party find refuge around the world. Here is one more account in Israel's *Haaretz* newspaper, of other Communist Party methods:

The camp's commanders set aside a room for torture, Sauytbay relates, which the inmates dubbed the "black room" because it was forbidden to talk about it explicitly. "There were all kinds of tortures there. Some prisoners were hung on the wall and beaten with electrified truncheons. There were prisoners who were made to sit on a chair of nails. I saw people return from that room covered in blood. Some came back without fingernails."

Why were people tortured?

"They would punish inmates for everything. Anyone who didn't follow the rules was punished. Those who didn't learn Chinese properly or who didn't sing the songs were also punished."

And everyday things like these were punished with torture?

"I will give you an example. There was an old woman in the camp who had been a shepherd before she was arrested. She was taken to the camp because she was accused of speaking with someone from abroad by phone. This was a woman who not only did not have a phone, she didn't even know how to use one. On the page of sins the inmates were forced to fill out, she wrote that the call she had been accused of making never took place. In response she was immediately punished. I saw her when she returned. She was covered with blood, she had no fingernails and her skin was flayed."[26]

In light of these things, what is the nature of our responsibility? John Quincy Adams famously said of America, "But she goes not abroad in search of monsters to destroy." No less than George Washington told us at the beginning: "It is our true policy to steer clear of permanent alliances with any portion of the foreign world."[27] (Though allies saved *us* at the beginning.) What is America meant to do? Should the nature of our national discussion turn away from what divides us and toward the question of our responsibilities in the world, we will have made great progress. I would propose these things: America must not deny these evils in the world and America must work so that no other can deny them. America must not ignore these evils in the world and America must work so that no other can ignore them. America must not enable these evils in the world and America must work so that no other can enable them. And America, with our Allies, must remain a place of refuge for the people of the world.

To win a battle of ideas, we must be prepared for the ways in which Beijing is attempting to undermine our influence, to subvert the very idea of America, and also to subvert the idea of America's leadership role in the world. To see how China's messaging to the world works, let us look to the meeting in Anchorage, Alaska, between Yang Jiechi and Wang Yi of the Chinese Communist Party and US secretary of state Anthony Blinken and US national security advisor Jake Sullivan. Yang speaks to China's long-term strategies, explaining that, "For China, we are now in a historic year where we will move from finishing the first centenary goal to the second centenary goal, and by the year 2035 China will surely achieve basic modernization. And by the year 2050, China will achieve full modernization."[28] He speaks to the relationship between the Communist Party and the Chinese people, stating that, "The Chinese people are wholly rallying around the Communist Party of China," and also of the *universal values of the Chinese Communist Party*. "Our values are the same as the common values of humanity. Those are: peace, development, fairness, justice, freedom, and democracy." He states that China, and by implication, not the United States, stands for international law,

What China and the international community follow or uphold is the United Nations-centered international system and the international order underpinned by international law, not what is advocated by a small number of countries of the so-called "rules-based" international order. And the United States has its style—United States-style democracy—and China has the Chinese-style democracy. It is not just up to the American people, but also the people of the world to evaluate how the United States has done in advancing its own democracy. In China's case, after decades of reform and opening up, we have come a long way in various fields.[29]

Yang presents China, as Communist Party leaders often do, as the country that is most responsible and benevolent within the international system, portraying the US and its Allies as a "small number of countries," positioning China and its adherents as the larger camp, while also taking a swipe at American democracy. This speech is part of a turn in which the Chinese Communist Party has begun to position itself as a comprehensive adversary of the United States and the world, which it, not China, played the lead role in building. China is an adversary and opponent, not only in terms of its investment in military systems designed to kill American and Allied sailors and soldiers, or its attempts to bend the world economy to its favor, but also, in ways that harken back much more closely to the Soviet Union: as an alternative to America as leader of the world's nations. Yang adds that, "The wars in this world are launched by some other countries, which have resulted in massive casualties. But for China, what we have asked for, for other countries, is to follow a path of peaceful development, and this is the purpose of our foreign policy." Like the Soviet Union, a nation that preached peace abroad but carried out brutal repression at home, the People's Republic of China, carrying out the first genocide by an industrialized nation since the Second World War, repeated military harassment of most of its neighbors, and the world's largest peacetime military build-up in decades, preaches that its foreign policy is for the sake of peace. China's neighbors know better, but its audience goes far beyond Asia, from the "useful idiots" that inhabit the peripheries of every consequential conflict in history, to the many nations of the world that have yet to make up

234 · THE DECISIVE DECADE

their minds about what China's rise means, particularly those that stand to benefit from Chinese loans and aid.

Yang's verbal attack on American leadership is even more explicit:

The United States itself does not represent international public opinion, and neither does the Western world. Whether judged by population scale or the trend of the world, the Western world does not represent the global public opinion. So we hope that when talking about universal values or international public opinion on the part of the United States, we hope the US side will think about whether it feels reassured in saying those things, because the US does not represent the world. It only represents the Government of the United States. I don't think the overwhelming majority of countries in the world would recognize that the universal values advocated by the United States or that the opinion of the United States could represent international public opinion, and those countries would not recognize that the rules made by a small number of people would serve as the basis for the international order.[30]

China's leaders and propagandists have been saying things like this for years, but never so explicitly as now. For example, as noted Communist Party diplomat and former ambassador to the United Kingdom Madame Fu Ying wrote in the *Financial Times* in 2016, "The US World Order is a suit that no longer fits . . . the Western-centered world order dominated by the US has made great progress and economic growth. But those contributions lie in the past."[31] While the Communist Party has always positioned itself rhetorically for an opening for China as world leader, only in recent years have officials been so publicly explicit in their attacks on American legitimacy. Importantly, the audience they see outside of China is one they believe will be bigger, in the end, than the US and our Allies. And this vision of "surrounding the cities with the countryside" by uniting the developing world against the developed world is one that goes back to the founding decades of the People's Republic of China.[32] Consider Mao's words to an Algerian delegation in 1958 in which he laid out his vision of Asia and Africa (and eventually Latin America) fighting together against the Western world:

In the circumstances of anti-imperialism, we here count as one front-line, that is the Eastern frontline, on the West Pacific. You are the Western front line. You are in a period of difficulty. . . . We have gone through many setbacks in the last twenty-two years; ultimately we won. India struggled against Britain for decades but won. Egypt has been independent for just a few years. Of course, their methods were different. Your struggle against the French now is a national liberation struggle, the time of the struggle may be long, hopefully yours won't take as long as ours.[33]

The Communist Party's diplomacy at the time emphasized military struggle and the use of violence. As Mao said to the Algerians, "We should support you because you are struggling against imperialism. It is the same as our struggle. This is our international mission. Algeria's contribution to the whole world is very big—you can pin down 800,000 French troops. . . . You will not lose. In five or ten years you will have victory." In 1962, he said a similar thing to a Vietnamese delegation: "You are Southeast Asia's front line. We are paying close attention to your situation and to the situation in Laos. You have already grabbed one of America's fingers. . . . If the [war in South Vietnam] goes on for five to ten more years then the US will think it is not worth it."[34]

In the words of historian John W. Garver, "At a minimum, [Mao] hoped to pressure the United States to cease supporting [Taiwan], blocking China's entry into the United Nations, and economically isolating China. Maximally, if several foreign revolutions actually succeeded, China might emerge as the leader of a revitalized world revolutionary movement and the structure of U.S. power in Asia would either collapse or be rolled back."[35]

China's leaders have never abandoned their idea of fighting the United States for leadership, nor have they abandoned their idea of doing this through appeals to and operations within the emerging nations of Asia, Africa, and Latin America. This strategy, during the Cold War, placed them at odds with both the United States and Soviet Union, and also shattered China's relationship with India, culminating in war in 1962. China today is pursuing a similar course of vilification of the West and of US-leaning or democratic-leaning Asian, African, and Latin American nations. Though

China has grown much more sophisticated, through its successful economic engagement with the world, in contrast to its unsuccessful ideological engagement during the Cold War, it has not abandoned the ideological roots of its strategy toward Asia, Africa, and Latin America. We must expect to hear the overarching themes of the support for the Chinese Communist Party by the Chinese people, the illegitimacy of the United States and other developed nations as a "small group" unrepresentative of "world opinion," as well as a deeper ideological thrust into the emerging world even as Beijing's diplomats and potentially its military attack regional neighbors. China's aggressive rhetoric and actions abroad are popular at home, at least among the many citizens who subscribe to the military nationalism of "the great rejuvenation of the Chinese nation." Yang Jiechi's remarks in Alaska—"Let me say here that, in front of the Chinese side, the United States does not have the qualification to say that it wants to speak to China from a position of strength"—became a popular T-shirt and slogan on the Chinese internet. Xi Jinping's remarks that foreigners will "bash their heads bloody on a steel great wall made of the flesh and blood of 1.4 billion Chinese people" was a popular applause line in his centennial speech.

As the Chinese Communist Party gins up militarism at home, a process that precedes Xi Jinping and has been part of the Communist Party's bloody history since it took control of China, the United States and our Allies must realize that we are dealing with an entity that is potentially much more dangerous than the Soviet Union, and likely to have less international appeal when it comes to its ideology and rhetoric. Even as America struggled in many parts of the world to win the battle of ideas with the Soviet Union, we should have a decisive advantage across the world when it comes to the battle of ideas with China. We must expose China's policies of genocide at home, its abuse of emerging nations through debt and financial coercion, and its persistent military harassment of its neighbors, including threats to use nuclear weapons against Australia and Japan. We are likely to have an advantage while sharing the ideals of America and the American System and also simply, methodically, and relentlessly pointing out the truth about Beijing.

If the United States is able to reduce or ultimately expel China's economic influence within the developed world, fight to win the economic competition agenda across the world's emerging continents, and restrain our own business leaders from mortgaging our geopolitical future through entrapment in the China market, we will have achieved the bulk of what this contest depends on. We will also need a robust campaign to defend and promote our ideals, and also to communicate with the Chinese people. Many alive in China today are not only aware of but have also lived through the Communist Party's bloody history, the wars, famines, and political pogroms that characterized Mao's China. Programs of organ harvesting, gulags, genocide, and political repression are also understood, even if they cannot be discussed openly. Even as the Communist Party attempts to steer much of its population toward a belief in "the great rejuvenation of the Chinese nation," there are millions of people who know and see the other side to the Party. Like Radio Free Asia and Voice of America during the Cold War, the United States and our Allies must maintain a constant and persistent vigil and testimony to these troubles inside China and its dominions, and offer an alternative to the Communist Party's version of history. The Communist Party's true objective, for whatever lies are spoken on the world stage, is to build their country into a clear and unified ideological whole.

While Russia has changed shape since the days of Soviet totalitarianism and the Chinese Communist Party has formed unique ideologies of its own, it is worth reminding ourselves of the vision of control at the heart of twentieth-century communism. Orlando Figes, historian of Russia, writes of Soviet architects in Moscow who "conceived of the city as a vast laboratory for organizing the behaviour and psyche of the masses, as a totally controlled environment where the egotistic impulses of individual people could be remoulded rationally to operate as one collective body or machine." He notes that, "It had always been the aim of the Bolsheviks to create a new type of human being. As Marxists, they believed that human nature was a product of historical development, and could thus be transformed by a revolution in the way people lived. . . . Trotsky waxed lyrical on the 'real scientific possibility' of reconstructing man. . . . 'Man must look at himself and see himself as a raw material, or at best as a semi-manufactured product, and say: "At last, my dear *homo sapiens*, I will work on you."'"[36]

Ideas play a central role in Beijing's confrontation with the world.[37] While this may not be the primary arena of victory, the Arena of Ideas is one in which we must also play to win. As much as they intend to project global military power from a position of dominance in Asia, China's leaders aspire to shape the mind of the world in ways that will accept and enable their rise to supremacy.

China's leaders are propagandists and seducers. How else could it be that in the midst of known and proven genocide, they continue to do business with the world? China's leaders have brought nations great and small to their side, as well as individuals and institutions of all statures. China cultivates a modern form of what John K. Fairbank once called "foreign nobles," people overseas who, in pursuit of the benefits conferred by China's imperial capital, are willing to be its advocates abroad. China's narratives of the inevitability of its rise to power have captured the minds of many. In the words of hedge fund manager Ray Dalio:

> Would you have not wanted to invest with the Dutch in the Dutch empire? Would you have not wanted to invest in the industrial revolution and the British empire? Would you not want to invest in the United States and the United States empire? I think it's comparable. . . .
>
> I believe China is a competitor of the United States or Chinese businesses are competitors of American businesses or other businesses around the world . . . and that therefore you want to be, if you're diversified, having bets on both horses in the race.[38]

We have already seen how American businesses and financiers are engaged with China as a market. Some are willing to engage with *the idea of China* as the world's dominant power. Fortunately, China's advocates in the United States are often called out with opprobrium. The Editorial Board of the *Wall Street Journal* took issue with other comments from Mr. Dalio:

> Asked about his investments in China and Beijing's human rights abuses, the billionaire drew in an equivalence with the US. "I look at the United States, and I say well, what's going on in the United States

and should I not invest in the United States" because of "our own human-rights abuses, or other things?"

[P]ressed on China's policy of "disappearing people," he added, "that is their approach, we have our approach." Tell that to publisher Jimmy Lai, who is locked in jail merely for asking China to live up to the promises it made about Hong Kong autonomy.

This is the sort of comment that sours Americans on Wall Street and opens executives to accusations of being "citizens of the world" before they are Americans.[39]

National Review reacted to comments from this investor with the headline, "We Can't Let Genocide Get in the Way of a Good Investment Opportunity, Right?"[40] Dalio is explicit in his own writing, for example in the *Financial Times* in 2021. With the subtitle "Anti-Beijing Bias Has Blinded Too Many for Too Long to Opportunities," he writes,

In the long run, timeless and universal truths determine why countries succeed or fail. In brief, empires rise when they are productive, financially sound, earn more than they spend, and increase assets faster than their liabilities. This tends to happen when their people are well educated, work hard and behave civilly. Objectively compare China with the US on these measures, as I chronicle in an ongoing study, and the fundamentals clearly favour China.

Prejudice and bias always blind people to opportunity. So, if you have been a China sceptic for reasons that don't square with what is happening there, I suggest you clear your mind.[41]

Around the world, Western institutions and even individuals have been willing to overlook Communist Party genocide, military build-up, expansionism and territorial claims, bloody rhetoric, and even blood spilled in reality in order to participate in China's rise. While China's advocates in the world's free states are many, Beijing plays an even more dangerous game among the world's emerging nations, where debt trap loans and infrastructure projects accompany efforts to sway the views of governments. This is accompanied by efforts at influence-building by the Chinese Communist Party's United Front Work Department, whose purpose is "mobilizing the party's friends to strike at the party's enemies" both inside China and around the world.[42] "United front work" was utilized by Mao Zedong and remains an essential tool of the Chinese Communist Party. As former Central Intelligence Agency analyst Peter Mattis explains, "Jiang Zemin, Hu Jintao, and Xi Jinping all have characterized united front work as a 'magic weapon' to facilitate China's rise in the midst of an international ideological battleground."[43] China's global influence operations include Communist Party–backed "friendship groups," Confucius Institutes, and other instruments of seduction, persuasion, and intimidation that also operate not only in America but around the world.[44] The Communist Party's vision of a new world order is one in which Beijing sits firmly in the center of human affairs, and, as its leaders say, "Backed by the invincible force of 1.4 billion people, we have an infinite stage for our era." An invincible force on an infinite stage. With a billion people living under history's most technologically advanced system of repression and coercion, the Communist Party of China seeks to dominate the world's seas, trade routes, and emerging continents, and to project its power from seabed to space. With its social credit system and vision of "social management," China's people are educated, managed, and shepherded by Beijing within the constructs of "the great rejuvenation of the Chinese nation" and "the Community of Common Destiny for Mankind," a vision of China's ascendancy and of China's power over virtually every other nation on Earth. If China's leaders are able to sway the world's great continents toward their orbit—even as global public opinion toward China deteriorates, worldwide economic engagement continues to thrive—then, regime by regime, fellow traveler by fellow traveler, and government by government, the world would be transformed in Beijing's image, much as America ushered in a period of great power peace and the relative proliferation of freedom that lasted from the Second World War until the twenty-first century.

In America, the true colossus of the modern world, we must remind ourselves that our good deeds and powerful ideals outweigh our shortcomings. What we are at our best is a place that can prevent places such as Nazi Germany, the Soviet Union, or the People's Republic of China from altering the course of history and of humanity.

OUR METHODS AND OUR PATH FORWARD

I n order to win a battle of ideas we must rebuild our own spirits and sense of national unity. We must project our shared ideals across our Alliance System and within other democracies. We must work to bring undecided nations to our side. We must counteract the narratives and strategies of our opponents. It is essential that we counter the Chinese Communist Party's ability to coerce, persuade, and operate inside the United States and within the Alliance System. We have not only the power of our ideals and their genuine universal, global resonance, but we also have the ways and means to spread them around the world. Institutions like Radio Free Europe, Radio Liberty, and Voice of America, think tanks with congressional participation such as the National Endowment for Democracies, the International Republican Institute, and the National Democratic Institute have all been the products of prior strategic competitions where the role of ideas was clearly understood. They must be revitalized and maximized again today. This will be one of the great missions of American national life. Institutions that oversee them, such as the US Agency for Global Media, could expand their mission to include public private partnerships in which the role of ideas and the power of American trade and enterprise could be brought together. We must build a message in which the world's nations large and small can understand that they should choose America and the Free World.

Additionally, American popular culture—which some have said is in fact our greatest export—would do well to become versed and skilled in the art of this crucial competition. While much has been written about Hollywood's pursuit of the China market and the moral compromises it has made, there is also a new side to American popular media that one can observe, a clever and persuasive view of US-China competition. For example, the Netflix special *Space Force* includes a comedic rendition of China as our primary rival, including competition for resources on the moon and a Chinese moon rover stealing the original American flag. The Showtime hit *Billions* goes well out of its way to depict a socially conscious billionaire protagonist who, hidden in the midst of the contemporary detail that defines the series, has a barely visible portrait of the Dalai Lama in his office. The American billionaire says this to a delegation of businesspeople from the People's Republic of China: "I'm going to have to pass on your offer. I can't do business with a group that has ties to a government with such a brutally poor record on human rights. I can't help enrich the oppressors. If you'd like to influence your government to start treating people like people, with decency and humanity, please give me a call. Otherwise, good night." *Top Gun: Maverick* was initially infamous for removing the Taiwanese and Japanese flags from the back of Tom Cruise's leather jacket in a film that had once been a symbol of American patriotism and daring, as well as a massive booster for US Navy recruitment in the 1980s. Removing the flags of two Asian democracies was outrageous to many. When the film was finally released in 2022, the flags were back, and the film has been a boon for Paramount Pictures—as the *Wall Street Journal* reported, "Paramount Revenue Gets Lift from 'Top Gun' Sequel, Streaming Service."[45] The China market continues to create scandals for film studios like Disney, whose film *Mulan* included a thank-you to Chinese police forces involved in Xinjiang genocide, and actors like *Fast and Furious* star John Cena, who apologized in tears in Chinese after calling Taiwan a country. By some accounts, the China market is drying up for Hollywood content. Chris Fenton, author of *Feeding the Dragon*, explains that "China was the golden goose that Hollywood looked to [in order] to really recoup some big investment dollars, and the huge capital it takes to make these big franchises." Now, according to Fenton, the China market is projected at zero for many Hollywood movies amid rising Communist Party censorship.[46]

Communist Party censors are bold in their desire to control the Arena of Ideas inside China: in 2021, censors demanded that the Statue of Liberty be removed from the latest Spider-Man film, which Sony Pictures refused to do. The loss of the China market may be a boon in the long run for American film studios, certainly when it comes to the important role of Hollywood in the global Arena of Ideas. Fenton adds, "The fact that China now is not as important to Hollywood is a fantastic thing for the creative expression of these filmmakers." [47]

China's consumers have given the world many examples of punishing companies that do not steer the course of nationalism in the markets of the People's Republic of China. American consumers can support our institutions and companies that do the right thing and make the right choice when it comes to standing up for freedom on the issue of US-China global competition. Netflix, Showtime, and Paramount, and those who have done the right thing in the famous saga of the National Basketball Association's travails in the China market, deserve American support. We should encourage cultural products that take an intelligent, contemporary view of the realities of US-China competition. We should support companies that begin to make the right, principled stands on human rights and values as well as on critical business issues such as supply chain strategy, intellectual property protection, and market prioritization. The popular culture products that could be created telling the stories of those who have lived through or escaped the dangers of modern China could be extraordinary and powerful. Such stories could broaden our national awakening on our most vital strategic challenge more profoundly than foreign policy discourse can.

We must remember and anticipate that attempts to stand up to the Chinese Communist Party may be labeled anti-Chinese and anti-Asian. But this is not the case. First, we must remember that American strategy towards the Chinese Communist Party and the People's Republic of China should never be mistaken for anti-Asian-American sentiment. Second, we must understand that American strategy and statecraft have as their primary theater in our lifetimes the *defense of Asia*. This defense is not only necessary, but it is an expression of our strongest principles and ideals. Our solidarity with Asia's democracies is essential to who we are. And our position as defender, not aggressor, in Asia is a direct inverse to Beijing's. We do this with consent and in concert with Asian nations from Japan to Korea to India to the Philippines. China itself was our ally once, in a fight against the brutalities of this world in the Second World War. That world ended when the Chinese Communist Party won the Chinese Civil War, driving Chiang Kai-shek and the Guomindang across the straits to establish their government on the island of Taiwan, known then and today as the Republic of China. In our time, those who carried the American flag on the front lines of the Communist Party's crackdown in Hong Kong and those who stand on the front lines now in Taiwan, in the shadow of the Communist Party's most strident military ambitions, show a different side to China's past, present, and perhaps someday its future, a side which we must remember and empower during our contest with this totalitarian regime.

We can understand that our experiment in bringing the Chinese Communist Party's authoritarian-totalitarian regime into the modern world through trade and commerce has failed to influence this state toward any semblance of amity to our way, our system, or our ideals, even though these same values are shared by nations and peoples of many origins in places all across the world. Across the strait, in Taiwan, is a vibrant Chinese democracy, one we have supported deeply in the past, and which once again has captured the attention of America. America should take confidence in the moral purpose that rests within our attention to the security and defense of Asia and our attention to Hong Kong, Taiwan, and mainland Chinese who share our universal cause in the Arena of Ideas. Our values transcend place and origin. Our tent is big and wide.

We must also work here at home to ensure that the Chinese Communist Party loosens and withdraws its grasp of anyone within our own borders. Those who arrive here, escaping this regime, should be defended and live here safe and free. Those who are pursued by Communist Party programs or influence operations should have recourse to American protection and justice. This means that it will be essential to counter and dismantle Communist Party influence operations, illegal and extralegal activities, and to ensure safe haven for those that need it. Attempts by the Chinese Communist Party to control or influence its citizens abroad should also be countered and dismantled, so that those who cross into America or the broader Free World are indeed free.

The world has watched as one authoritarian regime wages war against a democratic neighbor. In Ukraine, the murder of women and children, the use of flechette munitions on civilians, and the destruction of apartment blocks, hospitals, and cities by the Russian military has shown the world one side of the Russia-China "comprehensive strategic partnership of coordination for a new era." The Free World must now prepare for what may be coming in the Pacific. The Chinese Communist Party's pathologies will not remain inside the People's Republic of China unless contained by the United States and our Allies. As the Communist Party practices missile strikes on mock-up US aircraft carriers and naval bases in the same Xinjiang deserts where it carries out genocide against the Uyghurs, as it sends sorties of aircraft at an increasing pace into the Taiwan Strait, and as it exercises its naval and missile forces in unprecedented live-fire exercises surrounding the island of Taiwan, we must prepare for what also may come in the 2020s. A consensus is growing that the Chinese Communist Party may choose war in this decade.[48] With Russia at war in Europe and military exercises between these two dictatorships continuing by sea, air, and land, we may soon see what the world looks like as these two places probe the Free World's ramparts, in both Europe and in Asia.

The conquest of Taiwan sits at the ideological center of "the great rejuvenation of the Chinese nation." As Xi Jinping stated before the General Assembly of the People's Republic of China in 2021, "No one should underestimate the Chinese people's determination and strong ability to defend national sovereignty and territorial integrity! The historical task of the complete reunification of the motherland must be fulfilled, and it will definitely be fulfilled!"[49] Russia and China have pledged to each other mutual support on strategic goals in Europe and in Asia. The Chinese military is building up to the point that military action against Taiwan is feasible. In one assessment of Chinese military logistics from the US Naval War College:

> The PLA believes a future joint landing operation will include comprehensive employment of strategic deterrence; seizure of air, maritime, and information superiority in the area of operations; a focused blockade to seal and control the area around Taiwan; a large-scale joint firepower campaign; assault landings in Taiwan and possibly some of

the outer islands; and on-island operations. Throughout the campaign, information operations, precision strikes, and highly mobile forces will play critical roles. Additionally, operations will expand past the eastern part of Taiwan to seize advantage and strategic initiative to control the space around Taiwan and counter US intervention.[50]

An assessment published by US National Defense University points out that "evidence indicates that PLA urban combat training is increasingly oriented toward Taiwan." While the PLA is focused on "decapitation strikes," Chinese paramilitary forces with experience in Xinjiang could be employed in Taiwan "after a permissive environment was established."[51] In the meantime, China's State Council announced in an August 2022 White Paper on Taiwan that, "The wheel of history rolls on towards national reunification, and it will not be stopped by any individual or any force." The paper issued a warning to the United States and Allies:

> We Chinese will decide our own affairs. The Taiwan question is an internal affair that involves China's core interests and the Chinese people's national sentiments, and no external interference will be tolerated. Any attempt to use the Taiwan question as a pretext to interfere in China's internal affairs or obstruct China's reunification will meet with the resolute opposition of the Chinese people, including our compatriots in Taiwan. No one should underestimate our resolve, will and ability to defend China's sovereignty and territorial integrity.[52]

The world can see that China is preparing for military action, including the possible blockade, or invasion and occupation, of this island of twenty-four million people living under democratic government and self-rule. Should that moment come—should deterrence fail—we must remember the stakes for the Free World as a whole. As House Speaker Nancy Pelosi, whose visit to Taiwan in August 2022 was supported by twenty-six Republican senators including Minority Leader Mitch McConnell, stated in an op-ed in the *Washington Post*: "The Taiwan Relations Act set out America's commitment to a democratic Taiwan. . . . It fostered a deep friendship rooted in shared interests and values:

self-determination and self-government, democracy and freedom, human dignity and human rights. . . . Yet, disturbingly, this vibrant, robust democracy—named one of the freest in the world by Freedom House and proudly led by a woman, President Tsai Ing-Wen—is under threat. . . . By traveling to Taiwan, we honor our commitment to democracy: reaffirming that the freedoms of Taiwan—and all democracies—must be respected."[53]

A friend once said to me some years ago, "Taiwan is the Berlin of the Second Cold War." In that city, John F. Kennedy said his famous words, "Ich bin ein Berliner." In that city, Ronald Reagan said his famous words, "Mr. Gorbachev, tear down this wall." Berlin. The city of the Berlin Airlift. The city of the Berlin Wall. The city of the Berlin Crisis of 1961, where Soviet ultimatums brought the world to the brink of disaster just before the Cuban Missile Crisis in 1962. That city focused the mind. In that time, in that city, and around the world, the stakes were clear. In our time, the stakes remain the same.

As the Chinese Communist Party prepares itself and its country for a world that must never come, with military commanders that liken urban warfare to "killing rats in a porcelain shop," with diplomats who promise "reeducation" camps for the people of one of the world's free states, and with ideologists who refer to entire peoples whom the Communist Party has attempted to subjugate or destroy as the "five poisons," we must remember the meaning of America, its role in the world, its history, and its duty to humankind. It is not our economic power, our diplomatic potential, or our military might that make us different from other great countries. It is our role as the *guarantor* of human freedom, the place that can preserve and protect what humanity has aspired to for thousands of years.

Let right make might, and let us prevail in this, the hardest, most important contest of our time.

In this generation, we, too, are the Watchmen on the Walls of World Freedom.

CONCLUSION

The strategic vision laid out in this book aims not for accommodation of our enemies, nor the balancing of power. Rather, it seeks to create what Winston Churchill and Paul Nitze called "preponderance" in American power: the overwhelming ability to shape and influence world affairs. This strategy envisions the return of the United States of America as the head of a community of nations that have fought innumerable contests for freedom and prosperity, and that collectively refuse to surrender those gains to an ambitious, powerful, and ultimately delusional People's Republic of China.

The victories and achievements that define America's journey as a young nation—the American Revolution, the US Civil War, the Industrial Revolution, the Civil Rights Movement, the First and Second World Wars, the Cold War— are not a tired legacy. They are a cornerstone on which to build the future. America's journey has just begun. Often we are called upon to defeat or to defend against great evils that arise in different places around the world.

America's challenges draw upon our capabilities and our imagination as a nation. China's attempt to transform the world for the sake of its malignant vision of victory will require a counter so great and deep that, if we succeed, we will become the most capable version of ourselves the world has yet seen. America may be on the ropes or, by some objective measures, in decline. However, America is a nation of unique and proven ingenuity. Our greatest challenge is to reverse our weaknesses and failings and to rise again in the twenty-first century.

To find our Vision of Victory demands not only technical expertise, masterful usage of the tools and resources available, but also unity and fortitude that we have not seen in quite some time. Victory will require a uniquely American attribute: imagination. We must see the future in ways that the adversary cannot see. We must design and build the future in ways that the adversary can neither design nor build. We are a nation of creators and discoverers, of seekers and inventors, tied together by a confluence of world events. We are suited to lead the world through this period of peril in which history's most sophisticated dictatorships again pose their challenge to the free peoples of every nation.

Consider the full length of this description of "the present world crisis" by Paul Nitze in 1950, at the outset of one of the two defining strategic struggles in the twentieth century: the Cold War:

> Within the past thirty-five years the world has experienced two global wars of tremendous violence. It has witnessed two revolutions—the Russian and the Chinese—of extreme scope and intensity. It has also seen the collapse of five empires—the Ottoman, the Austro-Hungarian, German, Italian, and Japanese—and the drastic decline of two major imperial systems, the British and the French. During the span of one generation, the international distribution of power has been fundamentally altered. For several centuries, it had proved impossible for any one nation to gain such preponderant strength that a coalition of other nations could not in time face it with greater strength. The international scene was marked by recurring periods of violence and war, but a system of sovereign and independent states was maintained, over which no state was able to achieve hegemony.
>
> Two complex sets of factors have now basically altered this historical distribution of power. First, the defeat of Germany and Japan and the decline of the British and French Empires have interacted with the development of the United States and the Soviet Union in such a way that power has increasingly gravitated toward these two centers. Second, the Soviet Union, unlike previous aspirants to hegemony, is animated by a new fanatic faith, antithetical to our own, and seeks to impose its absolute authority over the rest of the world.[1]

Today, we face another crisis of world-changing proportions. We exist in a confluence of events whose roots go back a long way, and whose consequences are likely to be as serious as any prior world transformation if we do not address them. For thirty years of peace among the major powers since the collapse of the Soviet Union, we have lived through an era of economic globalization whose only precedent is the turn of the twentieth century ahead of the First World War. However, the factors that Nitze identified are still with us. The Russian and Chinese revolutions set these two nations on their paths as opponents and antagonists of the Western and Free World nations, and these two states continue to define the security challenges for America and the world's democracies from Europe to Asia. China and Russia spent much of the past thirty years since the end of the Cold War focused on economic development and social stability. Today we are witnessing a return to their most dangerous and expansionist authoritarian roots. For many who spent the past generation building businesses in China, the thirty-plus-year period of China's economic opening and engagement with the world is viewed as the norm, not an aberration. However, the Chinese Communist Party has defined their objectives clearly since the founding of the People's Republic of China.

The reality of "the China challenge" and even a "New Cold War" is clear. Not since the previous Cold War has America faced a "present world crisis," as Nitze described the world in NSC-68, in which so many factors combined to jeopardize the future of the Free World. In that time, the time of George F. Kennan's Long Telegram, Paul Nitze's NSC-68, and Dwight D. Eisenhower's "Solarium Project," America was able to set foundations for a winning, long-term grand strategy, a strategy that frames our objectives, and governs all underlying strategies. The architects of world order in that period focused primarily on one challenge above all and created a framework under which all other challenges would be met. America set the course not only for managing our adversary and the threat it presented to the world, but also the course for what America must do, what America must remain, and what America must become. While the United States was immediately handed the problem of communist aggression in the Korean War, the long-term project of Cold War architecture also meant unprecedented technological innovation, a "third Industrial Revolution," the Space Race, the spread of democracies around the world, and victory for the Free World over a totalitarian adversary. Today, as Beijing and Moscow again return to the aggression inherent to their twentieth-century revolutions and views of world order, we must devise a counterpoint of our own. In the face of Beijing's increasingly hostile and military creed, we must not only forge our own superior economic and technological progress, but also constrain and contain this adversary. We must cause China's power to contract from its positions across the world and confine its portion of the world economy, placing it in a position of stagnation and immobility behind a new Great Wall. America will have to achieve three fundamental things to win our contest with China and defend the world order against our authoritarian rivals: We must remain the world's largest economy. We must unite the world's democracies. We must maintain military deterrence over both China and Russia.

America must aim for these core outcomes in our contest:

- A Second Great Divergence in History—this time not between the West and the world but between the democracies and autocracies.

- An Alliance-Based Trading System—an economic community in which integration and cooperation builds between Allies and like-minded nations and in which Beijing is gradually separated from this economic community.

- A New Frontier of Economic Power—working backward from the world economy of 2100, 2050, and 2030, we must rapidly design and execute the advancements that will constitute economic power in the twenty-first century, and deny this progress to our adversaries to widen the gap between their economic power and our own.

- Secure Allied Supply Chains and a New Arsenal of Democracy— Beijing should no longer play a role in critical supply chains in either the United States or Allied World. We must innovate and build secure supply chains that reduce or terminate our reliance on China, while further diverting economic power away from Beijing. We must also revitalize our industrial base both to ensure advantages in key strategic industries and meet the demands of military competition with China and Russia.

- North American Economic Integration—the combined economy of the United States, Canada, and Mexico must create a new basis for competitive advantage in the twenty-first century. The contest with China will include a battle for dominance in the world economy. We must work with our neighbors to build an industrial and technological powerhouse here at home, while diverting the world's nations away from China using the superior pull of the US market.

- Engagement of America's CEOs and Business Leaders— America's executives are the officer corps of our economy. Our Fortune 500 and Fortune 1000 corporations have undergone a transformation in the thirty years of global peace since the Cold War and now consider themselves "multinational corporations" or "globally integrated enterprises." They must adapt to the realities of geopolitical competition between China and the United States and engage in building economic power for the United States and Allied World, not for our primary adversary. For the sake of their own interests and for the sake of their national loyalties, our companies must take the right side. Much of this contest will depend on the choices made by America's private sector.

- Economic Containment of China—America must focus and advance when it comes to strategic industries and emerging technologies. However, it will do us little good if our adversary receives our gains through economic engagement and espionage. America must deploy its tools of economic containment and economic warfare to hold back this opponent and deny it the gains that we are able to make.

Economic power will decide the outcome in the US-China contest, just as it was a decisive factor in both the Cold War and the Second World War.

Therefore, we must focus on this as the primary arena of victory, the one that enables all others. Second to this is military power because China and other adversaries have invested heavily in this arena. Our strategic crisis emanates from the accrual of economic power, military power, and hostile intent among these adversaries. We must pursue a constant strategy of "peace through strength," and not a naïve focus on economic power without military potential.

In short, we must achieve victory in the four arenas:

- In the Economic Arena: Containment of China and American and Allied Growth
- In the Diplomatic Arena: Rollback of China in the Allied System and the Emerging World
- In the Military Arena: American and Allied Preponderance
- In the Arena of Ideas: Triumph of the American and Free World Ideas

The Decisive Decade is built on a fundamental understanding of the People's Republic of China, its history, its strategy, its economic and military power, and its ambitions toward the world. Too few who work on US grand strategy are specialists on China. Too few specialists on China work on US grand strategy. George F. Kennan, who was responsible for the definitive articulation of the Soviet threat in his Long Telegram, was also responsible for the definitive articulation of the strategy that set America on the path to defeat the USSR: containment. Had Kennan not been keenly familiar with the USSR, a true Sovietologist, how could he have constructed his strategy of containment? Forty-five years later, under Ronald Reagan, a path that began with Harry Truman produced Kennan's aim of Soviet collapse. We must be vigilant in our understanding of our adversaries because this can make all the difference. Consider another American statesman and strategist who misunderstood our opponent and whose strategies have had profound consequences for this country. Henry Kissinger was a historian of Europe. His understanding of major power peace and world order came from studies of European diplomatic history, but, as the initial architect of American engagement with China, his misinterpretation of Beijing's aims and views of world order has had long-term effects for America. We are just beginning to live with the dangerous consequences of Kissinger's opening to Mao's China and the access to the world economy that the Chinese Communist Party gained as a result. This generation must always do the humble work of understanding the places that oppose us. One benefit of our period of rapprochement with China is the abundance of experience we now have with this country, spread among the many people who were able to live, work, study, and travel there. We did not have an equivalent advantage in the Cold War. It can now be applied to the work of American victory.

Today, we must also think beyond what Washington can do. Washington knows, Washington understands, the challenge that confronts us. But does America know what to do? This is my concern in writing this book. It is not a book for Washington alone. It is a book for America. My concern is that Washington, DC, versus the People's Republic of China is a contest we cannot win. My hope is that the United States of America, in the fullness of its economic strength, the discipline of its military, the power of its ideas, and the strength of its unique appeal to the nations and peoples of the world, can win the contest ahead.

Much depends on our business leaders, our financiers, and our CEOs. Without them, we cannot win our global contest with China. As China grows larger, richer, and more sophisticated, our hope of retaining our place in the world will diminish and ultimately plunge. We cannot win a strategic contest, we cannot maintain deterrence in Asia, if we are enabling our adversary's growth and efficiency. Our business leaders must pull back from China, rebuild and renew America, and win the economic contest with China in all key regions across the globe. We must do it in this decade. We must begin this journey: to rebuild America, to contain China's economic and military expansion, and to maintain deterrence in the Indo-Pacific and beyond. The decade ahead matters, not only because it is likely to be the time when essential economic and military contests are lost or won, but also because China's own economic struggles will reveal themselves as we begin to disengage.

America must remember our great capability in times of strategic crisis: the masterful utilization of national resources, our will and determination, and our innovative genius led us through the Cold War and the Second World War. We must find these strengths anew. From the workshops of Thomas Edison, the garages of Steve Jobs, Bill Hewlett, and David Packard, to the twenty-first-century factories of Elon Musk, and the countless roots and shoots that will form our new technologies and industries of the future. All the elements of our creative potential, from the past to the future, all these touchstones of American ingenuity, can show us how and where to go. And they can show us how to win. But we must work together as a united nation and bring out the best of all of us in this consequential challenge.

As Paul Nitze wrote in 1950, "From this idea of freedom with responsibility derives the marvelous diversity, the deep tolerance, the lawfulness of the free society. This is the explanation of the strength of free men. It constitutes the integrity and the vitality of the free system. The free society attempts to create and maintain an environment in which every individual has the opportunity to realize his creative powers." These principles of freedom and diversity, in contrast to our Russian enemy and to our adversaries in Beijing, form not only the ideal and practical character of our society, but also the basis for our position in the world. The world that America and our Allies built is the world that we must once again defend. As Nitze wrote, "[W]e must with our allies and the former subject peoples [in decolonizing nations] seek to create a world society based on the principle of consent." This system of free societies, based on inalienable rights, and with interlocking power, forms the structure of the American-led world. It is a structure whose design expresses the principles of America's own character. It is a structure that many of the world's free nations, as our consensual Allies, also value and adhere to. It is the world built by those who won the World Wars and ultimately repelled the designs of the Soviet Union in the Cold War. It is the world that must be strengthened and renewed to withstand and win the challenge posed by the People's Republic of China.

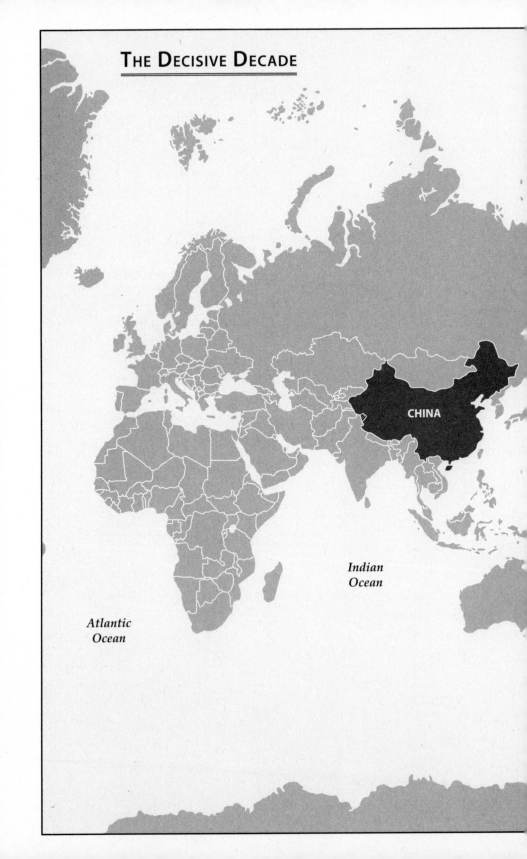

THE DECISIVE DECADE

CHINA

Indian
Ocean

Atlantic
Ocean

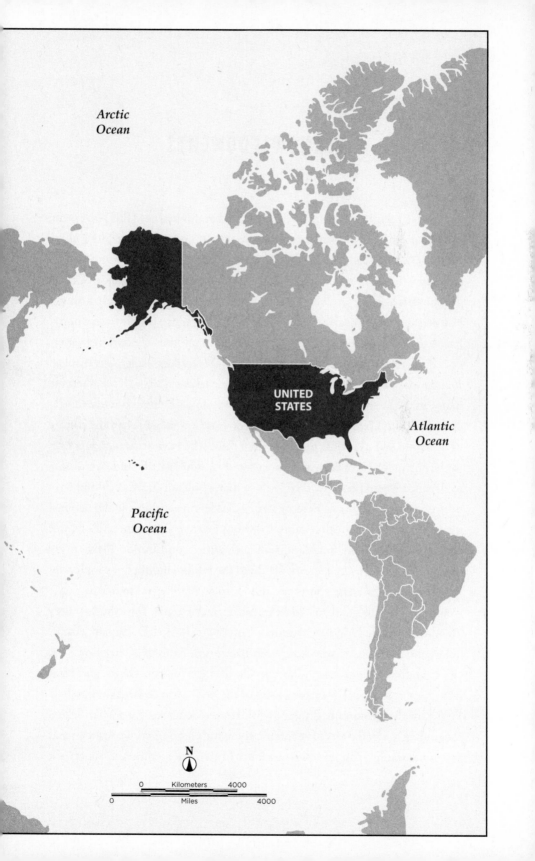

Arctic
Ocean

UNITED
STATES

Atlantic
Ocean

Pacific
Ocean

N

0   Kilometers   4000

0   Miles   4000

ACKNOWLEDGMENTS

There have been a great many people involved in this journey. This book is not just the product of a quest to answer the central questions raised by *China's Vision of Victory*—can the Chinese Communist Party's vision be stopped? Can America win this world-changing contest with the People's Republic of China? This book is also the product of many, many years of effort and many forms of learning and experience. It is the product, therefore, of the people from whom I have had the honor to learn so much in life. From my years of travel in a variety of continents and regions in my twenties and the studies of languages that laid foundations for a global understanding of the challenges we will face, there are many, many people whose memory will travel on with me. From my time at Columbia and Oxford, learning languages, humanities, and then the history of the world and its major countries, from those who have dedicated their lives to the pursuit of knowledge and understanding, from my time since returning to America where I have worked with so many brilliant individuals and have been honored to see my work recognized by leaders in government and national security, there are countless more to whom I am very grateful. All of these chapters of life are the foundations of any further contribution I have made here in *The Decisive Decade*. My thanks to the infinite number of people who have been a part of these efforts and this journey. With regard to this project, I would especially like to thank Toshi Yoshihara, Jack Devine, Tom Shugart, Jerry Hendrix, Michèle Flournoy, Admiral Scott Swift, Robert D. Kaplan, Ashley Tellis, and Tim Oliver, who have been mentors in national security over the years. Andrew Krepinevich, John Van Oudenaren, Andrew Gabel, and Peter Mattis for commenting on key pieces of the book. Nazak Nikakhtar, Clyde Prestowitz, Rob Atkinson, Robert Lighthizer, Derek Scissors, and Mike Sekora for guiding me in the arts of economic competition, competitive strategy, and economic warfare past and present. Rana Mitter, my mentor and supervisor in my master's and doctoral studies in the history of modern China at Oxford, as well as Robert Johnson, John Darwin, Hew Strachan, and Robert Service, who taught me military and global history there. Joshua Carlson, Namrata Goswami, Matt Padilla, who have shown me how to think about space. John Lyons, Tommie Lamont, Theodore Goodrich, William Polk, John Tyler, and Elson Harmon at Groton School. Donald Stoker, I couldn't have done this without you. Thank you for everything. Andrew May, for showing me how to think about the future. Rory Stewart, for providing the most inspiring example in both life and work. At Atlas Organization, Brie Hytovitz, Ishmael Maxwell, Rob MacInnis, and especially Soham Basu, my "crisis briefer" and extraordinary analyst who is wise beyond his years—we have accomplished some great things in the adventures of the past few years. Also, Chuck and Ellen Scarborough, Chad Scarborough, John Playforth, Herman and Elizabeth Playforth, Peter Temes, Arthur Klebanoff, Marshall Sonenshine, Michael Treacy, Lyel Resner, David Rowe, Bob Vitalo, Cliff Paige, Shane Keegan, Mac Marshall, Mac Rush, Jack Barry, Brigitta Schuchert, Tosh Barron, John Mauldin, David Kotok and all of the wonderful people at Camp Kotok, Barbara Smith, Willem de Vogel, Nancy Howar, Jason Glazer, Nancy Lazar, Michelle Watson, TS Allen, Linda Zhang, and Tom Romero (I wish you could have seen this book). Keith Wallman at Diversion Books, for making a tough and complex project enjoyable and for constant encouragement and optimism. Jane Glaser and Noah Perkins for keeping us on track for an ambitious publication schedule. Scott Waxman, for seeing the potential in my work since an early age. And all of my clients at Atlas Organization over the past five years—you have taught me so much and have shown me firsthand the importance of the strategic industries that create American economic power. It is through this journey above all and through the brilliant people I have worked with and encountered that I have come to understand the role that American business could ultimately play for the good in global competition with China. Finally, my family, my parents Anny and David, my brother Nicholas and sisters Becky and Sally, as well as their spouses Callum and Will, also Babur and Piney. And most importantly, to Nellie, my best friend and great companion—thank you for your tireless support, your strength and fortitude, and your infinite love and kindness, which have sustained me through the most challenging work I can imagine.

NOTES

Introduction

1. "VIDEO: Victor Gao on Australia's nuclear submarine deal," Australian Broadcasting Corporation, September 20, 2021, https://www.abc.net.au/news/2021-09-20 /victor-gao-on-australia's-nuclear-submarines-deal/13550288.

2. The Congressional Record, Senate, Vol. 166., No. 186, May 7, 2020, S2300.

3. I began using the phrase "the decisive decade" to describe US-China global competition on national television (February 2020) and with the US Department of Defense Joint Staff Strategic Multilayer Assessment program (July 2020). The importance of winning the 2020s, also explained in *China's Vision of Victory* (2019), has broad and multi-faceted use in the study of US-China competition. Retired US Navy Captain Jim Fanell first used the phrase "the decade of concern" in the 2010s to describe dangers to the US military in the Pacific as China expanded its forces. His articulation, "the decade of concern," has been deployed recently in public remarks by INDOPACOM Commander John Aquilino in 2022. Analysts including Andrew Erickson and Brendan Taylor have also written of the "dangerous decade" for various analytical purposes. Secretary of State Anthony Blinken now uses the phrase "the decisive decade" in discourse on China, initially in his 2022 speech "The Administration's Approach to the People's Republic of China." The ever-wider attention to the 2020s demonstrates a great step forward in our awareness, not only of the challenge we face from China but also of the *timeframe* in which this contest may be won or lost.

4. Paul Kennedy, *The Rise and Fall of the Great Powers: Economic Change and Military Conflict 1500–2000* (New York: Vintage, 1989), 330–33.

5. Robert D. Kaplan, *Earning the Rockies: How Geography Shapes America's Role in the World* (New York, 2017), 11.

6. Kennedy, *Rise and Fall of the Great Powers*, 330–33.

7. US Department of Defense, "Military and Security Developments Involving the People's Republic of China 2020: Annual Report to Congress."

8. "These Are the Top 10 Manufacturing Countries in the World," World Economic Forum, February 25, 2020, https://www.weforum.org/agenda/2020/02/countries -manufacturing-trade-exports-economics/.

9. Notable exceptions include Aaron Friedberg and Charles Boustany who have written on limiting economic engagement with China but explicitly stop short of containment, calling it, in early 2019, not "feasible or desirable at this point." See Aaron Friedberg and Charles Boustany, "Answering China's Economic Challenge: Preserving Power, Enhancing Prosperity," National Bureau of Asian Research, February 20, 2019. See also

Aaron Friedberg, "Rethinking the Economic Dimension of US China Strategy," American Academy of Strategic Education, August 2017. On the whole, the United States still needs an economic theory of victory in our contest with China. We do not yet have one and this book endeavors to show us a path.

10. Robert Gates, *Exercise of Power: American Failures, Successes, and a New Path Forward in the Post–Cold War World* (New York: Knopf, 2020), 10.

11. Henry A. Kissinger, "Reflections on Containment," *Foreign Affairs*, May/June, 1994.

12. HR McMaster, "Biden Would Do the World a Favor by Keeping Trump's China Policy," *Washington* Post, January 18, 2021, https://www.washingtonpost.com/opinions/2021/01/18 /mcmaster-biden-trump-china/.

13. Grand strategy often involves four parts, especially in the American tradition. These are often referred to as the "DIME," Diplomacy, Information, Military, and Economics. This book refers to these elements as "arenas" and revises their order for the purpose of the contest with China. See Terry L. Deibel, *Foreign Affairs Strategy: Logic for American Statecraft* (New York: Cambridge, 2007), for structural thinking on American statecraft and definitions of grand strategy.

Part One

1. "Joint Statement of the Russian Federation and the People's Republic of China on the International Relations Entering a New Era and the Global Sustainable Development," February 4, 2022.

2. David Lubin, "Huge Impact of 'Fortress Economics' in Russia and China," Chatham House, February 2, 2022, https://www.chathamhouse.org/2022/02 /huge-impact-fortress-economics-russia-and-china.

3. See Jeffrey A. Sonnenfeld, Steven Tian, Franek Sokolowski, Michael Wyrebkowski, and Mateusz Kasprowicz, "Business Retreats and Sanctions Are Crippling the Russian Economy," Yale School of Management, July 2022, https://www.ssrn.com /abstract=4167193, for a comprehensive account of effects on the Russian economy. This report also makes the point about the key consequences for Russia: Western sanctions and corporate flight.

4. Jim Pickard, "UK Prepares to Impose Sanctions on Russian Oligarchs in Event of Ukraine Invasion," *Financial Times*, January 30, 2022, https://www.ft.com /content/54614679-1e6b-43f6-9b7f-e209a12ec4b2.

5. *Bloomberg News*, "China Energy Giants in Talks for Shell's Russian Gas Stake," April 21, 2022, https://www.bloomberg.com/news/articles/2022-04-21 /china-state-energy-giants-in-talks-for-shell-s-russian-gas-stake?sref=JEAwJ9G5.

6. See Jeffrey Sonnenfeld and Yale Research Team, "1,000 Companies Have Curtailed Operations in Russia—But Some Remain," Chief Executive Leadership Institute, August 21, 2022, https://som.yale.edu/story/2022/over-1000-companies-have-curtailed-operations -russia-some-remain, for a comprehensive list of corporate activity in Russia.

7. *Bloomberg News*, "Beijing Tells Chinese in Russia to Help Fill Economic Void," March 22, 2022, https://www.bloomberg.com/news/articles/2022-03-22/beijing -tells-chinese-firms-in-russia-to-help-fill-economic-void?leadSource=uverify%20wall.

8. Yvonne Lau, "Samsung and Apple Exited Russia over Its Invasion of Ukraine. Chinese Smartphone Brands Have Already Seized Their Market Share," *Fortune,* July 7, 2022, https://fortune.com/2022/07/07/russia-ukraine-apple-samsung-china-smartphones-sales-realme-honor-xiaomi/.

9. See Jeffrey Sonnenfeld and Yale Research Team, "1,000 Companies."

10. Kevin Stankiewicz, "Howard Schultz Tells Cramer: China Will Overtake US as Starbucks' Biggest Market by 2025," CNBC, September 13, 2022, https://www.cnbc.com/2022/09/13/howard-schultz-tells-cramer-china-will-overtake-us-as-starbucks-biggest-market-by-2025.html.

11. Sara Germano, "Nike Chief Executive Says Brand Is 'of China and for China,'" *Financial Times*, June 24, 2021, https://www.ft.com/content/704a065d-f07d-4577-8133-7db3eb529299.

12. "A Guide to China: Outlook for the World's Second Largest Economy," JP Morgan Asset Management, September 9, 2022, accessed October 1, 2022, https://am.jpmorgan.com/br/en/asset-management/adv/insights/market-insights/guide-to-china/.

13. *Fox Business Network,* "JPMorgan CEO on Doing Business in China: 'America Will Still Be the Most Prosperous Nation on the Planet,'" August 8, 2021, https://www.foxnews.com/video/6267057940001.

14. Henry M. Paulson Jr., "China Wants to Be the World's Banker," *Wall Street Journal*, December 9, 2020, https://www.wsj.com/articles/china-wants-to-be-the-worlds-banker-11607534410.

15. Nicolas Rapp and Brian O'Keefe, "This Chart Shows China Will Soar past the US to Become the World's Largest Economy by 2030," *Fortune*, January 30, 2022, https://fortune.com/longform/global-gdp-growth-100-trillion-2022-inflation-china-worlds-largest-economy-2030/.

16. Callum Paton, "World's Largest Economy in 2030 Will Be China, Followed by India, with US Dropping to Third, Forecasts Say, *Newsweek,* January 10, 2019, https://www.newsweek.com/worlds-largest-economy-2030-will-be-china-followed-india-us-pushed-third-1286525.

17. Amanda Macias and Jessica Bursztynsky, "Elon Musk Says Chinese Economy Will Surpass US by 2 or 3 Times: 'the Foundation of War Is Economics,'" CNBC, February 28, 2020, https://www.cnbc.com/2020/02/28/musk-says-chinese-economy-will-surpass-the-us-by-two-or-three-times.html.

18. A. Wess Mitchell, "A Strategy for Avoiding a Two Front War," *National Interest*, August 22, 2021, https://nationalinterest.org/feature/strategy-avoiding-two-front-war-192137.

19. In *China's Vision of Victory*, I concluded with three objectives for the United States in light of the global grand strategy of the Chinese Communist Party: 1. We must realize that this contest is about economic power 2. We must gather and build the power of our friends and Allies around the world 3. We must maintain a favorable military balance over China and Russia.

20. Lijian Zhao, Twitter, November 29, 2019.

21. 毛泽东年谱 1949–1976 (北京, 2013), *A Chronological Record of Mao Zedong 1949–1976*, (Beijing, 2013), Vol. 2, 460, in Ward, *China's Vision of Victory.*

22. See for example Roland Rajah and Alyssa Leng, "Revising Down the Rise of China," Lowy Institute Analysis, March 2022, accounting for demographic decline, which is "essentially

locked in over the coming decades." The authors contend that "China would still become the world's largest economy." See Nicholas Eberstadt, "China's Demographic Outlook to 2040 and Its Implications: An Overview," American Enterprise Institute, January 2019, for a longer-term view with a population "peak" in 2028 or 2029. The Chinese Communist Party aims to offset demographic difficulties in the decade ahead with productivity boosts through technology, investment, and automation. Most observers expect that even as it slows, China's growth will continue.

23. Govind Bhutada, "The US Share of the Global Economy Over Time," Visual Capitalist, January 14, 2021, https://www.visualcapitalist.com/u-s-share-of-global-economy-over-time/.

24. Author's calculations with World Bank data, except US historic share of GDP, Visual Capitalist with World Bank data, ibid.

25. Author's calculations with World Bank data.

26. Author's calculations with Credit Suisse data, Credit Suisse Research Institute, Global wealth databook 2021. See also Derek Scissors, "137 Trillion Reasons We Can Lead," American Enterprise Institute, March 31, 2022.

27. Author's calculations with World Bank data.

28. See for example Bernard Marr, *Tech Trends in Practice: The 25 Technologies That Are Driving the 4th Industrial Revolution* (West Sussex (UK): Wiley, 2020), on Industry 4.0.

29. Kaplan, *Rockies*, 11.

30. Arthur Herman, *Freedom's Forge: How American Business Produced Victory in World War II* (New York: Random House, 2021), ix.

31. Herman, *Freedom's Forge*, ix.

32. For American companies in the war effort, see Herman, *Freedom's Forge*, as well as A.J. Baime, *The Arsenal of Democracy: FDR, Detroit, and an Epic Quest to Arm an America at War* (New York: First Mariner, 2014), and "Out-Producing the Enemy, American Production During WWII," The National WWII Museum, 2017, https://www.nationalww2museum.org/sites/default/files/2017-07/mv-education-package.pdf.

33. Herman, *Freedom's Forge*, 112.

34. Herman, *Freedom's Forge*, 115. See National WWII Museum, "Out-Producing the Enemy" for brief profiles of business leaders.

35. Kennedy, *Rise and Fall of the Great Powers*, 330–33.

36. David Lague and Benjamin Kang Lim, "China's Vast Fleet Is Tipping the Balance in the Pacific," Reuters, April 30, 2019, https://www.reuters.com/investigates/special-report/china-army-navy/.

37. World Economic Forum, "Top 10 Manufacturing Countries," 2020.

38. "A Conversation with Ambassador Katherine Tai, US Trade Representative," Center for Strategic and International Studies, October 4, 2021, https://www.csis.org/analysis/conversation-ambassador-katherine-tai-us-trade-representative.

39. "US-China Investment Ties: Overview," Congressional Research Service, January 15, 2021.

40. All statistics from US Department of Commerce Bureau of Economic Analysis. See "Activities of US Multinational Enterprises, 2019," US Department of Commerce BEA, November 12, 2021, https://www.bea.gov/news/2021/activities-us-multinational

-enterprises-2019, for an overview. Author's calculations as percentages of GDP and global totals.

41. Yahoo / Valuewalk, "10 Us Companies with Highest Revenue Exposure to China," August 2, 2020, https://www.yahoo.com/now/10-us-companies-highest-revenue-225350456.html.

42. Data from US Trade Representative (US-China trade) and World Bank (GDP).

43. See for example Henry Ashby Turner Jr., *General Motors and the Nazis: The Struggle for Control of Opel, Europe's Biggest Carmaker* (New Haven: Yale, 2005).

44. Geoffrey Jones, Grace Ballor, and Adrian Brown, "Thomas J. Watson, IBM and Nazi Germany," Harvard Business School, September 30, 2021.

45. Edwin Black, *IBM and the Holocaust: The Strategic Alliance Between Nazi Germany and America's Most Powerful Corporation,* (New York: Crown, 2001).

46. Vicky Xiuzhong Xu, with Danielle Cave, Dr. James Leibold, Kelsey Munro, Nathan Ruser, "Uyghurs for Sale: 'Re-Education', Forced Labour and Surveillance beyond Xinjiang," Australian Strategic Policy Institute, 2020.

47. "Global Supply Chains, Forced Labor, and the Xinjiang Uyghur Autonomous Region," Congressional Executive Commission on China, March 2020.

48. See US Customers Border Protection, "Xinjiang Supply Chain Business Advisory," July 2, 2020, https://www.cbp.gov/document/guidance/xinjiang-supply-chain-business-advisory.

49. William Mauldin, "US Warns Businesses Over Supply Chains Tied to Rights Violations in China," *Wall Street Journal,* July 1, 2020, https://www.wsj.com/articles/u-s-warns-businesses-over-supply-chains-tied-to-rights-violations-in-china-11593625904.

50. US Department of State, "Xinjiang Supply Chain Business Advisory," Updated July 13, 2021, https://www.state.gov/wp-content/uploads/2021/07/Xinjiang-Business-Advisory-13July2021-1.pdf.

51. Department of State, "Xinjiang Supply Chain."

52. Ana Swanson, "Nike and Coca-Cola Lobby Against Xinjiang Forced Labor Bill," *New York Times,* November 29, 2020, https://www.nytimes.com/2020/11/29/business/economy/nike-coca-cola-xinjiang-forced-labor-bill.html.

53. Neil L. Bradley, Chamber of Commerce of the United States of America, September 20, 2020, https://www.uschamber.com/sites/default/files/200922_h.r._6270_h.r._6210_uyghurforcedlabordisclosureandpreventionacts_house.pdf.

54. "China's Belt and Road Initiative: Hearing before the Subcommittee on International Trade, Customs, and Global Competitiveness of the Committee on Finance, United States Senate," June 12, 2019, https://www.govinfo.gov/content/pkg/CHRG-116shrg43886/html/CHRG-116shrg43886.htm.

55. *US-China Economic and Security Review Commission*, Chapter 3, Section 1, "The Belt and Road Initiative," in Annual Report to Congress, November 2018, 291.

56. Caterpillar Inc., "Capturing Opportunity with the Belt & Road Initiative," May 16, 2018, https://www.caterpillar.com/en/news/caterpillarNews/customer-dealer-product/capturingopportunitywiththebeltroadinitiative.html. Accessed September 30, 2022.

57. *US-China Commission*, "Belt and Road," 291.

58. Caterpillar Inc., "China Facilities," accessed October 1, 2022, https://www.caterpillar.com/en/company/global-footprint/apd/china/china-facilities.html.

59. Caterpillar Inc., "China Facilities," accessed October 1, 2022.

60. Alex Stone and Peter Wood, "China's Military-Civil Fusion Strategy: A View From Chinese Strategists," China Aerospace Studies Institute, 2020, 35.
61. Stone and Wood, "Military-Civil Fusion," 89.
62. Tsinghua University, official site, accessed October 16, 2021.
63. Kaveh Waddell, "The Devil's Bargain for AI Companies Working in China," *Axios*, July 15, 2018, https://www.axios.com/china-artificial-intelligence-ai-military-e274d4f6-71b6-4d76-b54a-c0510e7cc277.html.
64. You Zheng, "The Road of Military-Civil Fusion for Artificial Intelligence Development," June 8, 2018, translation by Elsa Kania available in full at The Elsa Kania Bookshelf: Sino-American Competition, Technological Futures & Approaching Battlefield Singularity, https://www.andrewerickson.com/2021/06/the-elsa-kania-bookshelf-sino-american-competition-technological-futures-approaching-battlefield-singularity/.
65. Zheng, "Military-Civil Fusion."
66. Zheng, "Military-Civil Fusion."
67. Julia Limitone, "China Is Ripping off Microsoft to the Tune of $10B," Fox Business, November 1, 2018, https://www.foxbusiness.com/business-leaders/china-is-ripping-off-microsoft-to-the-tune-of-10b.
68. Microsoft Corporation, "Microsoft Asia-Pacific R&D Group: Introduction," https://www.microsoft.com/en-us/ard/overview. Accessed September 30, 2022.
69. Microsoft Corporation, "About Microsoft's Presence in China," https://news.microsoft.com/about-microsofts-presence-in-china/. Accessed September 30, 2022.
70. US Department of State, "Huawei and Its Siblings, the Chinese Tech Giants: National Security and Foreign Policy Implications," Remarks by Dr. Christopher Ashley Ford, Assistant Secretary, Bureau of International Security and Nonproliferation, September 11, 2019, https://2017-2021.state.gov/huawei-and-its-siblings-the-chinese-tech-giants-national-security-and-foreign-policy-implications/index.html.
71. See Stone and Wood, "Military-Civil Fusion" for examples of industrial strategy and military innovation. See Anna Puglisi and Daniel Chou, "China's Industrial Clusters: Building AI-Driven Bio-Discovery Capacity," Georgetown Center for Security and Emerging Technology (CSET), June 2022, for an in-depth study of industrial clusters in one strategic industry.
72. State Council of the People's Republic of China, "China's Central SOEs Report Rising Profits in 2020 Amid Reforms," January 19, 2021.
73. *China Daily*, "State Capital Optimization Gets Impetus," February 24, 2021.
74. Trefor Moss, "China to Weld Its Biggest Shipbuilders into Single State-Run Giant," *Wall Street Journal*, July 2, 2019, https://www.wsj.com/articles/china-to-weld-its-biggest-shipbuilders-into-single-state-run-giant-11562067663.
75. Keith Zhai, "China Set to Create New State-Owned Rare-Earths Giant," *Wall Street Journal*, December 3, 2021, https://www.wsj.com/articles/china-set-to-create-new-state-owned-rare-earths-giant-11638545586.
76. General Office of the Chinese Communist Party Central Committee, "Opinion on Strengthening the United Front Work of the Private Economy in the New Era," September 15, 2020, translation by Center for Strategic and International Studies, https://interpret.

csis.org/translations/the-general-office-of-the-ccp-central-committee-issued-the-opinion
-on-strengthening-the-united-front-work-of-the-private-economy-in-the-new-era/.

77. General Office CCP Central Committee, "United Front Work of the Private Economy."

78. General Office CCP Central Committee, "United Front Work of the Private Economy."

79. See Ward, *China's Vision of Victory*, Part One: "The Great Rejuvenation of the Chinese Nation," 1–44.

80. Michael Mastanduno, "Strategies of Economic Containment: US Trade Relations with the Soviet Union," *World Politics*, Vol. 37, Issue 4, July 1985, 506.

81. Mastanduno, "Strategies of Economic Containment," 506.

82. Author's translation: (故上兵伐谋，其次伐交，其次伐兵，其上攻城). For alternatives, see Lionel Giles (1910) and Samuel B. Griffith (Oxford, 1963) English language translations.

83. Economies that are "squeezed between the low-wage poor-country competitors that dominate in mature industries and the rich-country innovators that dominate in industries undergoing rapid technological change." See Indermit S. Gill and Homi Kharas, "The Middle-Income Trap Turns Ten," Policy Research Working Paper 7403, The World Bank Group.

84. Michael Pettis, "The Only Five Paths China's Economy Can Follow," *Carnegie Endowment for International Peace Michael Pettis China Financial Markets blog*, April 27, 2022, https://carnegieendowment.org/chinafinancialmarkets/87007. Italics added.

85. See for example Stefan Link, *Forging Global Fordism: Nazi Germany, Soviet Russia, and the Contest over the Industrial Order* (Princeton: Princeton, 2020)

86. Russell Flannery, "China Theft of US Information, IP One of Largest Wealth Transfers in History: FBI Chief," *Forbes*, July 7, 2020, https://www.forbes.com/sites/russellflannery/2020/07/07/china-theft-of-us-information-ip-one-of-largest-wealth-transfers-in-history-fbi-chief/?sh=2f1195d14440.

87. William C. Hannas and Didi Kirsten Tatlow (eds.), *China's Quest for Foreign Technology: Beyond Espionage* (New York: Routledge, 2020), 23.

88. Hannas and Tatlow (eds.), *China's Quest*, xv–xvi.

89. Federal Bureau of Investigation, remarks as prepared for delivery, Robert S. Mueller, III, Director, March 1, 2012, https://archives.fbi.gov/archives/news/speeches/combating-threats-in-the-cyber-world-outsmarting-terrorists-hackers-and-spies.

90. State Council, 中国制造2025, "Made in China 2025" (2015), IoT ONE translation.

91. Karen M. Sutter, "Foreign Technology Transfer Through Commerce," in *China's Quest for Foreign Technology: Beyond Espionage*, 57.

92. Xi Jinping, "Certain Major Issues for Our National Medium- to Long-Term Economic and Social Development Strategy," *Qiushi*, November 1, 2020, Georgetown CSET translation.

93. Jason Douglas and Stella Yifan Xie, "Pandemic Bolsters China's Role as World's Manufacturer," *Wall Street Journal*, August 21, 2022, https://www.wsj.com/articles/pandemic-bolsters-chinas-position-as-the-worlds-manufacturer-11661090580.

94. See for example Alibaba Cloud Community, "What's New in Alibaba Cloud Database?" January 22, 2021, https://www.alibabacloud.com/blog/whats-new-in-alibaba-cloud-database_597203, Accessed October 1, 2022: "In 2009, Alibaba proposed a "de-IOE strategy" (IBM server, Oracle database, EMC storage) . . ."

95. See Chad P. Bown, "China Bought None of the Extra $200 Billion of US Exports in Trump's Trade Deal," Peterson Institute for International Economics, July 19, 2022, https://

www.piie.com/blogs/realtime-economic-issues-watch/china-bought-none-extra-200 -billion-us-exports-trumps-trade, for a record of China's imports from the US.

96. Katherine Tai, Center for Strategic and International Studies, 2021.

97. Clyde Russel, "Column: China's Mooted End to Australian Coal Ban Will Have Zero Market Impact," Reuters, July 25, 2022, https://www.reuters.com/markets/commodities /chinas-mooted-end-australian-coal-ban-will-have-zero-market-impact-2022-07-25/.

98. Geoffrey Barker, "Appeasement Is Not the Solution to the China Problem," Australian Strategic Policy Institute, December 1, 2021, https://www.aspistrategist.org.au /appeasement-is-not-the-solution-to-the-china-problem/.

99. Steven Nelson, "Chinese Paper Tags Australia as 'Target for a Nuclear Strike,'" *New York Post*, September 17, 2021, https://nypost.com/2021/09/17/chinese-paper-tags-australia -as-target-for-a-nuclear-strike/.

100. Congressional Record, Senate, Vol. 166., No. 186.

101. Mike Blanchfield, "Canada Urged to Join Allies in Tougher China Stance after Kovrig, Spavor Release," Canadian Broadcasting Company, October 11, 2021, https://www.cbc.ca /news/politics/canada-china-tougher-stance-1.6207251.

102. Regarding an alliance-based trading system, Jonathan Ward, various, including *Forbes* and Fox Business Network, 2019–2021. Regarding NATO for trade, see Robert D. Atkinson, "A Remarkable Resistance: Germany from 1900 to 1945 and China Today. Time for a NATO for Trade?," Information Technology and Industry Foundation, January 20, 2021, https://itif.org/publications/2021/01/20 /remarkable-resemblance-germany-1900-1945-and-china-today-time-nato-trade/.

103. Rana Foroohar, "Weaponized Supply Chains," *Financial* Times, October 11, 2021, https:// www.ft.com/content/eddaea67-b381-4eb7-88aa-3a879a744d6b.

104. Klint Finley, "The US Hits Huawei with New Charges of Trade Secret Theft," *Wired*, February 13, 2020, https://www.wired.com/story/us-hits-huawei-new-charges -trade-secret-theft/.

105. See "The International Emergency Economic Powers Act: Origins, Evolution, and Use," Congressional Research Service, March 25, 2022, https://crsreports.congress.gov/product /pdf/R/R45618/9 and "The Committee on Foreign Investment in the United States (CFIUS)," Congressional Research Service, February 26, 2020, https://crsreports.congress .gov/product/pdf/RL/RL33388/93.

106. "Lawyers: Industry Should Gird for Strict Enforcement of Xinjiang Import Ban," World Trade Online, January 14, 2022, https://insidetrade.com/share/173102.

107. Sydney H. Mintzer, Tamer A. Soliman, Yoshihide Ito, and Jing Zhang, "China Passes Broad New Anti-Sanctions Law to Counter Foreign Government Sanctions," Mayer Brown LLP, https://www.mayerbrown.com/en/perspectives-events/publications/2021/06 /china-passes-broad-new-anti-sanctions-law-to-counter-foreign-government-sanctions.

108. Michael Mastanduno, "Trade as a Strategic Weapon: American and Alliance Export Control Policy in the Early Postwar Period," *International Organization*, Vol. 42, No. 1, 1988, 141.

109. Mastanduno, "Strategic Weapon," 142

110. 罗援少将在2018军工榜颁奖典礼与创新峰会上的演讲. Author's translation.

111. Michael Mastanduno, *Economic Containment: CoCom and the Politics of East-West Trade*, (Ithaca: Cornell, 1992), 5.

112. *Bloomberg News*, "China Orders Government, State Firms to Dump Foreign PCs," May 5, 2022, https://www.bloomberg.com/news/articles/2022-05-06/china-orders -government-state-firms-to-dump-foreign-pcs.

113. *Bloomberg*, "China Orders."

114. Bob Davis and Lingling Wei, "The Soured Romance Between China and Corporate America," *Wall Street Journal*, June 5, 2020, https://www.wsj.com/articles/the-soured-romance -between-china-and-corporate-america-11591365699.

115. "President Xi's Speech to Davos in Full," World Economic Forum, January 17, 2017, https://www.weforum.org/agenda/2017/01/full-text-of-xi-jinping-keynote -at-the-world-economic-forum.

116. "Xi's speech in Davos," World Economic Forum. Italics added.

117. Michael Pettis, *The Great Rebalancing: Trade Conflict, and the Perilous Road Ahead for the World Economy*, (Princeton, 2013), 69 and 87.

118. Dr. Carl E. Walter, "Testimony Before the US-China Economic and Security Review Commission, China's Quest for Capital: Motivations, Methods and Implications," January 23, 2020.

119. The Department of Commerce and the inter-agency Committee on Foreign Investment in the United States (CFIUS) are two other essential institutions, especially as the US government begins to block not only inbound investment to the United States but also *outbound* investment to China.

120. Mastanduno, *Strategies of Economic Containment*, 1985, 507.

121. See US Department of the Treasury, "US Treasury Announces Unprecedented & Expansive Sanctions Against Russia, Imposing Swift and Severe Economic Costs," February 24, 2022, https://home.treasury.gov/news/press-releases/jy0608, and "US Treasury Escalates Sanctions on Russia for Its Atrocities in Ukraine," April 6, 2022, https://home.treasury.gov/news /press-releases/jy0705 for record of actions taken.

122. Juan C. Zarate, *Treasury's War: The Unleashing of a New Era of Financial Warfare* (Public Affairs, 2013).

123. Zarate, *Treasury's War*, 23–24.

124. Zarate, *Treasury's War*, 24–25.

125. See Executive Order 13959 of November 12, 2020, "Addressing the Threat from Securities Investments That Finance Communist Chinese Military Companies," https://www.govinfo .gov/content/pkg/FR-2020-11-17/pdf/2020-25459.pdf.

126. Edward Phillip Kinsey II, CPA, Chief Financial Strategy Officer, Senior Advisor to the Undersecretary of State for Economic Growth, Energy and the Environment, "Comments to the July 9, 2020: SEC Staff Roundtable on Emerging Markets," https://www.sec.gov /comments/emerging-markets/cll9-7400180-219051.pdf.

127. Yen Nee Lee, "China's $13 Trillion Bond Market Marks a Milestone. Here's What It Means," CNBC, April 1, 2019, https://www.cnbc.com/2019/04/01/china-bonds-debut-on -bloomberg-barclays-global-aggregate-index.html.

128. US Security and Exchange Commission, Division of Economic and Risk Analysis, "US Investors' Exposure to Domestic Chinese Issuers," July 6, 2020, https://www.sec.gov/files /us-investors-exposure-domestic-chinese-issuers_20200706.pdf. Italics added.

129. See also Gabriel Collins and Andrew S. Erickson, "Hold the Line Through 2035: A Strategy to Offset China's Revisionist Actions and Sustain a Rules-Based Order in the Asia-Pacific," Baker Institute for Public Policy, November 2020, for a similar end state, though a strategy that eschews containment.

130. See Ward, *China's Vision of Victory*, 107–110.

131. Klaus Schwab, *The Fourth Industrial Revolution* (New York: Crown Business, 2016), 1.

132. Schwab, *Fourth Industrial Revolution*, 7–8.

133. Marr, *Tech Trends*, 1–2.

134. Marr, *Tech Trends*, vii–viii.

135. "The Biden White House Plan for a New US Industrial Strategy," Atlantic Council, June 23, 2021, Brian Deese, National Economic Council Director, speech as prepared for delivery, atlanticcouncil.org/commentary/transcript/the-biden-white -house-plan-for-a-new-us-industrial-policy/.

136. "Biden White House Plan," speech as prepared for delivery.

137. CHIPS Act of 2022, https://www.govinfo.gov/content/pkg/BILLS-117hr4346enr/pdf /BILLS-117hr4346enr.pdf.

138. Dario Gil, Interview with Maria Bartiromo, Fox Business Network, September 28, 2020. Italics added.

139. Timothy Taylor, "The Curtain Opens on 20th Century," in *The Great Courses: History of the US Economy in the 20th Century* (The Teaching Company, 1996). Author's transcription of audio.

140. Schwab, *Fourth Industrial Revolution*, 7.

141. Winston S. Churchill, "Their Finest Hour," June 18, 1940.

142. Xi Jinping, "Secure a Decisive Victory in Building a Moderately Prosperous Society in All Respects and Strive for the Great Success of Socialism with Chinese Characteristics for a New Era," 19th Party Congress of the Communist Party of China, 2017.

143. Robert D. Atkinson, "Why Federal R&D Policy Needs to Prioritize Productivity to Drive Growth and Reduce the Debt-to-GDP Ratio," Information Technology and Innovation Foundation, September 2019.

144. Robert Atkinson and Jonathan Ward, "Ward and Atkinson: Amid US-China Trade Battle, Here Is How America Can Remain the World's Strongest Economy," Fox Business, November 15, 2019.

145. President's Council of Advisors on Science and Technology, "Report to the President: Revitalizing the US Semiconductor Ecosystem," September 2022, https://www.whitehouse .gov/wp-content/uploads/2022/09/PCAST_Semiconductors-Report_Sep2022.pdf.

146. James Pethokoukis, "Silicon Valley: An Unrepeatable Miracle? A Long-Read Q&A with Margaret O'Mara," October 4, 2019, https://www.aei.org/economics /silicon-valley-an-unrepeatable-miracle-a-long-read-qa-with-margaret-omara/.

147. Atkinson, "Federal R&D," 2019.

148. See especially Nancy Lazar on US manufacturing renaissance. For example, Leslie P. Norton, "Economist Nancy Lazar Is Betting on Middle America,"

Barron's, May 15, 2020, https://www.barrons.com/articles/economist-nancy-lazar
-is-betting-on-middle-america-51589568493.

149. The White House, "Executive Order on America's Supply Chains," February 24,
2021, https://www.whitehouse.gov/briefing-room/presidential-actions/2021/02/24
/executive-order-on-americas-supply-chains/.

150. "COVID-19 and Domestic PPE Production and Distribution: Issues and Policy Options,"
Congressional Research Service, 3.

151. Congressional Research Service, COVID-19 and Domestic PPE, 3.

152. Emily de La Bruyere and Nathan Picarsic, "Viral Moment: China's Post-COVID
Planning," March 2020, 9.

153. The President's Council of Advisors on Science and Technology, "Recommendations
for Strengthening American Leadership in Industries of the Future," June 2020, https://
science.osti.gov/-/media/_/pdf/about/pcast/202006/PCAST_June_2020_Report.pdf.

154. The White House, "Building Resilient Supply Chains, Revitalizing American
Manufacturing, and Fostering Broad-Based Growth: 100-Day Reviews under Executive
Order 14017," June 2021, 7.

155. Nicholas A. Lambert, *Planning Armageddon: British Economic Warfare and the First World
War* (Cambridge, MA: Harvard, 2012), 20.

156. Lambert, *Planning Armageddon*, 23.

157. Gordon H. Hanson, "Who Will Fill China's Shoes? The Global Evolution of Labor-
Intensive Manufacturing," National Bureau of Economic Research, December 2020, 18–19.

158. Hanson, "Who Will Fill China's Shoes?" 2020, 19.

159. Hanson, "Who Will Fill China's Shoes?" 2020, 16. See also Robert D. Atkinson,
"Innovation Drag: China's Economic Impact on Developed Nations," Information
Technology and Innovation Foundation, January 6, 2020.

160. Advanced Manufacturing National Program Office, "Manufacturing USA Strategic
Plan," November 2019, https://www.manufacturingusa.com/sites/manufacturingusa.com
/files/2021-01/2019%20MfgUSA%20Strategic%20Plan%2011-10-2020.pdf

161. "Manufacturing USA Strategic Plan," 2019.

162. Ro Khanna, *Entrepreneurial Nation: Why Manufacturing Is Still Key to America's Future*,
(New York: McGraw Hill, 2012), 17.

163. Federal Registrar, Vol. 86, No. 190, October 5, 2021 Notices, 55022–55023, https://www
.govinfo.gov/content/pkg/FR-2021-10-05/pdf/2021-21644.pdf.

164. Ibid.

165. Global GDP in 2021, World Bank, latest data as of October 1, 2022, data.worldbank.org.

166. Author's calculations with World Bank data.

167. Kent H. Hughes, "Small Business Is Big Business in America," Woodrow Wilson
International Center for Scholars, 2.

168. See Timothy Taylor, *History of the US Economy in the 20th Century*, for drivers of US growth.

Part Two

1. See Deibel, *Foreign Affairs Strategy*, 209, for a broad example of what diplomacy entails.

2. See Ward, *China's Vision of Victory,* 102–104 on Maoist strategies in the emerging world. See also John W. Garver, *Protracted Contest: Sino-Indian Rivalry in the Twentieth Century,* (Seattle: Washington, 2002) and Jonathan D. T. Ward, "China-India Rivalry and the Border War of 1962: PRC Perspectives on the Collapse of China-India Relations, 1958–62," DPhil Thesis, University of Oxford, 2017. See also Nadege Rolland, "A New Great Game? Situating Africa in China's Strategic Thinking," National Bureau of Asian Research, June 2021.

3. See Jeremy Friedman, *Shadow Cold War: The Sino-Soviet Competition for the Third* World (North Carolina, 2015). See John Lewis Gaddis, *We Now Know: Rethinking Cold War* History (Oxford, 1997), 152–188, for Maoist three worlds theory. See also, Rolland, "Situating Africa."

4. See Ward, "China-India Rivalry," and Garver, *Protracted Contest,* for historical reference.

5. "Meeting Asia's Infrastructure Needs," The Asian Development Bank, February 2017, https://www.adb.org/publications/asia-infrastructure-needs.

6. Derek Scissors, "China's Overseas Investment Remains Stuck in COVID Mud," American Enterprise Institute, January 2022.

7. Scissors, "China's Overseas Investment."

8. "Overview," US International Development Finance Corporation, accessed September 30, 2022, https://www.dfc.gov/who-we-are/overview.

9. Catherine Putz, "2020 Edition: Which Countries Are for or Against China's Xinjiang Policies?" *The Diplomat,* October 9, 2020, https://thediplomat.com/2020/10/2020-edition-which-countries-are-for-or-against-chinas-xinjiang-policies/.

10. John J. Mearshimer introduction to George F. Kennan, *American Diplomacy: Sixtieth-Anniversary Expanded Edition* (Chicago, 2012), xi.

11. Edward J. Drea, Ronald H. Cole, Walter S. Poole, James F. Schnabel, Robert J. Watson, and Willard J. Webb, *History of the Unified Command Plan: 1946–2012,* Joint History Office, Office of the Chairman of the Joint Chiefs of Staff (Washington, DC, 2012).

12. Gaddis, *We Now Know,* 66–67.

13. Victor D. Cha, "Powerplay: Origins of the US Alliance System in Asia," *International Security,* Vol. 34, No. 3 (Winter 2009/2010).

14. See *China's Vision of Victory,* Part Five: "A Community of Common Destiny for Mankind," 177–223.

15. See Elbridge A. Colby, *The Strategy of Denial: American Defense in an Age of Great Power Conflict* (Yale, 2021)

16. "OECD 60 Years," accessed September 30, 2022, https://www.oecd.org/60-years/.

17. Dzirhan Mahadzir, "US, UK Aircraft Carriers Drill with Japanese Big Deck Warship in the Western Pacific," *USNI News,* October 4, 2021, https://news.usni.org/2021/10/04/u-s-u-k-aircraft-carriers-drill-with-japanese-big-deck-warship-in-the-western-pacific.

18. Ankita Garg, "Garena Free Fire to TikTok: All the 273 Chinese Apps That Indian Govt Banned so Far," *India Today,* February 15, 2022, https://www.indiatoday.in/technology/news/story/garena-free-fire-to-tiktok-all-the-273-chinese-apps-that-indian-govt-banned-so-far-1913141-2022-02-15.

19. "Indian Navy and RAN Begin Fourth Edition of AUSINDEX Exercise," *Naval Technology,* September 6, 2021, https://www.naval-technology.com/news/indian-navy-ran-begin-ausindex-exercise/.

20. See for example French support for South China Sea Patrols at the Shangri-la Dialogue in 2016, in Ankit Panda, "French Defense Minister to Urge EU South China Sea Patrols," *The Diplomat*, June 6, 2016, https://thediplomat.com/2016/06/french-defense-minister-to-urge-eu-south-china-sea-patrols/.

21. See for example Wang Yiwei, *The Belt and Road Initiative: What Will China Offer the World in Its Rise?* (Beijing: New World, 2016).

22. See Ward, "China-India Rivalry" and Garver, *Protracted Contest*. See also Nadege Rolland, "Situating Africa."

23. Wang Yiwei, *Belt and Road*, 18.

24. Du Debin and Ma Yahua, "'The Belt and Road': The Grand Geostrategy of the Great Rejuvenation of the Chinese Nation," *Geographical Research*, June 2015.

25. See also Rolland, "Situating Africa," which makes this point referencing twenty-first-century Chinese strategists.

26. See also Nadege Rolland, "China's Southern Strategy," *Foreign Affairs*, June 9, 2022, https://www.foreignaffairs.com/articles/china/2022-06-09/chinas-southern-strategy.

27. See for example bilateral trade data with Latin America, Asia, and Africa, Observatory of Economic Complexity.

28. John F. Kennedy, "Remarks of Senator John F. Kennedy, Conference on India and the United States, Washington, DC, May 4, 1959," John F. Kennedy Presidential Library and Museum, jfklibrary.org/archives/other-resources/john-f-kennedy-speeches/india-and-the-us-conference-washington-dc-19590504.

29. Author's calculations, Credit Suisse statistics.

30. "PM Lee Hsien Loong's Q&A Session at the 27th International Conference on the Future of Asia," Prime Minister's Office Singapore, May 26, 2022, https://www.pmo.gov.sg/Newsroom/PM-Lee-Hsien-Loong-Q-and-A-session-at-the-27th-International-Conference-on-the-Future-of-Asia.

31. Jonathan Ward, "The Emerging Geopolitics of the Indian Ocean Region," East West Center, June 28, 2017, https://www.eastwestcenter.org/publications/the-emerging-geopolitics-the-indian-ocean-region.

32. See Walter R. Borneman, *MacArthur at War: World War II in the* Pacific (New York: Little, Brown, 2016), 184–204 on the "West-Coast-to-Australia lifeline."

33. See for example Euan Graham, "Assessing the Solomon Islands' New Security Agreement with China," International Institute for Strategic Studies, May 5, 2022, https://www.iiss.org/blogs/analysis/2022/05/china-solomon-islands.

34. Rolland, "Situating Africa," 23.

35. Rolland, "Situating Africa," 2.

36. Roland, "Situating Africa," 13.

37. Jagannath Panda, "The Asia-Africa Growth Corridor: An India-Japan Arch in the Making?" *Focus Asia*, No. 21, August 2017, https://isdp.eu/content/uploads/2017/08/2017-focus-asia-jagannath-panda.pdf.

38. "5G Smart Farming Lands in Brazil," Huawei Blog, January 5, 2021, https://blog.huawei.com/2021/01/05/5g-smart-farming-brazil/, accessed October 1, 2022.

39. "A New Era for Brazil's Digital Economy Powered by ICT," Huawei Technologies Co. Ltd., https://www.huawei.com/us/executives/articles/Brazil-Digital-Economy-ICT-Innovation, Italics added.

40. "A New Era for Brazil's Digital Economy," Huawei Technologies.

41. "Mapping China's Tech Giants," Australian Strategic Policy Institute, database and archive, accessed June 6, 2022.

42. See Executive Order 13959 of November 12, 2020.

43. Mark Kane, "BYD Han EV Reaches Latin America: The First Batch Has Arrived," October 31, 2021, https://insideevs.com/news/544329/byd-han-ev-latin-america/.

44. *Jawaharlal Nehru's Speeches*, Vol. I (Delhi, 1949), 235–36.

45. Arthur M. Schlesinger, *A Thousand Days: John F. Kennedy in the White House* (Houghton Mifflin, 1965), 454.

46. Jonathan D. T. Ward and Jagannath Panda, "Why a US-India Partnership Must Succeed," *National Interest*, February 25, 2020, https://nationalinterest.org/feature/why -us-india-partnership-must-succeed-126857.

47. "India-China Clash: 20 Indian Troops Killed in Ladakh Fighting," BBC, June 16, 2020, https://www.bbc.com/news/world-asia-53061476.

48. "US Security Cooperation with India: Fact Sheet," US Department of State, January 20, 2021, https://www.state.gov/u-s-security-cooperation-with-india/.

49. "Charter of the Shanghai Cooperation Organization," *United Nations Treaty Series*, Volume 2896. The organization has arguably been hollowed out in recent years through the admission of opposing states India and Pakistan.

50. "Joint Statement of the Russian Federation and the People's Republic of China," 2022.

51. See Richard Weitz, "Assessing Chinese-Russian Military Exercises: Past Progress and Future Trends," Center for Strategic and International Studies, July 2021, for military exercises till 2021.

52. See for example, Vladimir Putin, "The Real Lessons of the 75th Anniversary of World War II," *National Interest*, June 18, 2020, https://nationalinterest.org/feature/vladimir-putin -real-lessons-75th-anniversary-world-war-ii-162982.

53. "Joint Statement of the Russian Federation and the People's Republic of China," 2022.

54. "Joint Statement of the Russian Federation and the People's Republic of China," 2022.

55. Peter Perdue, *China Marches West: The Qing Conquest of Central Eurasia* (Cambridge, MA: Belknap, 2010), 173.

56. Jonathan Ward, M.St. Global and Imperial History, Advanced Option papers, University of Oxford, 2012.

57. See Wang Huiyao, "It's Time to Offer Russia an Offramp. China Can Help with That: Guest Essay," *New York Times*, March 13, 2022.

58. Demetri Sevastopulo, Kathrin Hille, and Kana Inagaki, "Chinese and Russian Nuclear Bombers Fly over Sea of Japan as Biden Visits Tokyo," *Financial Times*, May 24, 2022, https://www.ft.com/content/2b77473c-44d8-4b27-98f8-07c096f5302c.

59. "China to send troops to Russia for 'Vostok' exercise," Reuters, August 17, 2022, https://www.reuters.com/world/china/chinese-military-will-send-troops-russia-joint -exercise-2022-08-17/.

60. See Sergey Radchenko, *Two Suns in the Heavens: The Sino-Soviet Struggle for Supremacy, 1962–1967* (Stanford: Stanford, 2009) and Lorenz Luthi, *The Sino-Soviet Split: Cold War in the Communist World* (Princeton: Princeton, 2008) for the two best works on the Sino-Soviet split.

61. Rayhan Demytrie, "Russia Faces Brain Drain as Thousands Flee Abroad," BBC, March 13, 2022, https://www.bbc.com/news/world-europe-60697763.

62. Jack Devine, *Spymaster's Prism: The Fight Against Russian Aggression* (Lincoln, Nebraska: Potomac Books, 2021), 59.

63. Andrew Osborn, "As if Things Weren't Bad Enough, Russian Professor Predicts End of US," *Wall Street Journal*, December 29, 2008, https://www.wsj.com/articles /SB123051100709638419.

64. Osborn, "Russian Professor."

65. Karen Gilchrist, "A Second Wave of Russians Is Fleeing Putin's Regime," CNBC, July 14, 2022, https://www.cnbc.com/2022/07/14/russians-flee-putins-regime-after-ukraine-war -in-second-wave-of-migration.html.

66. See Jeffrey Sonnenfeld and Yale Research Team, "1,000 Companies."

67. With thanks to Dr. Kanchan Gupta of India's Observer Research Foundation, who coined this phrase while interviewing me after the China-India border clashes in 2020.

Part Three

1. George Washington, "First Annual Address to Congress," January 8, 1790.

2. "Remarks of Senator John F. Kennedy in the United States Senate, National Defense, Monday, February 29, 1960," John F. Kennedy Presidential Library and Museum.

3. See Ward, *China's Vision of Victory*, 37–44, on "preparing to fight and win wars." See also, Xi Jinping, "Secure a Decisive Victory," 19th Party Congress, 2017.

4. John Feng, "Chinese Movie About US Military Defeat Set to Break Box Office Records," *Newsweek*, October 19, 2021, https://www.newsweek.com/chinese-movie-about -us-military-defeat-set-break-box-office-records-1640342.

5. John Lewis Gaddis, *We Now Know: Rethinking Cold War History*, (New York: Oxford, 1997), 78.

6. Gaddis, *We Now Know*, 81–82. Italics original.

7. Christian Brose, *The Kill Chain: Defending America in the Future of High-Tech Warfare* (New York: Hachette, 2020), xiii–xv.

8. Brose, *Kill Chain*, xvi–xvii.

9. *Selected Works of Mao Tsetung*, Vol. 5 (Peking, 1977), 18.

10. "同时，中国人民也绝不允许任何外来势力欺负、压迫、奴役我们，谁妄想这样干，必将在14亿多中国人用血肉筑成的钢铁长城面前碰得头破血流！"Author's translation of Xi Jinping's speech on CCP 100th Anniversary. For official English language translation, which softens this line, see, "Full Text of Xi Jinping's Speech on the CCP's 100th Anniversary," *Nikkei Asia*, July 1, 2021, https://asia.nikkei.com/Politics /Full-text-of-Xi-Jinping-s-speech-on-the-CCP-s-100th-anniversary.

11. 中华人民共和国对外关系文件集(1962)第九集，(世界知识出版社编辑，北京) Collected Documents on the Foreign Relations of the People's Republic of China, Collection No. 9 (World Knowledge Publishing House, Beijing), 44.

12. See Ward, *China's Vision of Victory*, 37–44, on "fighting the bloody battles of our era." See also Thomas Gibbons-Neff and Steven Lee Myers, "China Won't Yield 'Even One Inch' of South China Sea, Xi Tells Mattis," *New York Times*, June 27, 2018, https://www.nytimes.com/2018/06/27/world/asia/mattis-xi-china-sea.html.

13. Franklin Delano Roosevelt, Fireside Chat, February 23, 1942, https://www.presidency.ucsb.edu/documents/fireside-chat-6.

14. Chiang Kai-shek, *China's Destiny and Chinese Economic Theory* (Roy Publishers, 1947), 36. Modern spellings of Taiwan, Xinjiang and Manchuria inserted to replace antiquated English spellings.

15. See Peter Perdue, *China Marches West*, on genocide of Junghur Mongols.

16. Andrew S. Erickson and Joel Wuthnow, "Barriers, Springboards and Benchmarks: China Conceptualizes the Pacific 'Island Chains,'" *China Quarterly*, January 2016.

17. Louis Morton, *Strategy and Command: The First Two Years [United States Army in World War II: The War in the Pacific* (Center of Military History, United States Army, 1962).

18. Isaac Kardon, "Research & Debate-Pier Competitor: Testimony on China's Global Ports," *Naval War College Review*, Vol. 74.

19. Toshi Yoshihara and Jack Bianchi, "Seizing on Weakness: Allied Strategy for Competing with China's Globalizing Military," *Center for Strategic and Budgetary Assessments*, 2021.

20. "Statement of General Stephen J. Townsend, United States Army, Commander, United States Africa Command, Before the Senate Armed Forces Committee [sic]," March 15, 2022, https://www.armed-services.senate.gov/imo/media/doc/AFRICOM%20FY23%20Posture%20Statement%20%20ISO%20SASC%2015%20MAR%20Cleared.pdf.

21. Jim Gomez and Aaron Favila, "AP Exclusive: US Admiral Says China Fully Militarized Isles," Associated Press, March 21, 2022, https://apnews.com/article/business-china-beijing-xi-jinping-south-china-sea-d229070bc2373be1ca515390960a6e6c.

22. Author's conversation with US naval strategist Thomas Shugart (Ret.)

23. Congressional Research Service, "China Naval Modernization: Implications for US Navy Capabilities-Background Issues for Congress," March 8, 2022, https://crsreports.congress.gov/product/pdf/RL/RL33153/261, 2.

24. CRS, "China Naval Modernization," March 2022, 3.

25. See Odd Arne Westad, *The Global Cold War: Third World Interventions and the Making of Our Times* (Cambridge: Cambridge, 2011) and Gaddis, *We Now Know*.

26. Andrew F. Krepinevich Jr., "How to Deter China: The Case for Archipelagic Defense," *Foreign Affairs*, March/April 2015.

27. Andrew F. Krepinevich Jr., "Preserving the Balance: A US Eurasia Defense Strategy," Center for Strategic and Budgetary Assessments, 2017, 81–83.

28. Jonathan D. T. Ward, "The Influence of Seapower on China," US Naval Institute Proceedings, Vol. 145, August 2019.

29. Kardon, "Pier Competitor," 3.

30. Kardon, "Pier Competitor," 3.

31. Jerry Hendrix, "Want Infrastructure? Build Shipyards," *Wall Street Journal*, April 21, 2021, https://www.wsj.com/articles/want-infrastructure-build-shipyards-11619044766.

32. See CRS, "Navy Force Structure and Shipbuilding Plans: Background and Issues for Congress," September 19, 2022, for a discussion of US shipbuilding requirements and challenges.

33. Commander Bryan G. McGrath, "1,000 Ship Navy and Maritime Strategy," USNI Proceedings, January 2007, https://www.usni.org/magazines/proceedings/2007 /january/1000-ship-navy-and-maritime-strategy.

34. US Marine Corps, "Force Design 2030," March 2020, https://www.hqmc.marines.mil /Portals/142/Docs/CMC38%20Force%20Design%202030%20Report%20Phase%20I %20and%20II.pdf?ver=2020-03-26-121328-460, 2.

35. USMC, "Force Design 2030," 4.

36. Author's conversation with Admiral Jonathan Greenert (Ret).

37. Dominic Nicholls and Danielle Sheridan, "Ben Wallace: Submarines Rather Than Ships Could Be the Royal Navy's Future," *The Telegraph*, September 2, 2022, https:// www.telegraph.co.uk/politics/2022/09/02/ben-wallace-submarines-rather-ships -could-royal-navys-future/.

38. CRS, "Navy Large Unmanned Surface and Undersea Vehicles: Background and Issues for Congress," https://crsreports.congress.gov/product/pdf/R/R45757/56 , 17.

39. CRS, "Navy Force Structure," 4.

40. CRS, "Navy Force Structure," 4.

41. CRS, "Navy Large Unmanned," 1–2.

42. "A Conversation with the Chairman of the Joint Chiefs of Staff on the Military Challenges of the 21st Century," 2021 Aspen Security Forum, November 3, 2021, https://www .aspensecurityforum.org/_files/ugd/93f0e1_aac7c2c1af36429ebeac447f6d0f866a.pdf.

43. See Colby, *Strategy of Denial.*

44. "Full transcript of notes of a speech by Winston Churchill broadcast on BBC radio, 10pm, 15 November 1934," UK Parliament, https://www.parliament.uk/globalassets/documents /parliamentary-archives/Churchill-for-web-Mar-2014.pdf.

45. See Donald Stoker, *Purpose and Power: A History of U.S. Grand Strategy from the Revolutionary Era to the Present* (Cambridge: Cambridge, 2023), Chapter 10.

46. "A Report to the National Security Council – NSC 68," April 12, 1950, President's Secretary's File, Truman Papers, 12.

47. See Stoker, *US Grand Strategy.*

48. Norman A. Bailey, "The Strategic Plan That Won the Cold War: National Security Decision Directive 75" (Potomac Foundation, 1998).

49. "National Security Decision Directive on US Relations with the USSR" (NSDD-75), January 17, 1983, 1.

50. NSDD-75, 2.

51. NSDD-75, 7.

52. See The White House, "National Security Strategy of the United States of America," December 2017 for reference to China, Russia, North Korea, and Iran. See The White House, "Interim National Security Strategic Guidance," March 2021, for continued reference to these states.

53. Krepinevich, "Preserving the Balance," x.

54. Abraham Denmark and Caitlin Talmadge, "Why China Wants More and Better Nukes," *Foreign Affairs*, November 19, 2021.

55. Ward, *China's Vision of Victory*, 67–68.

56. US Department of Defense, "Military and Security Developments Involving the People's Republic of China 2021: Annual Report to Congress," i.

57. Department of Defense, "China 2021," viii.

58. On missile defense, including against hypersonics, see Tom Karako and Masao Dahlgren, "Complex Air Defense: Countering the Hypersonic Missile Threat," CSIS, February 2022, and Ian Williams, Masao Dahlgren, Thomas G. Roberts, and Tom Karako, "Boost-Phase Missile Defense: Interrogating the Assumptions," CSIS, June 2022.

59. US Department of Defense, "2022 Nuclear Posture Review," 1.

60. Department of Defense, "China 2021," 64.

61. Department of Defense, "China 2021," 66–68.

62. US Space Force, "Space Capstone Publication, Spacepower: Doctrine for Space Forces," June 2020, vi.

63. Space Force, "Spacepower," 28.

64. Sandra Erwin, "Hyten Blasts 'Unbelievably' Slow DoD Bureaucracy as China Advances Space Weapons," *Space News*, October 28, 2021, https://spacenews.com/hyten-blasts-unbelievably-slow-dod-bureaucracy-as-china-advances-space-weapons/.

65. Erwin, "Hyten Blasts 'Unbelievably' Slow DoD Bureaucracy."

66. Thomas Newdick, "China Acquiring New Weapons Five Times Faster Than US Warns Top Official," *The Drive*, July 6, 2022, https://www.thedrive.com/the-war-zone/china-acquiring-new-weapons-five-times-faster-than-u-s-warns-top-official.

67. Colby, *Strategy of Denial*, 148.

68. Erwin, "Hyten Blasts 'Unbelievably' Slow DoD Bureaucracy."

69. Jeffrey W. Hornung, Scott Savitz, Jonathan Balk, Samantha McBirney, Liam Mclane, and Victoria M. Smith, "Preparing Japan's Multi-Domain Defense Force for the Future Battlespace Using Emerging Technologies," RAND Corporation, July 2021.

70. Colby, *Strategy of Denial*, 175.

71. Author conversation with US naval strategist Thomas Shugart (Ret.)

72. Colby, *Strategy of Denial*, 176.

73. See for example Rebeccah L. Heinrichs, "How to Strengthen US Deterrence and Weaken the Attempts of Rival Nuclear Coercion," Hudson Institute, September 2022, and Patty-Jane Geller, "Russia, China and the Power of Nuclear Coercion," The Heritage Foundation, September 13, 2022.

74. See Colby, *Strategy of Denial*, 173–179 on horizontal and vertical escalation in US-China conflict.

75. US Cyber Command, "Achieve and Maintain Cyberspace Superiority: Command Vision for US Cyber Command," April 2018, https://www.cybercom.mil/Portals/56/Documents/USCYBERCOM%20Vision%20April%202018.pdf, 2.

76. US Department of Defense, "Summary: Department of Defense Cyber Strategy," 2018.

77. US Cyber Command, "Cyberspace Superiority."

78. Frank Konkel, "CIA Awards Secret Multibillion-Dollar Cloud Contract," Nextgov, November 20, 2020, https://www.nextgov.com/it-modernization/2020/11/exclusive-cia-awards-secret-multibillion-dollar-cloud-contract/170227/.

79. Brian Schimpf, "Anduril Boss: In an Era of Strategic Competition, We Need Artificially Intelligent Systems," *Defense News,* December 6, 2021, https://www

.defensenews.com/outlook/2021/12/06/anduril-boss-in-an-era-of-strategic-competition
-we-need-artificially-intelligent-systems/.

80. Alexander C. Karp, "In Defense of Europe: A Letter from the Chief Executive Officer," Palantir, March 10, 2022, https://www.palantir.com/newsroom/letters /in-defense-of-europe/en/.

81. See for example, Joseph Votel and James Geurts, "Forging the Industrial Network the Nation Needs," *National Interest*, June 24, 2022.

82. Peter L. Singer, "Federally Supported Innovations: 22 Examples of Major Technology Advances That Stem from Federal Research Support," ITIF, February 2014.

83. US Department of Defense, "Review of Critical Minerals and Materials," in The White House "Building Resilient Supply Chains, Revitalizing American Manufacturing, and Fostering Broad-Based, Growth," June 2021, 157.

84. House Armed Services Committee, "Report of the Defense Critical Supply Chain Task Force," July 22, 2021, 2.

85. Quoted in Bonji Ohara, "The Effect of the Spread of COVID-19 on the US-China Political Warfare and the International Order," Sasakawa Peace Foundation China Observer, April 7, 2020, https://www.spf.org/spf-china-observer/en/document-detail025.html.

86. "The Defense Production Act of 1950, as Amended," August 2018, https://www.fema.gov /sites/default/files/2020-03/Defense_Production_Act_2018.pdf.

87. "The Biden White House plan," Brian Deese at Atlantic Council, 2021.

88. Department of the Interior, "2022 Final List of Critical Minerals," *Federal Register*, Vol. 87, No. 37, February 24, 2022, https://www.govinfo.gov/content/pkg/FR-2022-02-24 /pdf/2022-04027.pdf.

89. Department of Defense, "Review of Critical Minerals and Materials," 162.

90. Namrata Goswami and Peter A. Garretson, *Scramble for the Skies: The Great Power Competition to Control the Resources of Outer Space* (Lanham, MD: Rowman & Littlefield, 2020), 19.

91. See Goswami and Garretson, *Scramble for the Skies*, and Joshua Carlson, *Spacepower Ascendant: Space Development Theory and a New Space Strategy*.

92. See Goswami and Garretson, *Scramble for the Skies*, and Carlson, *Spacepower Ascendant*.

93. Goswami and Garretson, *Scramble for the Skies*, 8.

94. Buzz Aldrin (foreword) in James Trefil, *Space Atlas, Second Edition: Mapping the Universe and Beyond* (Washington, DC: National Geographic, 2018), 23–26.

95. Carlson, *Spacepower Ascendant*.

96. With thanks to Namrata Goswami, Joshua Carlson, Matt Padilla, and all others who have guided me in the study of space.

97. Winston S. Churchill, "We Shall Fight on the Beaches," June 4, 1940. Kirstin Hunt, writing in *Smithsonian* in 2017, points out Churchill's appeal to America in this speech. Emphasis added.

98. See Michelle Shevin-Coetzee and Jerry Hendrix, "From Blue to Black: Applying the Concepts of Sea Power to the Ocean of Space," Center for a New American Security, November 2016, for an in-depth discussion of space and oceans.

Part Four

1. See Joseph Ellis, *Revolutionary Summer: The Birth of American Independence* (New York: Vintage, 2014), and Joseph Ellies, *The Cause: The American Revolution and Its Discontents, 1773–1783* (Liveright, 2021).

2. Julien Nocetti, "The Outsider: Russia in the Race for Artificial Intelligence," French Institute for International Relations, December 2020, 9.

3. Todd Harrison, Kaitlyn Johnson, Thomas G. Roberts, Tyler Way, and Makena Young, "Space Threat Assessment 2020," CSIS, March 2020.

4. "NSC-68," 4. Italics added.

5. "Communiqué on the Current State of the Ideological Sphere (Document No. 9)," Rogier Creemers translation, 2013.

6. See Samantha Hoffman, "Managing the State: Social Credit, Surveillance and the CCP's Plan for China," The Jamestown Foundation, August 17, 2017, https://jamestown.org/program/managing-the-state-social-credit-surveillance-and-the-ccps-plan-for-china/, on "social management."

7. Elena Gorokhova, *A Mountain of Crumbs: A Memoir* (New York: Simon & Schuster, 2011), 172.

8. UNIAN News Agency (Ukraine); for English-language coverage of this interview, see, for example, Sam Clench, "'I Feel Shame': Captured Russian Soldier's Powerful Denunciation of Ukraine Invasion," news.com.au, https://www.news.com.au/world/europe/i-feel-shame-captured-russian-soldiers-powerful-denunciation-of-ukraine-invasion/news-story/4fea7b000dc4f44a0f7456c1fc4adf6a.

9. Abraham Lincoln, "The Gettysburg Address," November 19, 1863.

10. Martin Luther King Jr., "I Have a Dream," August 28, 1963.

11. Langston Hughes, "Let America Be America Again," *The Collected Poems of Langston Hughes* (Knopf, 1994).

12. John F. Kennedy, "Remarks Prepared for Delivery at the Trade Mart in Dallas, TX, November 22, 1963 [Undelivered]," John F. Kennedy Presidential Library and Museum.

13. Ronald Reagan, "Remarks on East-West Relations at the Brandenburg Gate in West Berlin," June 12, 1987, Ronald Reagan Presidential Foundation & Institute.

14. Martin Luther King Jr., "I've Been to the Mountaintop," April 3, 1968.

15. Simon Denyer, "Former Inmates of China's Muslim 'Reeducation' Camps Tell of Brainwashing, Torture," *Washington Post*, May 17, 2018, https://www.washingtonpost.com/world/asia_pacific/former-inmates-of-chinas-muslim-re-education-camps-tell-of-brainwashing-torture/2018/05/16/32b330e8-5850-11e8-8b92-45fdd7aaef3c_story.html.

16. Franklin Delano Roosevelt, "The Four Freedoms," January 6, 1941.

17. Original cable at The National Archives, Kew, United Kingdom. See summary for example in Adam Lusher, "At Least 10,000 People Died in Tiananmen Square Massacre, Secret British Cable from the Time Alleged," *The Independent*, December 23, 2017, https://www.independent.co.uk/news/world/asia/tiananmen-square-massacre-death-toll-secret-cable-british-ambassador-1989-alan-donald-a8126461.html.

18. See Joseph Riley, "Hedging Engagement: America's Neoliberal Strategy for Managing China's Rise in the Post–Cold War Era," DPhil Thesis, University of Oxford, 2016, for verbatim accounts of China engagement theory.

19. Chen Jian, *Mao's China and the Cold War* (Chapel Hill, NC: North Carolina, 2001), 7.

20. Qiang Zhai, *China and the Vietnam Wars, 1950–1975* (Chapel Hill, NC: North Carolina, 2000), 4.

21. Darren Byler, *In the Camps: China's High-Tech Penal Colony* (New York: Columbia, 2021).

22. See for example Byler, *In the Camps* and Raymond Zhong, "As China Tracked Muslims, Alibaba Showed Customers How They Could, Too," *New York Times*, December 16, 2020, https://www.nytimes.com/2020/12/16/technology/alibaba-china-facial-recognition -uighurs.html. See also US Department of State, "Huawei and Its Siblings."

23. See BlackRock iShares China A ETF and BlackRock MSCI Emerging Markets ETF, accessed September 2, 2022, https://www.blackrock.com/us/individual/products/273318 /ishares-msci-china-a-etf and https://www.blackrock.com/us/individual/products/239637 /ishares-msci-emerging-markets-etf.

24. Byler, *In the Camps*, 88.

25. Byler, *In the Camps*, 89.

26. David Stavrou, "A Million People Are Jailed at China's Gulags. I Managed to Escape. Here's What Really Goes on Inside," *Haaretz*, October 17, 2019, https://www.haaretz.com/world -news/2019-10-17/ty-article-magazine/.premium/a-million-people-are-jailed-at-chinas -gulags-i-escaped-heres-what-goes-on-inside/0000017f-e216-d804-ad7f-f3fe73670000.

27. George Washington, "Farewell Address," September 17, 1796.

28. US Department of State, "Secretary Anthony J. Blinken, National Security Advisor Jake Sullivan, Director Yang and State Councilor Wang at the Top of Their Meeting," March 18, 2021, https://www.state.gov/secretary-antony-j-blinken-national-security-advisor-jake- sullivan-chinese-director-of-the-office-of-the-central-commission-for-foreign-affairs-yang -jiechi-and-chinese-state-councilor-wang-yi-at-th/.

29. Department of State, "Blinken, Sullivan, Yang and Wang Meeting," 2021.

30. Department of State, "Blinken, Sullivan, Yang and Wang Meeting," 2021.

31. Fu Ying, "The US World Order Is a Suit That No Longer Fits," *Financial Times*, January 6, 2016, https://www.ft.com/content/c09cbcb6-b3cb-11e5-b147-e5e5bba42e51.

32. See Rolland, "Situating Africa," Ward, "China-India Rivalry," and Garver, *Protracted Contest*.

33. 毛泽东年谱 1949–1976, Vol. 3, 555, in Ward, *China's Vision of Victory*.

34. 毛泽东年谱 1949–1976, Vol. 5, 163, in Ward, *China's Vision of Victory*.

35. John W. Garver, *Foreign Relations of the People's Republic of China* (Pearson, 1993), 137.

36. Orlando Figes, *Natasha's Dance: A Cultural History of Russia* (New York: Metropolitan Books, 2002), 446–47.

37. See Ward, *China's Vision of Victory*, Part One: "The Great Rejuvenation of the Chinese Nation," 1–44, and Part Five: "A Community of Common Destiny for Mankind," 177–223.

38. Elliot Smith, "Bridgewater's Ray Dalio Backs China despite Trade War Escalation," CNBC, August 7, 2019, https://www.cnbc.com/2019/08/07/bridgewaters-ray-dalio-backs-china -despite-trade-war-escalation.html.

39. The Editorial Board, "Ray Dalio's China Equivalence," *Wall Street Journal*, December 2, 2021, https://www.wsj.com/articles/ray-dalios-china-equivalence-bridgewater -xi-jinping-wall-street-america-11638486891.

40. Jim Geraghty, "We Can't Let Genocide Get in the Way of a Good Investment Opportunity, Right?" *National Review*, December 2, 2021, https://www.nationalreview.com/corner /we-cant-let-genocide-get-in-the-way-of-a-good-investment-opportunity-right/.

41. Ray Dalio, "Don't Be Blind to China's Rise in a Changing World," *Financial Times*, October 23, 2020, https://www.ft.com/content/8749b742-d3c9-41b4-910e-80e8693c36e6.

42. Peter Mattis, Prepared Statement, "China's Digital Authoritarianism: Surveillance, Influence, and Political Control," Hearing Before the House Permanent Select Committee on Intelligence, May 16, 2019.

43. Mattis, Prepared Statement, 2019.

44. See Mattis, Prepared Statement, 2019. See also Alexander Bowe, "China's Overseas United Front Work: Background and Implications for the United States," US-China Economic and Security Review Commission, August 24, 2018, and Toshi Yoshihara and Jack Bianchi, "Uncovering China's Influence in Europe: How Friendship Groups Coopt European Elites," Center for Strategic and Budgetary Assessments, 2020.

45. Lillian Rizzo and Connor Hart, "Paramount Revenue Gets Lift from 'Top Gun' Sequel, Streaming Service," *Wall Street Journal*, August 4, 2022, https://www.wsj.com/articles/paramount-revenue-rose-19-on-top-gun-streaming-service-11659614982.

46. Alexandra Canal, "China No Longer the 'Golden Goose' for Movies Studios: Hollywood Producer," Yahoo! Finance, September 5, 2022, https://finance.yahoo.com/news/china-no-longer-the-golden-goose-for-movie-studios-hollywood-film-producer-182035259.html.

47. Canal, "China No Longer the 'Golden Goose.'"

48. See Rep. Mike Gallagher, "Battle Force 2025: A Plan to Defend Taiwan Within the Decade," *Foundation for Defense of Democracies*, February 17, 2022 for a good overview. See also "the Davidson Window," for example in Kathrin Hille and Demetri Sevastopulo, "Taiwan: Preparing for a Potential Chinese Invasion," *Financial Times*, June 7, 2022, https://www.ft.com/content/0850eb67-1700-47c0-9dbf-3395b4e905fd.

49. "Xi Jinping: Speech at the General Assembly Commemorating the 100th Anniversary of the Revolution of 1911," China Aerospace Studies Institute translation.

50. Kevin McCauley, "Logistics Support for a Cross-Strait Invasion: The View from Beijing," US Naval War College China Maritime Studies Institute, China Maritime Report No. 22, July 2022, 3.

51. Sale Lilly, "'Killing Rats in a Porcelain Shop: PLA Urban Warfare in a Taiwan Campaign," in Joel Wuthnow, Derek Grossman, Phillip C. Saunders, Andrew Scobell, and Andrew N.D. Yang, *Crossing the Strait: China's Military Prepares for War with Taiwan* (Washington, DC: National Defense University, 2022), 140.

52. The Taiwan Affairs Office of the State Council and The State Council Information Office (PRC), "The Taiwan Question and China's Reunification in the New Era," August 2022.

53. Nancy Pelosi, "Why I'm Leading a Congressional Delegation to Taiwan," *Washington Post*, August 2, 2022, https://www.washingtonpost.com/opinions/2022/08/02/nancy-pelosi-taiwan-visit-op-ed/.

Conclusion

1. NSC 68.

INDEX

ABOUT THE AUTHOR

Jonathan D.T. Ward has been studying Russia, China, and India for nearly twenty years since his undergraduate days in Russian and Chinese language at Columbia University. Dr. Ward is the author of *China's Vision of Victory*, a guide to the global grand strategy of the Chinese government, which has been widely read in US government and national security circles, as well as by audiences in business and finance. He earned his PhD at the University of Oxford, where he specialized in China-India relations, after initially being admitted to Oxford for a doctorate in Russia-China relations during the Cold War. He has traveled widely in Russia, China, India, Latin America, and the Middle East, and speaks Russian, Chinese, Spanish, and Arabic, among other languages. As a subject matter expert, Dr. Ward has been an advisor to the US Department of Defense on Chinese long-term strategy and has briefed numerous US government audiences that have included US Strategic Command, US Indo-Pacific Command, the US Department of Commerce, the US Defense Intelligence Agency, and the Strategy Division of the US Naval Staff. Through his consulting company, Atlas Organization, Dr. Ward helps Fortune 500 companies and financial institutions understand US-China global competition, improve their risk assessments on China, and build new global strategies that can withstand historic geopolitical change. He is a frequent commentator on national and international television and radio, with appearances on Bloomberg, CNBC, Fox Business, Fox, MSNBC, and CNN International, among other networks. He lives in Washington, DC.